Grammar
Strand 2

TAPESTRY

The **Tapestry** program of language materials is based on the concepts presented in *The Tapestry of Language Learning:* The Individual in the Communicative Classroom by Robin C. Scarcella & Rebecca L. Oxford.

Each title in this program focuses on:

Individual learner strategies and instruction

The relatedness of skills

Ongoing self-assessment

Authentic material as input

Theme-based learning linked to task-based instruction

Attention to all aspects of communicative competence

TAPESTRY

GRAMMAR STRAND 2

Nancy Herzfeld-Pipkin

Heinle & Heinle Publishers
An International Thomson
Publishing Company
Boston, Massachusetts, 02116, USA

I(T)P

The publication of *Grammar Strand 2* was directed by the members of the Heinle & Heinle Newbury House ESL/ELT Publishing Team:

Erik Gundersen, Editorial Director
Bruno Paul, Market Development Director
Maryellen Eschmann Killeen, Production Editor

Also participating in the publication of this program were:

Publisher: Stanley J. Galek
Manufacturing Coordinator: Mary Beth Hennebury
Full Service Project Manager/Compositor: PC&F, Inc.
Art: Dave Blanchette and PC&F, Inc.
Interior Design: Maureen Lauran
Cover Design: Maureen Lauran
Photo/Video Specialist: Jonathan Stark

Copyright © 1997 by Heinle & Heinle Publishers

All rights reserved. No part of this publication may be reproduced or transmitted in any form or by any means, electronic or mechanical, including photocopy, recording, or any information storage and retrieval system, without permission in writing from the publisher.

Manufactured in the United States of America

ISBN: 0-8384-2301-9

Heinle & Heinle Publishers is an International Thomson Publishing Company.

10 9 8 7 6 5 4 3 2 1

To language learners everywhere who think that grammar is a necessary evil, in the hopes that you may come to find a more positive place for grammar in your learning.

PHOTO CREDITS

1, 2, 7 left and right, 11 center, 13, 14, 34, 81, 87, 95, 113, 114, 115, 121, 134, 135, 147, 148, 174, 181, 191, 202, 213, © Jonathan Stark/Heinle & Heinle Publishers; 7, © Judy Gelles/Stock Boston; 11 left, © Bob Kramer/Stock Boston; 11 right, © Addison Geary/Stock Boston; 20, © Peter Menzel/Stock Boston; 33, © Michael Dwyer/Stock Boston; 55 left and center, AP/Wide World Photos; 55 right, FPG; 74 left, © Michael Dwyer/Stock Boston; 74 right, © Lee Balterman/FPG; 95, © Spencer Grant/Stock Boston; 101, Ken Mattsson; 105, © Willie L. Hill, Jr./Stock Boston; 114 bottom left, Jean-Claude Lejeline/Stock Boston.

TEXT CREDITS

2, Student interview by Rica Ajuilar.

4, Student interview by Noriko Otani.

25, Cartoon, "Fred Bassett," © 1996. Reprinted by permission of Tribune Media Services.

26, Facts adapted from *National Geographic Picture Atlas of Our World,* Washington, D.C.: The National Geographic Society, 1979, pp. 53, 59, 110, 167. Courtesy of National Geographic Society.

28, Paragraph on Chad adapted from *National Geographic Picture Atlas of Our World,* Washington, D.C.: The National Geographic Society, 1979, p. 221. Courtesy of National Geographic Society.

28, Paragraph on earthquakes adapted from *National Geographic Picture Atlas of Our World,* Washington, D.C.: The National Geographic Society, 1979, p. 11. Courtesy of National Geographic Society.

28, Paragraph on our Earth adapted from *National Geographic Picture Atlas of Our World,* Washington, D.C.: The National Geographic Society, 1979, p. 16. Courtesy of National Geographic Society.

30, Information on mountain forming adapted from *National Geographic Picture Atlas of Our World,* Washington, D.C.: The National Geographic Society, 1979, p. 12. Courtesy of National Geographic Society.

30, Information on Bolivia adapted from *National Geographic Picture Atlas of Our World,* Washington, D.C.: The National Geographic Society, 1979, p. 95. Courtesy of National Geographic Society.

41, Cartoon, "Mother Goose and Grimm," © 1996. Reprinted by permission: Tribune Media Services.

44, E-mail message by Dottie Fagg.

55-56, Application responses by Seth Pipkin.

86, Menu adapted from Tom's "Back East" Sub Shop, San Diego, California, Tom Iammarino.

92, Cartoon, "Family Circus." Reprinted with permission of King Features Syndicate.

102, Information adapted from *San Diego Exempt Employee Information Guide,* T Systems International, Inc. 1993. pp. 5-6. Reprinted with permission.

122, 125, Information adapted from Kanner, Bernice. "New Tastes, Old Favorites, New Twists," Parade Magazine, Nov. 12, 1995, pp. 4-5. Reprinted with permission from Parade, copyright © 1995 and Bernice Kanner.

128, Information adapted from Hales, Dianne, "What America Eats . . . Our Survey Shows," Parade Magazine, Nov. 12, 1995, p. 4. Reprinted with permission from Parade, copyright © 1995 and Dianne Hales.

129, Chart on Clinton's diet taken from Ciabattari, Jane, "Parade's Special Intelligence Report, 'Eating Wisely at the White House,'" Parade Magazine, Nov. 12, 1995. Reprinted with permission from Parade, copyright © 1995.

137, 138-139, Questions and answers about Native Americans adapted from "Images of the American Indian," Boys' Life, December, 1993, p. 36. By permission of BOYS' LIFE, published by the Boy Scouts of America.

141, Interview information adapted from Daniel, Douglass, "A Changing Image for American Indians," Boys' Life, December 1993, pp. 38-39. By permission of BOYS' LIFE, published by the Boy Scouts of America.

157, Map and legend adapted from Mission Valley Shopping Center, San Diego, California, 1995. Reprinted with permission.

163, Cartoon, "Laugh Parade," © 1996. Reprinted courtesy of Bunny Hoest and Parade.

168, Cartoon, DENNIS THE MENACE® used by permission of Hank Ketcham and © by North American Syndicate.

179, Oral history instructions adapted from Zimmerman, William, "Keeper of the Past," Boys' Life, December, 1993, p. 69. By permission of William Zimmerman and BOYS' LIFE, published by the Boy Scouts of America. Original source: "How to Tape Instant Oral Biographies" (Guarionex Press) by Bill Zimmerman. Write to Guarionex Press, Attn: Bill Zimmerman, 201 West 77 St., New York, NY 10024

181, Story adapted from Ingram, Leah, "Getting into Guinness," Boys' Life, September 1993, pp. 27-28. By permission of Leah Ingram and BOYS' LIFE, published by the Boy Scouts of America.

183, The Six Golden Rules of Record Breaking adapted from the *Guinness Book of Records 1996.* Copyright © Guinness Publishing Ltd. 1995.

184, Authentic Longevity Records taken from the *Guinness Book of Records 1996.* Copyright © Guinness Publishing Ltd. 1995.

187, Facts on languages. Records taken from the *Guinness Book of Records 1996.* Copyright © Guinness Publishing Ltd. 1995.

199, 203, Chunnel information adapted from Henricks, Mark, "A Tunnel Under the Sea," Boys' Life, October 1993, pp. 19-21. By permission of Mark Henricks and BOYS' LIFE, published by the Boy Scouts of America.

205, Cartoon, "Family Circus." Reprinted with permission of King Features Syndicate.

Welcome to Tapestry

*E*nter the world of Tapestry! Language learning can be seen as an ever-developing tapestry woven with many threads and colors. The elements of the tapestry are related to different language skills like listening and speaking, reading and writing; the characteristics of the teachers; the desires, needs, and backgrounds of the students; and the general second language development process. When all these elements are working together harmoniously, the result is a colorful, continuously growing tapestry of language competence of which the student and the teacher can be proud.

This volume is part of the Tapestry Program for students of English as a second language (ESL) at levels from beginning to "bridge" (which follows the advanced level and prepares students to enter regular postsecondary programs along with native English speakers). Upper level materials in the Tapestry Program are also appropriate for developmental English courses—especially reading and composition courses. Tapestry levels include:

Beginning	Advanced
Low Intermediate	High Advanced
High Intermediate	Bridge

Because the Tapestry Program provides a unified theoretical and pedagogical foundation for all its components, you can optimally use all the Tapestry student books in a coordinated fashion as an entire curriculum of materials. (They will be published from 1993 to 1996 with further editions likely thereafter.) Alternatively, you can decide to use just certain Tapestry volumes, depending on your specific needs.

Tapestry is primarily designed for ESL students at postsecondary institutions in North America. Some want to learn ESL for academic or career advancement, others for social and personal reasons. Tapestry builds directly on all these motivations. Tapestry stimulates learners to do their best. It enables learners to use English naturally and to develop fluency as well as accuracy.

Tapestry Principles

The following principles underlie the instruction provided in all of the components of the Tapestry Program.

EMPOWERING LEARNERS

Language learners in Tapestry classrooms are active and increasingly responsible for developing their English language skills and related cultural abilities. This self direction leads to better, more rapid learning. Some cultures virtually train their students to be passive in the classroom, but Tapestry weans them from passivity by providing exceptionally high interest materials, colorful and motivating activities, personalized self-reflection tasks, peer tutoring and other forms of cooperative learning, and powerful learning strategies to boost self direction in learning.

The empowerment of learners creates refreshing new roles for teachers, too. The teacher serves as facilitator, co-communicator, diagnostician, guide, and helper. Teachers are set free to be more creative at the same time their students become more autonomous learners.

HELPING STUDENTS IMPROVE THEIR LEARNING STRATEGIES

Learning strategies are the behaviors or steps an individual uses to enhance his or her learning. Examples are taking notes, practicing, finding a conversation partner, analyzing words, using background knowledge, and controlling anxiety. Hundreds of such strategies have been identified. Successful language learners use language learning strategies that are most effective for them given their particular learning style, and they put them together smoothly to fit the needs of a given language task. On the other hand, the learning strategies of less successful learners are a desperate grab-bag of ill-matched techniques.

All learners need to know a wide range of learning strategies. All learners need systematic practice in choosing and applying strategies that are relevant for various learning needs. Tapestry is one of the only ESL programs that overtly weaves a comprehensive set of learning strategies into language activities in all its volumes. These learning strategies are arranged in eight broad categories throughout the Tapestry books:

Forming Concepts
Personalizing
Remembering New Material
Managing Your Learning
Understanding and Using Emotions
Overcoming Limitations
Testing Hypotheses
Learning with Others

The most useful strategies are sometimes repeated and flagged with a note, "It Works! Learning Strategy . . ." to remind students to use a learning strategy they have already encountered. This recycling reinforces the value of learning strategies and provides greater practice.

RECOGNIZING AND HANDLING LEARNING STYLES EFFECTIVELY

Learners have different learning styles (for instance, visual, auditory, hands-on; reflective, impulsive; analytic, global; extroverted, introverted; closure-oriented, open). Particularly in an ESL setting, where students come from vastly different cultural backgrounds, learning styles differences abound and can cause "style conflicts."

Unlike most language instruction materials, Tapestry provides exciting activities specifically tailored to the needs of students with a large range of learning styles. You can use any Tapestry volume with the confidence that the activities and materials are intentionally geared for many different styles. Insights from the latest educational and psychological research undergird this style-nourishing variety.

OFFERING AUTHENTIC, MEANINGFUL COMMUNICATION

Students need to encounter language that provides authentic, meaningful communication. They must be involved in real-life communication tasks that cause them to *want* and *need* to read, write, speak, and listen to English. Moreover, the tasks—to be most effective—must be arranged around themes relevant to learners.

Themes like family relationships, survival in the educational system, personal health, friendships in a new country, political changes, and protection of the environment are all valuable to ESL learners. Tapestry focuses on topics like these. In every Tapestry volume, you will see specific content drawn from very broad areas such as home life, science and technology, business, humanities, social sciences, global issues, and multiculturalism. All the themes are real and important, and they are fashioned into language tasks that students enjoy.

At the advanced level, Tapestry also includes special books each focused on a single broad theme. For instance, there are two books on business English, two on English for science and technology, and two on academic communication and study skills.

UNDERSTANDING AND VALUING DIFFERENT CULTURES

Many ESL books and programs focus completely on the "new" culture, that is, the culture which the students are entering. The implicit message is that ESL students should just learn about this target culture, and there is no need to understand their own culture better or to find out about the cultures of their international classmates. To some ESL students, this makes them feel their own culture is not valued in the new country.

Tapestry is designed to provide a clear and understandable entry into North American culture. Nevertheless, the Tapestry Program values *all* the cultures found in the ESL classroom. Tapestry students have constant opportunities to become "culturally fluent" in North American culture while they are learning English, but they also have the chance to think about the cultures of their classmates and even understand their home culture from different perspectives.

INTEGRATING THE LANGUAGE SKILLS

Communication in a language is not restricted to one skill or another. ESL students are typically expected to learn (to a greater or lesser degree) all four language skills: reading, writing, speaking, and listening. They are also expected to develop strong grammatical competence, as well as becoming socioculturally sensitive and knowing what to do when they encounter a "language barrier."

Research shows that multi-skill learning is more effective than isolated-skill learning, because related activities in several skills provide reinforcement and refresh the learner's memory. Therefore, Tapestry integrates all the skills. A given Tapestry volume might highlight one skill, such as reading, but all other skills are also included to support and strengthen overall language development.

However, many intensive ESL programs are divided into classes labeled according to one skill (Reading Comprehension Class) or at most two skills (Listening/Speaking Class or Oral Communication Class). The volumes in the Tapestry Program can easily be used to fit this traditional format, because each volume clearly identifies its highlighted or central skill(s).

Grammar is interwoven into all Tapestry volumes. However, there is also a separate reference book for students, *The Tapestry Grammar,* and a Grammar Strand composed of grammar "work-out" books at each of the levels in the Tapestry Program.

Other Features of the Tapestry Program

PILOT SITES

It is not enough to provide volumes full of appealing tasks and beautiful pictures. Users deserve to know that the materials have been pilot-tested. In many ESL series, pilot testing takes place at only a few sites or even just in the classroom of the author. In contrast, Heinle & Heinle Publishers have developed a network of Tapestry Pilot Test Sites throughout North America. At this time, there are approximately 40 such sites, although the number grows weekly. These sites try out the materials and provide suggestions for revisions. They are all actively engaged in making Tapestry the best program possible.

AN OVERALL GUIDEBOOK

To offer coherence to the entire Tapestry Program and especially to offer support for teachers who want to understand the principles and practice of Tapestry, we have written a book entitled, *The Tapestry of Language Learning. The Individual in the Communicative Classroom* (Scarcella and Oxford, published in 1992 by Heinle & Heinle).

A Last Word

We are pleased to welcome you to Tapestry! We use the Tapestry principles every day, and we hope these principles—and all the books in the Tapestry Program—provide you the same strength, confidence, and joy that they give us. We look forward to comments from both teachers and students who use any part of the Tapestry Program.

Rebecca L. Oxford
University of Alabama
Tuscaloosa, Alabama

Robin C. Scarcella
University of California at Irvine
Irvine, California

WEAVING THE GRAMMAR STRANDS INTO THE TAPESTRY SERIES

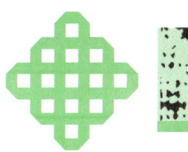

Grammar Strands is a four-level grammar series in the Tapestry Program. These materials are designed to supplement any course in which grammar is needed to address the specific needs of learners. The work-text format allows for greater flexibility for both in-class and out-of-class use. *Grammar Strand 1* and *Grammar Strand 2* feature a complete and comprehensive presentation of structures while *Grammar Strand 3* and *4* may be supplemented with *The Tapestry Grammar,* the Tapestry Program grammar reference, for a more in-depth study. The grammatical content for the Grammar Strands books was selected on the basis of needs of students at the proficiency levels covered by particular books and also on the basis of grammar issues raised in other materials at that level.

Their title reveals the purpose of the Grammar Strands in the Tapestry series: a focus on English grammar that is woven throughout the Tapestry materials making grammar one strand of thread interwoven with many other strands of language study. This approach to language learning enriches the study of grammar by putting it into the context of learning to communicate in English—rather than learning linguistic facts about English. Learning English grammar in context is a fundamental aspect of the "tapestry of language" that is contained in this coherent series of materials.

While these books differ from the other books in the Tapestry series because of this focus on grammar, they take the same approach to language learning. The Grammar Strands have thematic unity through presentation of grammar in the context of particular themes that run through a chapter. The students work with authentic language in authentic contexts. In addition, information about and practice with learning strategies is embedded throughout each of the Grammar Strands. While these books are focused on issues in English grammar, they also help students to become more skillful in all areas of language learning.

Grammar Strands at Levels 1 and 2

At Levels 1 and 2, the Grammar Strands are complete grammar textbooks that can be used with other Tapestry materials or alone as the complete text for a lower proficiency level grammar course.

To provide for the needs of students at Levels 1 and 2, more explanatory material is included than in the Grammar Strands at the upper levels. The grammar explanations given in *Grammar Strand 1* and *2* are based on the same approach used in *The Tapestry Grammar* and prepare students for the use of that reference when they reach the appropriate proficiency level. In *Grammar Strand 1* and *2*, terminology and explanations are presented, however, in language and examples more appropriate to the communication skills of students at the lower proficiency levels. As a result of having more explanatory materials in addition to a full range of examples and exercises, *Grammar Strand 1* and *2* are somewhat longer than *Grammar Strand 3* and *4*.

Teachers who work with students at these lower proficiency levels will find *Grammar Strand 1* and *2* wonderful new resources. All too often, materials at this level provide either too much grammar and not enough communication—or random communication activities that do not provide a coherent understanding of how English works. These grammar books are a useful balance of communication with grammar study. Moreover, they treat the lower proficiency students with respect and provide content that is worthy of adult learners. As part of a total series of materials, *Grammar Strand 1* and *2* can be used to help students move in a coherent sequence to higher levels of proficiency in English.

Grammar Strands at Levels 3 and 4

At Levels 3 and 4, the Grammar Strands are grammar workbooks designed to be used with the reading, writing, listening, speaking, and/or culture books in the Tapestry series. For example, in a course that combines reading with grammar, the teacher can use the appropriate Tapestry reading book along with the Grammar Strand for that proficiency level. This approach to grammar materials is another example of the innovative design developed for the Tapestry series. While the grammatical explanations and terminology come from *The Tapestry Grammar,* the Grammar Strands are not designed to be used as a supplement for this reference text. Rather than providing materials that would have students focus on grammar in isolation, the Tapestry approach has led to the development of these Grammar Strands that can be woven into classes that are focused on communication and on content.

Explanations, Examples, and Exercises

THE BALANCE IN *GRAMMAR STRANDS* 3 AND 4

All grammar textbooks are built on various combinations of the three "E's"— explanations, examples, and exercises. At Levels 3 and 4, the Grammar Strands are true workbooks, emphasizing the exercises and examples rather than the explanations. Cross references are provided to the relevant sections of *The Tapestry Grammar* for students and teachers who would like more grammatical explanation. At these upper levels, the Grammar Strands provide supplementary and complementary learning activities rather than additional discussion of the grammar topic. For a more complete grammar course, or for the richest possible combination of materials, a teacher will include *The Tapestry Grammar* in the selection of textbooks for courses using the Grammar Strands at Levels 3 and 4.

Patricia Byrd
Department of Applied Linguistics and ESL
Georgia State University

PREFACE

During the initial stage of this project, Tapestry grammar team members participated in a weekend grammar retreat courtesy of Heinle & Heinle in Boston. At one of the sessions of this retreat, an ESL student commented that grammar is a necessary part of language study although it has no actual use or meaning in the "real" world outside the classroom. I thought about this comment often while writing this book; showing the relevance of grammar study to actual use of the language became one of my main goals. This is not to say that this text was written to help learners in any situation they may face when using the language. Rather, it is my hope that this book will provide students with some basic knowledge about the structure of English as well as various strategies and tools to help them use these structures on their journey toward language proficiency outside the classroom.

Grammar Strand 2 is designed to be used with intermediate level students of English. This text consists of thirty-two lessons, which have been divided into seven chapters according to grammatical focus. Some lessons may be a review of a particular grammatical item for students at this level, but have been included to provide a more comprehensive picture of the structure of English.

The bulk of each lesson is made up of exercises/activities that afford students as much active involvement as possible. A wide variety of contexts has been incorporated into the lessons in order to familiarize students with typical situations encountered by native speakers and/or students studying in English-speaking countries. Many of the lessons incorporate authentic texts and student-generated writing.

To the Student

How many of you like to study grammar? Probably some of you are smiling or even laughing at this question. Why do so many people think that grammar is difficult or uninteresting? Are you one of those people?

How much do you know about English grammar? You probably know more than you think. Every time you say something or listen to someone, you are using your knowledge of grammar. Maybe you do not know all of the words to describe grammar, but that's not always the most important thing to know. Being able to **use** the grammar of a language when you read, write, speak, or listen is very important!

In this book you will find many exercises and activities to help you understand and use different grammatical items in various situations or contexts. Through these exercises and activities you will also be practicing your listening, speaking, reading, and writing skills. Each lesson in this book has several parts. In most of these parts you will be participating by discussing and practicing the grammar presented. In many cases, you will be using authentic materials and some of these may have unfamiliar words. Try not to be too concerned with these new words. Instead, try to understand the general meaning and complete the activity as best you can. Don't be afraid to try, even if you make some mistakes. Often you can learn much from your mistakes.

Finally, do you think grammar is something you find only in a classroom? Think about some of the topics and themes in this book and try to use the grammar you learned when you are not in class. In addition, when you are outside the class, try to find other situations that use some of the grammatical structures in this book and practice using them as much as possible.

To the Teacher

Grammar Strand 2 presents and provides practice with various grammatical structures divided into seven areas of focus. Each of these seven chapters includes two to eight lessons, each focusing on a particular structure within the chapter's general focus.

There are thirty-two lessons in this text. Each is divided into several sections, ending in different kinds of activities that provide students with practice of the particular structure(s) highlighted in the lesson. These activities progress from more structured, controlled exercises to more creative, open-ended activities.

The following descriptions and suggestions are to help you, the teacher, understand the organization of the text and provide specific ideas on how to utilize it.

GENERAL NOTES ABOUT MATERIALS/ACTIVITIES IN THIS BOOK

- Many authentic materials have been included in this text; some are adapted and others are not. In some cases difficult vocabulary has been glossed in the margins. In other cases, students should try to focus on general meaning and/or grasping meaning from context. In either case, students might be discouraged from getting bogged down with vocabulary and encouraged to focus on more general meaning and usage.
- Each lesson provides a variety of activities/exercises. It is hoped this will afford students many opportunities to participate as well as a chance to express themselves in different ways using different language skills. Due to the variations in time and purpose of individual classes, it is not necessarily expected that every teacher will cover everything in each lesson. Teachers should feel free to choose those activities that best suit the needs and abilities of their particular students.
- Many of the exercises have more than one possible answer.
  - In some of the more structured activities the directions explicitly tell students that more than one answer may be appropriate.
  - In the less structured exercises, of course, many answers will be possible.

  These types of exercises have been included to show students that several variations may be acceptable. It is hoped this will help them when dealing with English outside the classroom where they may encounter such variations. It is also hoped that this approach will help students to really use and manipulate the language.
- Examples are given for a few exercises. For those exercises where no example has been given, the teacher might want to do the first one or two questions with the class as a whole to be sure each student understands exactly how to complete the exercise.

Following is a more detailed description of all the sections and suggestions on how to present or follow up on them.

Chapter Organization

PREVIEW

This section introduces the topic or theme of the lesson through either a discussion or a short activity. In many cases some artwork has also been included to serve as a vehicle for eliciting discussion as a preview of the chapter. This part of the lesson is also meant as a lead-in to the presentation of the particular grammatical structure that immediately follows. It is hoped that in some cases, this structure might be elicited during the preview activity. In several lessons students are asked to refer back to this section in order to complete an activity presented later in the lesson.

PRESENTATION

After the Preview is completed, the grammatical structure of the lesson is introduced through a specific context. Teachers may want to discuss the content of this material before asking students to answer the questions that follow.

Immediately following this presentation, students are asked to look at specific questions. These questions focus on the grammar of the lesson and ask students to analyze parts of the presentation. This section is meant as an inductive exercise for students to figure out (or state as review) the grammar of the lesson.

The teacher may want to stress to the class that these questions are meant to help them figure out grammar on their own. If the students get frustrated by some of the questions, they should be encouraged to discuss them with others in the class or simply do the best they can until the class discussion. Then when the exercise is discussed with the class as a whole, they will get more information. Furthermore, the Explanation section always follows these questions to be sure that students clearly see the main grammar point(s) of the lesson.

If the questions are too difficult for a particular group of students, the teacher may want to skip over them to the explanation that follows as it gives the information that will answer the questions.

EXPLANATION

This section provides rules, charts, and discussion of the grammatical focus of the lesson. This is the only section of the lesson that does not ask students to complete an exercise or activity. Explanations have been kept to a minimum wherever possible.

Teachers will notice that Chapters 2 through 4 provide information about forming negative sentences and questions. These explanations have been kept to a minimum in these chapters because there is a complete review of these kinds of sentences in Chapter 5. In addition, most of the exercises and activities in Chapters 2 through 4 do not ask students to specifically use questions or negative sentences. Teachers who feel their students need more practice with these, should feel free to adapt the activities in these chapters to include this practice.

PRACTICE

Each lesson presents a wide variety of activities and exercises ranging from more controlled to more open and creative. The activities follow the focus or topic that was presented in the Preview and Presentation sections.

MORE CONTROLLED EXERCISES

The first few activities of each lesson are more controlled and may be more traditional in that they are often fill in the blanks or choosing the correct form. Sometimes students are asked to find errors or create sentences with given words or phrases as well. Usually these activities focus on review of a particular form or provide basic practice of the grammatical focus of the lesson.

LISTENING ACTIVITIES

Many lessons also have listening activities. There is no tape that accompanies this book; listening scripts are provided in the appendix. Some teachers may want to use these scripts for listening practice only. Others may want to refer students to the appendix after completing a particular activity.

These activities often focus on more informal forms that are found in the spoken language such as contractions and reduced forms. Sometimes these activities ask students to listen for specific forms, while others may serve as short dictation exercises.

MORE OPEN-ENDED ACTIVITIES

Each lesson also has some activities that ask students to be more creative and independent. In these activities, the students must use the particular grammatical structure from the lesson as much as possible. In this way, students are asked to apply what they learned by using the new grammatical item in a particular situation.

Some of these activities may be somewhat challenging for students. Teachers may want to review parts of the lesson, provide examples, or take students step-by-step through some of these exercises.

SELF-ASSESSMENT CHECKLISTS

At the end of each lesson students are asked to do some self-assessment by going over their own work. After the last one or two activities, students are given a short checklist that highlights the main features of the lesson. They then check their responses to the activity for the specific forms and usage included on the checklist.

Acknowledgments

First, I would like to thank Dr. Suzette Elgin, my mentor from graduate school days, for providing me with many important lessons and insights about teaching and curriculum development that I have kept with me over the years.

I am extremely grateful to friends and family for their understanding and support while I spent harried days and nights working on this book. As always, I thank my boys, Jack, Seth, and Scot, for not only having confidence in me but always making me proud of my wonderful family. I especially want to thank my friend Jean Riley for her unfailing friendship and never-ending ability to listen and provide help, even with the details of a grammar text. In addition, I thank Anne Ediger, my friend and colleague, for taking time out of her own busy schedule to help me work out some important last-minute details.

I also want to thank the many wonderful colleagues and students I have worked with over the years in the areas of ESL, developmental writing, and teacher training. They have always supported my efforts to make the study of grammar more meaningful and accessible and shown genuine enthusiasm for my materials. I especially want to thank my colleagues at the ALI at San Diego State University for their willingness to listen and provide suggestions during the production of this text.

Many thanks go to people at Heinle & Heinle. In particular, I thank Dave Lee for bringing me into this project, and Ken Mattsson and Pat Byrd for all their help and enthusiasm along the way. I would also like to thank reviewers on the Tapestry team, especially Melissa Derr, Melanie Schneider and Alice Deakins for their help and advice at the beginning stages of this project. In addition, my thanks go to Erik Gundersen, Maryellen Eschmann Killeen, and Elaine Hall for their help and guidance during the production of this text.

Finally, I thank the following reviewers for their helpful comments and suggestions during the development of this text:

Lucia Adrian, EF International;

Kristina Grey, Northern Virginia Community College;

Arron Grow, Mississippi State University;

Philip Less, University of Arkansas at Little Rock;

Valerie Pierce, Indiana University; and

Helen Solorzano, Northern University.

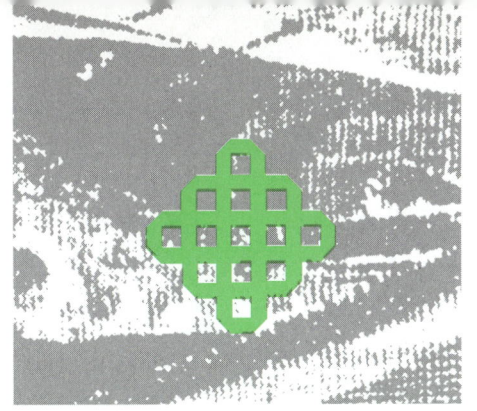

CONTENTS

1 Sentence Patterns — 1

LESSON 1: INTERVIEWS—IDENTIFYING AND DESCRIBING PEOPLE — 2
Focus: subjects and predicates — 2

LESSON 2: HOBBIES AND INTERESTS—DESCRIBING FREE-TIME ACTIVITIES — 7
Focus: subject-verb-object pattern — 7

2 Simple Verbs — 13

LESSON 3: INSTRUCTIONS AND DIRECTIONS—USING COMMANDS/IMPERATIVES — 14
Focus: base form of the verb — 14

LESSON 4: PEOPLE AND EVENTS BEFORE OUR TIME—TALKING ABOUT THE PAST — 20
Focus: simple past (base + -ed) — 20

LESSON 5: DISCUSSING CUSTOMS/HABITS AND FACTS—USING GENERAL TIME — 25
Focus: simple present (base/base + -s) — 25

3 Expanded Verbs — 33

LESSON 6: WHAT'S HAPPENING NOW?—DISCUSSING THE PRESENT — 34
Focus: present progressive (continuous) (be + base + -ing) — 34

LESSON 7: WHAT'S IN YOUR FUTURE?—MAKING PREDICTIONS — 40
Focus: will + base/be going to + base — 40

LESSON 8: WHAT'S ON THE PROGRAM?—PLANNING AND SCHEDULING — 44
Focus: be + base + -ing/be going to + base/ base + -s — 44

LESSON 9: ONGOING EVENTS IN THE PAST—DESCRIBING PAST CONTINUOUS EVENTS — 49
Focus: past progressive (continuous) [be (past) + base + -ing] — 49

LESSON 10: ACCOMPLISHMENTS—DESCRIBING EXPERIENCES—UNSPECIFIED TIME — 55
Focus: present perfect (have/has + past participle) — 55

LESSON 11: MORE ACCOMPLISHMENTS—EXPERIENCES—PAST RELATED TO PRESENT — 62
Focus: present perfect (have/has + past participle) — 62

LESSON 12: ACCOMPLISHMENTS—DESCRIBING EXPERIENCES FROM PAST TO PRESENT—PART ONE — 69
Focus: present perfect (have/has + past participle with for/since) — 69

LESSON 13: THE ENVIRONMENT—DESCRIBING EXPERIENCES FROM PAST TO PRESENT—PART TWO — 74
Focus: present perfect progressive (continuous) (has/have + been + base +-ing) — 74

4 Modals and Semi-modals — 81

LESSON 14: EVERYDAY ACTIVITIES—DISCUSSING POSSIBILITIES — 82
Focus: might/may/could — 82

LESSON 15: SKILLS/TALENTS/CAPABILITIES—DISCUSSING ABILITIES — 88
Focus: can/could/be able to — 88

LESSON 16: TRAVEL IDEAS—GIVING SUGGESTIONS/RECOMMENDATIONS/ADVICE — 95
Focus: should/ought to/had better/could/might — 95

LESSON 17: WHAT'S NECESSARY?—DISCUSSING OBLIGATIONS AND REQUIREMENTS — 102
Focus: must/have to/have got to — 102

LESSON 18: DRAWING CONCLUSIONS—MAKING INFERENCES AND ASSUMPTIONS — 109
Focus: must — 109

LESSON 19: GETTING HELP AND PERMISSION—MAKING REQUESTS — 115
Focus: would/could/will/can/may — 115

5 Negatives/Question Formation — 121

LESSON 20: EATING HABITS/HEALTHY EATING—MAKING NEGATIVE STATEMENTS — 122
Focus: be/have/do/modal + not — 122

LESSON 21: QUESTIONNAIRES/APPLICATIONS—ASKING AND ANSWERING QUESTIONS—PART ONE — 130
Focus: yes/no questions — 130

LESSON 22: NATIVE AMERICANS—ASKING AND ANSWERING QUESTIONS—PART TWO — 137
Focus: wh- questions — 137

6 Noun Phrases — 147

LESSON 23: TAKING INVENTORY—DISCUSSING QUANTITY — 148
Focus: nouns—singular/plural/countable/uncountable — 148

LESSON 24: SHOPPING AT THE MALL—INDICATING SPECIFIC AND NON-SPECIFIC NOUNS — 157
Focus: articles—the/a/an/zero article — 157

LESSON 25: MUSIC AND DANCE—MAKING REFERENCES — 164
Focus: pronouns—subject/object/reflexive — 164

LESSON 26: ADVERTISING AND CONSUMERS—SHOWING OWNERSHIP/POSSESSION—PART ONE — 170
Focus: possessive nouns — 170

LESSON 27: FAMILY TIES/ GENEALOGY—SHOWING OWNERSHIP/POSSESSION—PART TWO 175
   Focus: possessive pronouns 175

LESSON 28: SETTING RECORDS— DESCRIBING AND COMPARING 181
   Focus: adjectives—comparatives/ superlatives 181

7 Prepositions

LESSON 29: SCHEDULES— EXPRESSING TIME RELATIONSHIPS 192
   Focus: prepositions of location—time 192

LESSON 30: GOING PLACES— EXPRESSING SPATIAL RELATIONSHIPS 198
   Focus: prepositions of location—place 198

LESSON 31: WEDDINGS—OTHER NOUN/VERB RELATIONSHIPS 208
   Focus: prepositions—for/with/by/of 208

LESSON 32: SPECIAL DAYS AND GIFTS—REVIEW AND CHANGING WORD ORDER 213
   Focus: preposition review and deleting— for/to (indirect objects) 213

Sentence Patterns

CHAPTER 1

LESSON 1: INTERVIEWS—IDENTIFYING AND DESCRIBING PEOPLE

Focus: subjects and predicates

Preview

Ask your teacher the following questions and listen carefully to the answers. Write the answers below the questions.

1. What is your nationality?

   _____

2. What do you usually do after school in your free time?

   _____

3. How can you describe yourself in one or two words? (What do you look like? What kind of person are you?)

   _____

Now answer the same questions about yourself.

1. What is your nationality?

   _____

2. What do you usually do after school in your free time?

   _____

3. How can you describe yourself in a few words? (What do you look like? What kind of person are you?)

   _____
   _____

Presentation

Today is the first day of class for Noriko Otani and Rica Ajuilar. They have just met and are getting to know each other. Below you will find some of the things Rica learned about Noriko. Read the paragraph and follow the directions about the chart. Then answer the questions after the chart.

(1) Noriko Otani is my new friend. (2) She is from Kanagawa-ken, Japan. (3) Her native language is Japanese. (4) She likes English, but she also wants to learn the German language. (5) She is a Systems Engineer in a computer company in Japan. (6) When she returns to Japan, she wants to work for a new company. (7) Noriko is single. (8) She has only one brother. (9) She plays golf very well. (10) She traveled to Hawaii and Singapore last year.

Look at the chart. It divides the information in several sentences from the paragraph into two pieces.

1. One column shows who or what the sentence is talking about.
2. The other column lists the information about that person or thing.

SENTENCE #	WHO OR WHAT	INFORMATION GIVEN
1	Noriko Otani	is my new friend
2	She	is from Kanagawa-ken, Japan
3	Her native language	is Japanese
5	She	is a Systems Engineer
7	Noriko	is single
9	She	has only one brother
10	She	traveled to Hawaii and Singapore

QUESTIONS

1. Look at the two columns in the chart (*who or what* and *information given*). Do you think each group is necessary for a good English sentence? Can you have a good sentence without one of these pieces?
2. Look carefully at the verbs in the chart above. What verb do you find more than once? What kind(s) of information do you find in the sentences with this verb?
3. What kinds of information did you find in your teacher's answers and in your own answers in the Preview? What verbs are in these sentences?

Explanation

1. Every English sentence must have a **subject** and a **predicate.**
2. A subject is the person or thing that the speaker (or writer) is talking about. A subject can be just one word or it can be more than one word.

    Noriko Otani is my new friend.
    She is from Kanagawa-ken, Japan.
    Her native language is Japanese.

3. A predicate is information about the subject. A predicate must always have a verb. [For more information about verbs see Chapter 2 (Lessons 3-5) and Chapter 3 (Lessons 6-13).]
4. There are different predicate patterns in English. Two common predicate patterns are:
    a. verb + object

    She **plays golf** very well.
      verb   object

    NOTE A sentence *may* include just a subject and a verb, but this is unusual. Very often other words (such as an object) follow the verb. For more information about objects see Lesson 2.

LESSON 1: INTERVIEWS—
IDENTIFYING AND
DESCRIBING PEOPLE

b. verb + complement

In the following examples the information after the verb is called a complement. The complement gives more information about the subject. There are three common complements in English as follows:

She is **from Kanagawa-ken, Japan.** [This complement is a prepositional phrase. For more information about prepositions, see Chapter 7 (Lessons 29-32).]
This information tells you where the subject is from.

Noriko is **single.** [This complement is an adjective. For more information about adjectives, see Chapter 6 (Lesson 28).]
This information describes the subject.

She is **a Systems Engineer.** [This complement is a noun phrase. For more information about noun phrases, see Chapter 6 (Lessons 23-28).]
This information tells you who the subject is/what she does.
It is a kind of identification.

5. **IMPORTANT:** When your sentence contains a complement, you will need a linking verb. **BE** (is/am/are/was/were) is the most common linking verb.
   Other examples of linking verbs are:

become	go	look	sound
feel	grow	seem	stay
get	keep	smell	taste

Do not forget to include a linking verb when you have a complement in the sentence.

She	**is**	from Kanagawa-ken, Japan.
Noriko	**is**	single.
She	**is**	a Systems Engineer.

6. Speakers often use short forms with the subject and the linking verb *be*. These short forms are called **contractions** and they are common in everyday speech. (In writing, these forms include an apostrophe to show that a letter was removed.)

   She's single.
   You're a Systems Engineer.
   I'm from New York City.

Practice

ACTIVITY ONE

Below you will find some information about Rica. Find the subject and predicate of four of these sentences. Complete the chart below with the information you find in this paragraph.

(1) My friend's name is Rica Ajuilar. (2) She is from Ciudad Juarez Chihuahug in Mexico. (3) Her native language is Spanish and she is studying English now. (4) Rica also wants to study Japanese. (5) Her job is a lawyer. (6) She is single, but next April she will get married. (7) She has one younger brother and one younger sister. (8) Her interests are swimming and scuba diving. (9) She likes the beach.

SENTENCE #	WHO OR WHAT (SUBJECT)	INFORMATION GIVEN (PREDICATE)
_____	_____	_____
_____	_____	_____
_____	_____	_____
_____	_____	_____

LEARNING STRATEGY

Managing Your Learning: Identifying problems in grammar can help you overcome making these mistakes yourself.

ACTIVITY TWO

Below you will find another student's paragraph about a new friend in his class. Some of the sentences in this paragraph are not correct. Find the problems in these sentences and correct them. Look for these kinds of problems:

1. a sentence with no subject
2. a problem with the predicate
3. a sentence with no verb

(You may find these problems in more than one sentence.)

My classmate's name is Frank. He 26 years old. He is from Germany. His native language is. He is studying English for his job in Germany. He an accountant in his country. Can also speak French. His hobby is. He also likes to play soccer. He New York and Miami before he came here.

ACTIVITY THREE

Listen carefully as your teacher reads some sentences to you. She or he will read each sentence two times.

- Some of them will follow the verb + complement pattern and will include a contraction. When you hear a contraction and a complement, write these in the space provided below.
- If you do not hear a contraction and a complement in the sentence, leave the space blank.

1. _____
2. _____
3. _____
4. _____
5. _____
6. _____
7. _____
8. _____

Share your answers with a partner. If necessary, ask your teacher to repeat the sentences.

ACTIVITY FOUR

WHO AM I? WHAT IS IT?

Work in a group of three people for this activity.

- Choose one person in your classroom. Describe this person in a few short sentences (three to five sentences). Do not tell the name of the person.
- Choose one thing in your classroom and describe it in a few short sentences (three to five sentences). Do not tell the name.
- Tell one of your descriptions to the other people in the class. They must guess the person or object you are describing.

EXAMPLE This object is in my kitchen.
It is very cold on the inside.
Sometimes it is very large but sometimes it can be small.
People keep food in it.
(ANSWER: a refrigerator)

ACTIVITY FIVE

Your teacher will give you a partner and you will interview each other. You will learn about each other by asking questions. Below are some questions you can ask. Then make notes about your partner's answers.

Interview Questions*

1. Where are you from? What is your native language?
2. Are you a student? (If the answer is yes, what do you study?)
3. Do you work? (If the answer is yes, what kind of work do you do?)
4. Why are you studying English? Have you studied it before?
5. What will you do after you finish your English studies?
6. What do you like to do in your free time? Do you have any hobbies or favorite sports?
7. Can you describe your personality a little? (What kind of person are you?)

---

*You may want to learn other information about your partner. These are not the only questions possible for this activity. You may ask other questions as well.

LEARNING STRATEGY

Remembering New Material: Learning how to take good notes helps you remember what was said.

After the interview, you and your partner:

- will introduce each other to the class. Tell the class what you learned about each other during the interview.
- will each write this information in a paragraph to give to your teacher. (You will write about your partner and your partner will write about you.)

After you write your paragraph, check your work for the following:

❏ Each sentence has a subject.
❏ Each sentence has a predicate.
❏ Each sentence has a verb.
❏ Each sentence with a complement has a linking verb.

LESSON 2: HOBBIES AND INTERESTS— DESCRIBING FREE-TIME ACTIVITIES

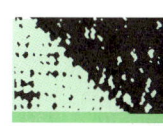

Focus: subject-verb-object pattern

Preview

Answer the following questions using complete sentences. Write your answers and then share them with the person sitting next to you. Be prepared to share your answers with the class. Write down some of the other students' answers as well.

1. What do you like to do in your free time? Do you have any hobbies? What are they?

   _____

2. What was the last book you read or movie you saw?

   _____

CHAPTER 1
SENTENCE PATTERNS

Presentation

Students in Mr. Levine's English class interviewed each other yesterday. They all talked about what they like to do in their free time. Below you will see their answers to some of the questions in the preview above. Read these answers.

Rica: I like the beach very much. I practice swimming and scuba diving.
Noriko: I play golf. I also use my computer a lot.
Hsueh-hua: My hobby is Chinese painting. I paint pictures whenever I have the time.
Yusei: I have several pets and I like to take care of them.
Cho-Jung: I like music and I play the violin and the piano.
Mubarak: I travel often. I've visited England, France, and parts of Asia.

A. Answer the following questions about the students' information above. Then complete the chart by writing your answers in the second column (after the subject and verb on the chart). The first one has been done for you as an example.

1. What does Rica like? What does she practice?
   (Answer: the beach) (Answer: swimming/scuba diving)
2. What does Noriko play? What does she use?
3. What does Hsueh-hua paint?
4. What does Yusei have?
5. What does Cho-Jung like? What does she play?
6. What places has Mubarek visited?

SUBJECT AND VERB	YOUR ANSWER
1. Rica likes	*the beach*
She practices	*swimming and scuba diving*
2. Noriko plays	
She uses	
3. Hsueh-hua paints	
4. Yusei has	
5. Cho-Jung likes	
She plays	
6. Mubarek has visited	

B. Look at the answers you wrote in the second column. What kinds of words did you write?

What predicate pattern from Lesson 1 do the sentences in the chart follow?

Explanation

1. In Lesson 1 you learned about two common predicate patterns in English:
   - linking verb + complement
   - verb + object

      In this lesson you will learn more about the verb + object pattern.

2. As you saw in Lesson 1, a sentence *may* include just a subject and a verb, but this is unusual. (For example: What kind of work do you do? **I teach.**)

   More often, you will find the pattern: subject + verb + object.

Rica	likes	the beach.
subject	verb	object

Yusei	has	several pets.
subject	verb	object

Cho-Jung	plays	the violin.
subject	verb	object

3. Although the subject + verb + object pattern is common, you will not always find an object after a verb. Some verbs need an object and other verbs do not. Some verbs can even be used with or without an object.

   NOTE If you are not sure about this, you can find the verb in a dictionary. Sometimes you will see the letter **t** or the letters **vt** next to a verb in the dictionary. This means that verb needs an object (verb transitive). Other times you will see the letter **i** or the letters **vi** next to a verb in the dictionary. This means that verb does not need an object (verb intransitive).

4. Of course, sometimes you will find other words after the object as well. [For more information about words that often follow an object see Chapter 7.]

   I paint pictures whenever I have the time.
      object

   Cho-Jung plays the violin at school.
      object

   Remember that other words do not usually go between the verb and the object.

   > I **like the beach very much.**
   > (NOT: I like very much the beach.)

   > I also **use my computer a lot.**
   > (NOT: I also use a lot my computer.)

   > I **enjoy the pizza** at that restaurant.
   > (NOT: I enjoy at that restaurant the pizza.)

LESSON 2: HOBBIES AND INTERESTS—DESCRIBING FREE-TIME ACTIVITIES

Practice

ACTIVITY ONE

The following paragraph is about stamp collecting. Almost all of the sentences follow the subject-verb-object pattern. One sentence does not follow this pattern.

- Find the sentences that have verbs and objects. Circle these words (verbs and objects).
- Find the sentence that does not have an object. Put a line under this sentence.

Many people collect stamps. In fact, stamp collecting is one of the most popular hobbies in the world. A beginner can start a collection with little money. This hobby requires some special equipment. A collector needs an album for his stamps. She or he also needs something to attach the stamps to the pages. In addition, many collectors have a pair of tongs. With the tongs, they don't touch (or damage) the stamps.

ACTIVITY TWO

Read the short paragraph below. Some of the sentences are correct and some of them are not correct. Which sentences have a problem? Find each problem. Then show how to change the sentence to make it correct. The problem can be about anything you learned about sentence patterns in Lessons 1 and 2.

EXAMPLES Cho-Jung likes music. He plays (at school) the violin.

IT WORKS!
Learning Strategy:
Identifying
Problems in
Grammar

My friend's name is Martin. He was born on May 9 and he 26 years old now. His native language is German, but he speaks often French. He a banker, so he needs to study for his job English. He has in his family one sister. He plays many sports in his country. Now he is studying in the United States, so he doesn't have here much time to play sports. Sometimes he plays soccer on Saturdays.

ACTIVITY THREE

Work in small groups for this exercise. Each student in the group should look back at his or her answers from the Preview section at the beginning of this lesson. Answer these questions:

1. Which sentences follow the subject + verb + object pattern?
2. What verbs did you find in the sentences with the objects? Make a list of these verbs.

Now each student should share his or her list of verbs with the others in the group.

LEARNING STRATEGY

Overcoming Limitations: Using a dictionary helps you fill in the gaps in your knowledge about the language.

ACTIVITY FOUR

Below you will find several common verbs in English. With a partner do the following:

1. Decide whether each of these verbs needs an object (a transitive verb) or does not need an object (an intransitive verb). Circle the transitive verbs.
    (If you are not sure about some of the verbs, you may want to use a dictionary to help you.)
2. Write a sentence for each transitive verb you find. (If the verb is intransitive, do not write a sentence.)

| find | own | run | eat | travel | touch | take |
| swim | learn | begin | walk | cook | sleep | use |

LEARNING STRATEGY

Remembering New Material: Making up your own sentences helps you remember basic sentence patterns.

ACTIVITY FIVE

1. Look at the photographs below.
   - Write one or two sentences for each picture. Your sentence(s) should describe the picture or talk about what the person is doing in the picture. You may also want to talk about what these people do in their free time.
   - Use some of the verbs from the list below in your sentences. You may also use other transitive verbs.

     buy   watch   see   play   like   enjoy   read   practice   study

   - You should use the subject + verb + object pattern for each sentence you write.

Check your work for the following:

❏ All of your sentences have a subject and a predicate.

❏ All of your sentences have a verb.

❏ Your sentences include the subject + verb + object pattern.

❏ You do not have other words in between the verb and the object of a sentence.

After you check your work, share your answers with the class.

2. Look back at the photographs in the Preview part of this lesson. Think about the scene and the people you see in each picture. Choose one of these pictures and write a paragraph about it as follows:

- Write a story about (or description of) this scene and the person (or people) in it. Be sure to include at least one or two sentences that follow the subject + verb + object pattern in your paragraph.

OR

- Write a story about (or a description of) your own experience in one of these places or doing one of these activities. Be sure to include at least one or two sentences that follow the subject + verb + object pattern in your paragraph.

Check your work for the following:

❏ All of your sentences have a subject and a predicate.

❏ All of your sentences have a verb.

❏ Some of your sentences include the subject + verb + object pattern.

❏ You do not have other words in between the verb and the object of a sentence.

Simple Verbs

CHAPTER 2

LESSON 3: INSTRUCTIONS AND DIRECTIONS— USING COMMANDS/IMPERATIVES

Focus: base form of the verb

Preview

Is there something that you know how to do very well? For example, can you cook something or can you make something? Think of something that is easy to do and you can explain easily to other people. Explain how to do this to one of your classmates.

Presentation

Read the following recipe for making a seven-layer dip.

INGREDIENTS:
one large can of bean dip	1/2 package of taco mix seasoning
2 or 3 medium avocados	1 1/2-2 cups of cheddar cheese
1-2 teaspoons of lemon juice	1 small can of chopped black olives
1/2 cup of mayonnaise	2 tomatoes
1/2 cup of sour cream	one bunch of green onions (scallions)

Use a 9 inch by 13 inch pan. Make each layer as follows:

distribute/put all over

Layer 1 *Spread* the can of bean dip on the bottom of the pan.

crush/press into a mass

Layer 2 *Mash* the avocados with the lemon juice. Put the avocado layer on top of the bean layer in the pan.

Layer 3 Mix the mayonnaise, the sour cream and the taco mix seasoning together. Spread this mixture on top of the avocado layer.

make into small pieces by rubbing against a rough surface

Layer 4 *Grate* the cheddar cheese. Put the cheese on top of layer 3.

remove the water/liquid

Layer 5 *Drain* the olives in the can. Spread the olives on top of the cheese.

cut into small pieces

Layer 6 *Chop* the tomatoes and put them on top of the layer of olives.

Layer 7 Chop the green onions (including the tops) and put them on top of the last layer.

Chill the dip. Serve with chips or vegetables.

QUESTIONS

1. Find as many verbs as you can in the recipe above. Write them below. Do you notice anything about these verbs?

   _____

   _____

2. Now look at the sentences where you found these words. Do these sentences follow all of the sentence pattern rules talked about in Lessons 1 and 2? Why or why not?

3. What is the subject in each of the sentences in this recipe?

Explanation

1. In Lesson 1 you learned that every sentence must have a subject (*who* or *what* you are talking about) and a predicate (*information about the subject*).

   In the recipe above, you probably noticed that these sentences do not have subjects. That is because these verbs are IMPERATIVES (COMMANDS) and the subject is an **understood you.** This means that the reader or listener knows the subject is **you,** so we do not need to include it in the sentence.

2. An imperative verb uses the base form of the verb only. (Some people call this the "simple form" of the verb.) This form is called a **simple verb** because it is only one word.

   Make each layer as follows.
   (simple verb)
   Spread the can of bean dip on the bottom of the pan.
   Mash the avocados with the lemon juice.

3. We often use the imperative form of the verb when we give instructions on how to make or do something.

   Read the following recipe for making a seven-layer dip.
   Chill the dip. **Serve** with chips or vegetables.

4. We also use these forms as commands. Often we use these commands in more serious situations when we want to be very direct.

   Sit quietly in your chair!
   Watch the cars! **Be** careful when you cross that busy street!

5. When you want to use imperative forms as commands, you should be careful. In some situations you may want to be more polite and not so direct. In these cases, to be more polite, other words (such as "please") are necessary.

   Please sit down in your chair now.

   We will talk more about making polite requests later when we talk about modal auxiliaries. (See Lesson 19.)

6. To make a negative imperative or command, add the auxiliary **do** and the word **not** before the verb. [For more information and practice with negative sentences, see Lesson 20.]

   Follow this pattern: Do + not + verb (base form)

   Do not serve the dip warm.
   Do not cross that street in the middle of the block.

   Native speakers often use contractions with the *do* and the *not*.

   Don't serve the dip warm.
   Don't cross that street in the middle of the block.

LESSON 3: INSTRUCTIONS AND DIRECTIONS—USING COMMANDS/IMPERATIVES

CHAPTER 2
SIMPLE VERBS

Practice

ACTIVITY ONE

A. Look at the instructions for the Preview section of this lesson. Find as many imperative verb forms as you can. List them below.

_____

Look at the three questions that follow the recipe in the Presentation part of this lesson. Find the imperative verb forms there as well. Write all of these forms in the space below.

_____

B. Now your teacher is going to read some instructions for some everyday things many people do. Listen to the instructions and write down any imperative verb forms you hear for each one. Then say what you think these instructions are for. (Answers are at the end of the lesson.)

1. _____
2. _____
3. _____
4. _____

ACTIVITY TWO

Below you will find two paragraphs of instructions about how to grow greens from bean seeds. Above each paragraph you will find a list of verbs. Fill in the blank spaces of each paragraph with the verbs from the list above it. Write the verb you think best fits in each space, using the imperative form each time.

GROW SOME GREENS

You will need: alfalfa or mung bean seeds
a quart glass jar with a large opening
an old nylon stocking
a rubber band

PART A

VERBS: hold   cover   put   let   fill

_____ two tablespoons of seeds in a quart jar. _____ the jar half full of *lukewarm* water. _____ it with *fabric* from the stocking. _____ the stocking in place with the rubber band. _____ the seeds *soak* for 24 hours.

not too hot/not cold
cloth/material

keep in water for a long time

PART B

VERBS: continue   lay   cover   rinse   pour   fill   drain   replace

_____ the water out of the jar. _____ the seeds four times with cool water. _____ them completely (so that there is no water left). _____ the nylon. _____ the jar on its side. _____ it with a cloth. (Don't cover the open end. Air that enters through the nylon helps your seeds sprout.) _____ to *rinse* and drain the seeds at least once a day for three or four days.

rewash in clean water

LEARNING STRATEGY

Forming Concepts: Knowing the purpose of a grammatical construction helps you understand when to use it.

ACTIVITY THREE

A. In small groups, look at each picture below and decide what message or instruction each person is giving. Write the message on the line below each picture. Use an imperative verb form in each of your answers.

1

Picture 1: (the man's message/instruction)

_____

2

Picture 2: (the librarian's message/instruction)

_____

3

Picture 3: (the doctor's message/instruction)

_____

B. With the same group, look at the following pictures and answer the questions under each picture. Your answers should be complete sentences and you should use the imperative form of the verb in each answer. Try to use as many different verbs in your answers as possible.

1

1. What do you think the passenger is saying to the driver of the car?
2. What do you think the girl is saying to the little boy?

2

1. What do you think the lady is saying to the thief?
2. What do you think the thief is saying to the lady?
3. What do you think the people across the street are saying?

3

1. What do you think the man at the stove is saying?
2. What do you think the other person is saying?

4

What do you think the woman at the front of the bus is saying to some of the children? (You should have at least two answers.)

ACTIVITY FOUR

Work in small groups for this activity. Each person in the group is going to give instructions to the others by choosing <u>one</u> of the following situations. (Each person in the group should choose a different situation.)

- First, write down the instructions for your situation. Be sure to use imperatives.
- Then give your instructions to the other people in your group.

A. Someone from your country needs to get a passport and a visa to go to another country to study for six months.

B. Someone wants to know how to find out about your school and how to register to take classes there.

C. Someone wants to know how to get a driver's license in the city where you are now living.

D. Someone wants to know how to mail a package to his or her country from the country in which you are now living.

LEARNING STRATEGY

Understanding and Using Emotions: Having a good time when you learn can increase your chances of learning a language well.

ACTIVITY FIVE

What's your favorite recipe? Think of something that you like to cook (or eat) and write a recipe for it. Be sure to use imperative verb forms in your recipe. Share this recipe with your class. If you have time, make this dish and bring it to school to share with your classmates.

NOTE If everyone wants to bring some food to share, you can have a "pot-luck" party.

Look back at your instructions in the last two activities (Activity Four and Activity Five). Check your instructions for the following:

❏ You have several steps in each of your instructions.
❏ All of your verbs are in the imperative form.

Answers to listening—Activity One B

1. using a public (coin) telephone
2. starting a computer
3. putting a CD in a player or disk drive
4. using a vending machine

LESSON 4: PEOPLE AND EVENTS BEFORE OUR TIME—TALKING ABOUT THE PAST

Focus: simple past (base + -ed)

Preview

1. Who were the first people to live in your native country? Do you know the name of these people? Where did they live? What do you know about how they lived?
2. Look at the photograph below. What do you know about this place? Do you know anything about the people who built these pyramids?

Presentation

The Aztecs lived in Mexico before the Europeans arrived there. Read the following paragraph about them. Then answer the questions that follow.

> The Aztec Indians believed that one of their gods had white skin and a beard. This god sailed away on a raft made of snakes but promised to return. In 1519 Montezuma II, king of the Aztec people, learned that white-skinned men with beards were near his land. Montezuma believed that this was the return of his god.

QUESTIONS

1. What are some of the verbs in this paragraph? Write them in the space below.
   _____
   _____

2. What is the same about many of these verbs? What do you find at the end of many of these verbs?
3. What is the time in this paragraph? What information can you learn about the time from the verbs? Are there any other words in this paragraph that tell you something about the time?

Read the following paragraph about the earlier groups of people of Mexico. Then answer the questions.

Some of the early Indians were the Olmec, the Zapotec, the Maya and the Toltec. Most of them were farmers. Their main crop was maize (corn). About the year A.D. 1200, the Tenocha people moved into the Valley of Mexico. After many battles with their neighbors, they settled on an island in the middle of Lake Texcoco—"The Lake of the Moon." From this island they built a powerful nation. The Spaniards came to this land and found these people. The Spaniards called these people the Aztecs.

QUESTIONS

1. What is the time in this paragraph? How do you know?
2. What are some of the verbs in this paragraph? Write them in the space below.

_____

_____

3. Do most of the words in your answer to #2 have the same endings? How do some of these verbs look different from many of the verbs you found in the first paragraph about the Aztecs?

Explanation

1. A verb + the **ed** ending (base + -ed) means past time. Verbs that have the **ed** ending for past time are called **regular** verbs.

    This form of the verb is often called "simple past" and is a simple verb form. (As you learned in Lesson 3, a simple verb has only one word.)

    This god **sailed** away on a raft made of snakes.
      simple verb
    The Spaniards **called** these people the Aztecs.

2. Sometimes you must make a spelling change in the verb when you add the **ed** ending.

    EXAMPLE A verb that ends in the letter **e** will only add the **d**.
    Montezuma **believed** that this was the return of his god.

    You will find a review of some of these changes at the back of this book on page 230.

3. Some verbs do not use the **ed** ending for past time. These verbs are called **irregular** verbs.

    Their main crop **was** maize (corn).
    From this island they **built** a powerful nation.
    The Spaniards **came** to this land and **found** these people.

    You must memorize these irregular forms. You will find a list of irregular verbs at the back of this book on page 228. This chart shows the verbs in groups according to the kind of change the verb makes.

    EXAMPLES buy   bought
              think thought
              fight fought
              teach taught
              catch caught

LESSON 4: PEOPLE AND EVENTS BEFORE OUR TIME—TALKING ABOUT THE PAST

LEARNING STRATEGY

Remembering New Material: Putting words into groups with similar endings helps you remember.

4. Other words in a sentence can also tell you past time. Some of these time words are:

   yesterday
   last week/last month/last year
   ago (three days ago/long ago)
   a specific year (1519) or another specific point in time

5. To make a negative sentence with these simple verbs, add the auxiliary **did** and the word **not** before the verb. Then use the base form of the verb. Do not add the -ed ending to the verb (or use the irregular past form) in this case. [For more information and practice with negative sentences, see Lesson 20.]
   Follow this pattern: did + not + verb (base form)

   They **did not build** a powerful nation.
   The Tenocha people **did not move** into the Valley of Mexico.

   Native speakers often use contractions with the *did* and the *not*.

   They **didn't build** a powerful nation.
   The Tenocha people **didn't move** into the Valley of Mexico.

6. To make a question with these simple verbs, you must add the auxiliary **did** before (to the left of) the subject. Use the base form of the verb. Do not add the -ed ending to the verb (or use the irregular past form) in this case. [For more information and practice with this kind of question, see Lesson 21.]
   Follow this pattern: did + subject + verb (base form)

   Did they build a powerful nation?
   Did the Tenocha people move into the Valley of Mexico?

Practice

ACTIVITY ONE

Complete the following paragraphs using the simple past form of the verbs given in parentheses.

A. The ancient Egyptians (build) _____ the pyramids of Egypt for a very serious reason. These people (believe) _____ strongly in life after death. The kings, called Pharaohs, (want) _____ their bodies

continue to exist   to *last* forever. They (tell) _____ their people to build the pyramids

defend/keep from danger or harm   to *protect* their bodies after death. Each pyramid (hold) _____ a

pharaoh's body. When the pharaoh (die) _____, the people

keep in good condition   (*preserve*) _____ his body. They (make) _____ his body

into a mummy. Then they (put) _____ the mummy in the pyramid.

LESSON 4: PEOPLE AND EVENTS BEFORE OUR TIME—TALKING ABOUT THE PAST

B. In about 1333 B.C. Tutankhamun (become) _____ Pharoah when he (be) _____ about nine years old. He (die) _____ ten years later. In 1922, after many years of *digging,* the *archaeologist* Howard Carter and his workmen (discover) _____ a *sealed* entrance to King Tut's tomb. In this tomb they (find) _____ many beautiful things and the king's mummy. Four *coffins* (protect) _____ this mummy. In order to make the third coffin, the Egyptians (use) _____ almost 2,500 pounds of gold!

break up or turn over the earth

scientist who studies human life and civilizations

tightly/completely closed

casket/box for burying a dead body

LEARNING STRATEGY

Forming Concepts: Guessing meanings from context improves your comprehension.

ACTIVITY TWO

A. You are going to hear some information about four women from the United States. Listen to the information and then write each past tense verb you hear.

1. Grandma Moses—Artist
   _____

2. Harriet Beecher Stowe—Writer
   _____

3. Sacagawea—Native American Woman/Explorer
   _____

4. Barbara Jordan—Politician/Educator
   _____

Compare answers with a partner. Ask your teacher to repeat the paragraphs if necessary.

B. Name a famous person from your country (man or woman). Why is this person famous? What did this person do to become famous? Write two to three sentences about this person and share this information with your class.

LEARNING STRATEGY

Personalizing: Telling personal information is a good way to improve your language ability.

ACTIVITY THREE

A. Write some sentences about your own past. Below each line you will find a past time word. Write a sentence about your past on each line, using the time word or expression given.

_____
(last week)

_____
(several years ago)

_____
(yesterday)

_____
(in 19___)
     year

B. Think about your country's more recent past (within the last 100 years). What important or famous things happened then? Use the time line below to mark down a few famous events. (An example is on the time line.)

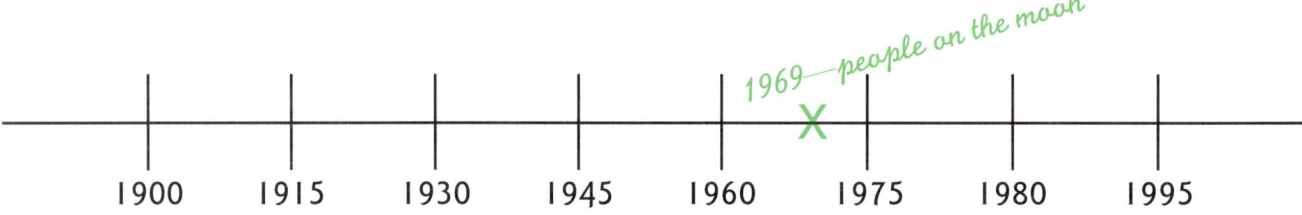

Write a few sentences describing these events. Use time words and expressions of the past in some of your sentences. Share your answers with the class.

ACTIVITY FOUR

Do this activity in small groups. Think of one famous event or person (from any country). Write a few sentences describing the event or the events in this person's life. Do not write the name of the person or the event. Read your description to the class. The class will try to guess the event or the name of the person you are describing.

EXAMPLE This event took place in July, 1969. It happened on the moon. Neil Armstrong did this.
    (Answer: The event was the first person walking on the moon.)
    OR
This person was the first human to walk on the moon. He was an astronaut on the Apollo 11 spacecraft. He made this famous walk in July, 1969.
    (Answer: This person was Neil Armstrong.)

ACTIVITY FIVE

A. Choose one of the following topics.
1. Do you have a favorite time in history? Is there a culture or group of people from the past that you think is very interesting? Describe what you know about life at that time. Discuss why you think that time or culture was interesting.
2. Think about one special or important day in your life. Why do you remember this particular day? Did something especially good or unusual happen on this day? Describe what happened.

B. Work in small groups for this part of the activity. Each student should tell the others in the group his or her answer to the question above.

C. Write two to four sentences describing what you learned from one of the other students in your group.

D. Write a paragraph about your answer to the question in A above. When you finish, check your work for the following:

❏ Each sentence has a verb.
❏ The regular simple past verb forms have *base + ed*.
❏ The irregular simple past forms are correct.
❏ You have some past time words in your paragraph.

LESSON 5: DISCUSSING CUSTOMS/HABITS AND FACTS—USING GENERAL TIME

Focus: simple present (base/base + -s)

Preview

Look at the cartoon. What is the message? (What does this cartoon say about these people and television?) Is television popular in your country? Do people spend much time watching television in your country? What are some typical customs and habits where you come from?

FRED BASSET *by ALEX GRAHAM*

CHAPTER 2
SIMPLE VERBS

Presentation

Read the following about life in some countries. Then answer the questions that follow.

large piece of ice floating in the sea
out of the country/overseas
plaster material used for building
an edible kind of water animal with ten arms/legs

1. Residents of Greenland usually see plenty of ice, even in August. One village chops *icebergs* into cubes and ships them *abroad* to chill drinks.
2. People see volcanoes from almost any place in El Salvador. There are also many earthquakes there. People often build low houses with large *stucco* walls there.
3. Each year fishermen in South Korea catch tons of *squid,* a favorite snack food. They hang the squid out to dry in the sun before they eat it.
4. On the western coast of Gotaland, the name for southern Sweden, a herring fisherman begins his workday at 2 A.M. Skilled workers build large ships at the port of Goteborg. A few workers go to jobs far underground.

QUESTIONS

1. Look at the information in #1 above. What do the people in one village in Greenland do? When do they do this? What time word tells you how often people in Greenland see ice?
2. Look at the information in #2 above. Can you find any time words in the third sentence?
3. Look at the information in #3 above. What do South Korean fishermen do? When do they do this? What time expression can you find in the first sentence?
4. Below you will find some of the verbs found in the information above. Find the subject of each of these verbs. Write it in the space next to the word. What ending can you find on some of these verbs? When do you use this ending?

SUBJECT | SUBJECT

1. chops _____   ships _____
2. see _____   build _____
3. catch _____   hang _____
4. begins _____   build _____

Explanation

1. Customs or habits are things people do regularly or as a routine. The time in a sentence about habits and customs may be **general** or **habitual** time.
2. When you want to talk about general or habitual time in English, often the verbs have no endings (base alone).

   Residents of Greenland usually **see** plenty of ice, even in August.
   Each year fishermen in South Korea **catch** tons of squid.

      If the subject is third person singular (he/she/it), you will find the **s** ending (base + -s).

   On the western coast of Gotaland, a herring fisherman **begins** his workday at 2 A.M.
   One village **chops** icebergs into cubes and **ships** them abroad to chill drinks.

   This form of the verb is a simple form. (See Lesson 3 for more information about a simple verb form.) The verb forms in these sentences are sometimes called "the present tense" or the "simple present."

LESSON 5: DISCUSSING CUSTOMS/HABITS AND FACTS—USING GENERAL TIME

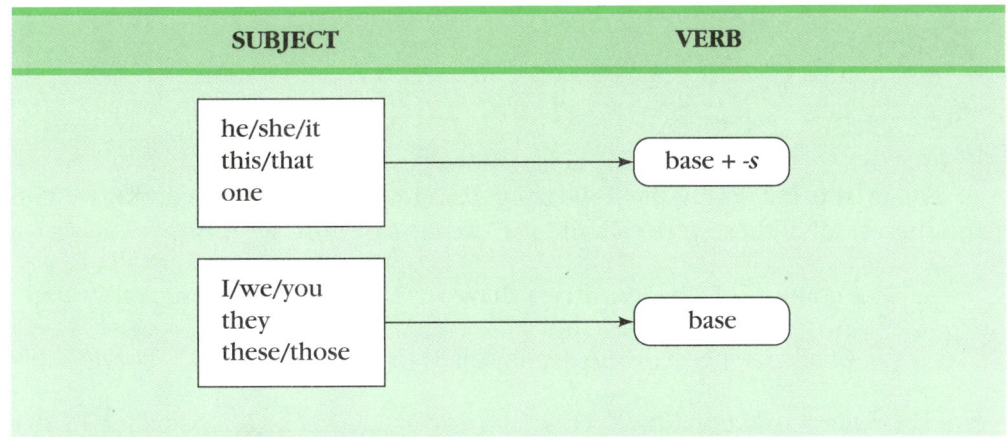

3. Sometimes you must make a spelling change when you add the **s** ending. You will find a review of some of these changes at the back of this book on page 230.

    A fisherman in South Korea **catches** many squid.
    A worker in Sweden **goes** to his job far underground.

4. We also use these forms (base or base + -s) to talk about scientific facts.

    Water **boils** at 100°C and **freezes** at 0°C.

5. There are several time words or expressions (called frequency words) that you may find in the sentence when the time is habitual or general. Some of these words and expressions are:

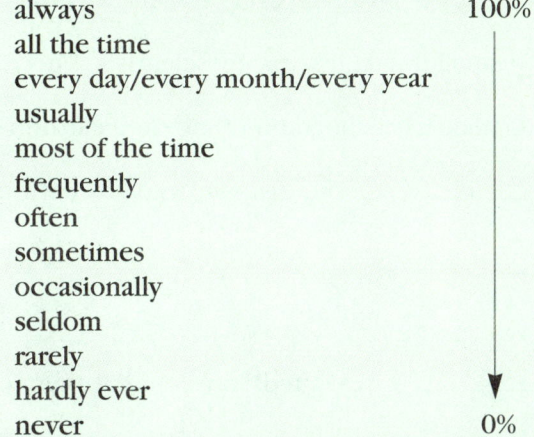

always — 100%
all the time
every day/every month/every year
usually
most of the time
frequently
often
sometimes
occasionally
seldom
rarely
hardly ever
never — 0%

6. To make a negative sentence with these simple verbs, add the auxiliary **do** or **does** and the word **not** before the verb. Then use the base form of the verb. Do not add the -s ending to the verb in this case. [For more information and practice with negative sentences, see Lesson 20.]

    Follow this pattern: do/does + not + verb (base form)

Residents of Greenland usually **do not see** ice in August.
A fisherman in South Korea **does not catch** many squid.
Native speakers often use contractions with the *do/does* and the *not*.
Residents of Greenland usually **don't see** ice in August.
A fisherman in South Korea **doesn't catch** many squid.

7. To make a question with these verb forms, you must add the auxiliary **do** or **does** before (to the left of) the subject. Use the base form of the verb. Do not add the -s ending to the verb in this case. [For more information and practice with this kind of question, see Lesson 21.]

    Follow this pattern: do/does + subject + verb (base form)

Do residents of Greenland see ice in August?
Does a fisherman catch many squid in Korea?

CHAPTER 2
SIMPLE VERBS

Practice

ACTIVITY ONE

Fill in the blanks in the following paragraphs using the verbs given in parentheses. All of these verbs should use the *base* or *base + s* form.

edge of land next to the sea

A. The country of Chad in Africa (have) _____ no *seacoast* at all. Yet some Chadians (people who live in Chad) (live) _____ comfortably on the water of Lake Chad. This lake (get) _____ smaller in dry weather and larger in wet weather. People (build) _____ villages on top of floating islands. These islands (come) _____ from reeds and water plants.

shake (usually with noise)
several different things/a number of

B. Earthquakes (happen) _____ in many parts of the world. In fact, they (*rattle*) _____ Earth's surface every day from a *variety* of causes. Most earthquakes are too small to feel, except by scientists. They (use) _____ an instrument called a seismograph to measure earthquakes. This instrument (indicate) _____ the distance and strength of an earthquake.

earth/world

fast turning motion

turn quickly around and around

slant/be not quite upright

C. Our Earth (be) _____ a seasoned traveler. Autumn (cool) _____ into winter and spring (warm) _____ up to summer as we (travel) _____ with the *globe* on its year-long trip around of the sun. This (happen) _____ because the *whirling* Earth doesn't stand up straight. The Earth *(spin)* _____ around the sun and *(lean)* _____ at an angle of 23½ degrees. Without that tilt, we would have no seasons.

ACTIVITY TWO

Next to each number below you will find words about things that some people often or sometimes do and some that people never do. Write two sentences about these activities as follows:

1. Make a sentence about your personal habits. Use the words given and one of the frequency words or expressions listed below.
2. Make another sentence about somebody you know (someone in your family or a friend) and his or her habits, using the same words given. Try to use as many different frequency words and expressions as possible.

EXAMPLE   brush teeth in the morning

a. *Every day I brush my teeth in the morning.*

b. *My brother never brushes his teeth in the morning.*

| always | every day/every morning/every week | usually | frequently |
| seldom | sometimes | rarely | often | hardly ever | never |

1. read a newspaper

    a. _____

    b. _____

2. take a bus or subway to work or school

    a. _____

    b. _____

3. go to the movies on the weekend

    a. _____

    b. _____

4. watch television at night

    a. _____

    b. _____

5. drink coffee with breakfast

    a. _____

    b. _____

LEARNING STRATEGY

Managing Your Learning: Cooperating and discussing things with others is one of the best ways to learn.

ACTIVITY THREE

Work with a partner to choose the correct form of the verb in parentheses. Think carefully about the time in each sentence. Some of the answers will be in past time and other answers will be in general/habitual time. Circle the correct word.

IT WORKS!
Learning Strategy:
Guessing Meaning
from Context

MOUNTAINS

The restless Earth (build / built / builds) mountains in several ways. The Himalayas and the Appalachians (were / are / is) typical of "folded" mountains. This type of mountain (form / formed / forms) when one landmass (moved / moves / move) and (meets / met / meet) another area of land. Millions of years ago India (is / were / was) on a separate piece of land. Then, that land (moves / moved / move) closer to Asia. When this land (hit / hits) Asia, it (pushes / push / pushed) up the land and (makes / made / make) "wrinkles." These wrinkles (is / are / were) the highest mountains on earth (the Himalayas).

The Rocky Mountains in the United States (is / are / were) another type of mountain, called "block" mountains. In order to make "block" mountains, big pieces of the earth's crust (break / breaks / broke) loose and then (tilt / tilts / tilted). That's how some of the Rocky Mountains (form / forms / formed). These mountains (rise / rose / rises) above the land around them.

BOLIVIA

It (was / were / is) hard to start a fire in La Paz, Bolivia. At 11,900 feet (3, 627m), this city (is / was / are) the highest capital in the world. The thin air (provide / provides / provided) less oxygen than at sea level, and fires (needs / needed / need) oxygen. Also because of the altitude, planes at La Paz's airport (need / needed / needs) more time to get in the air, so the runways (are / is / were) extra long. The people of the altiplano, the area around La Paz, (have / had / has) larger-than-normal hearts and lungs to help them breathe.

About 70 percent of the population of Bolivia (live / lives / lived) on the altiplano. These people (were / is / are) mostly Quechua and Aymara Indians and mestizos. Spaniards (come / came / comes) to this area in 1538. They (finds / found / find) Indians when they (arrived / arrives / arrive). Some of these Indians (was / were / are) farmers and (grew / grow / grows) the white or "Irish" potato, a plant native to the Americas. Some of the first Europeans (marries / marry / married) the native Indians; the mestizos (are / was / is) their descendants.

ACTIVITY FOUR

Look at the following list of natural disasters. Do you know what all of them are? Do any of them happen where you come from? How often do they happen? Can you remember a recent or famous example of any of them in your native area?

tornado	avalanche
hurricane	flood
earthquake	blizzard
drought/famine	typhoon
volcano	wildfire

Choose two of the disasters from the list and write two sentences about each one.
- Your first sentence should be about how often that disaster happens in your native area. Include a frequency word or expression in this sentence.
- Your second sentence should be about a specific disaster in the past.
  (Be sure to use the correct form of the verb in each of your sentences.)

EXAMPLES

a. *Hurricanes sometimes hit Florida.*

OR

Sometimes Florida has hurricanes.

b. *In 1992, Hurricane Andrew caused much destruction there.*

1. a. _____

   b. _____

2. a. _____

   b. _____

Share your answers with the class.

LEARNING STRATEGY

Understanding and Using Emotions: Becoming aware of a classmate's culture helps you get to know this person and people in general.

LESSON 5: DISCUSSING CUSTOMS/HABITS AND FACTS—USING GENERAL TIME

ACTIVITY FIVE

A. With a partner, have a short discussion about some of the customs and habits in your country. You should choose one of the following topics to talk about:

Eating Habits
- kinds of meals people eat
- types of food that are most popular
- time of day for meals

Family Life
- how many children in a family
- how often children do things with their parents
- how old children are when they leave home to live on their own
- relationship of family to "extended" family (aunts/uncles/grandparents, etc.)
- how often people move far away from their family

Work Habits
- hours and days people go to work
- relationship between workers and boss
- how people dress for work
- how often people change jobs

School
- relationship between student and teacher
- hours and days people go to school
- how hard students work in school
- how much homework is required
- how students dress for school

B. After your discussion, you should tell the class what you learned from your partner.

C. Write a paragraph about what you told your partner about the customs in your native country.

After you write your paragraph, check your work for the following:

❏ Some sentences have frequency words or expressions.

❏ If the time of the sentence is habitual or general time, the verb form is *base* or *base + -s*.

❏ Your verb forms agrees with the subject of your sentence. (Be sure the verb has the *-s* ending if your subject is third person singular.)

Expanded Verbs

CHAPTER 3

LESSON 6: WHAT'S HAPPENING NOW?— DISCUSSING THE PRESENT

Focus: present progressive/continuous (be + base + -ing)

Preview

Imagine you are having a conversation with someone. This person asks you, "What do you do?" What will you answer? Are you a student now? Do you work? What kind of job do you have or do you want to have?

Presentation

The following pictures show people at their jobs. Look carefully at each picture and do two things:

1. Write the name of the job you think this person has.
2. Write a sentence about what each person is doing.
   Follow the example below and write your answers in the blanks provided.

EXAMPLE   job: _taxi (cab) driver_

He is driving his taxi.

OR

He is taking a passenger (fare) somewhere.

OR

He is waiting for a passenger (fare).

1. picture #1   job: _____
   _____

2. picture #2   job: _____
   _____

3. picture #3   job: _____
   _____

Share your answers with the class. Write some of your classmates' answers if they are different from yours.

Your teacher will write some of the students' answers on the board.

QUESTIONS

1. Write down the subject and the verb from some of the sentences you and your classmates discussed. Follow the answers from the example sentences.

SUBJECT	VERB
He	*is driving*
He	*is taking*
He	*is waiting*

2. Look carefully at the verbs in the chart above. What do you find at the end of these verbs? Do you find any other words that work with the verbs in these sentences?
3. What do you think is the time of these sentences? Is the action in each of these sentences finished or not finished?

Explanation

1. In Chapter 2 (Lessons 3–5) you learned about simple verbs (one word). In this chapter you will learn about **expanded verbs.** An expanded verb has at least two words.
2. When we want to talk about actions in present time, we use an expanded verb. This expanded verb is often called the *present continuous* or *present progressive* tense.

   In this case the expanded verb has two words: a form of the auxiliary **be** (am/is/are) and the verb.

   He **is driving** his taxi.
   (be) + (verb) = expanded verb

3. When you use this expanded verb form, the verb must have an **ing** ending. This ending tells you the action is not finished or is continuous.

   In addition, the form of **be** (am/is/are) must agree with the subject of the sentence.

   I **am studying** grammar now.
   The teacher **is explaining** grammar to the class right now.
   We **are trying** to learn the rules.
   The students **are listening** to the teacher.

4. Sometimes you must make a spelling change when you add the -ing ending to a verb.

   The children are **running** in the playground.
   We are **writing** the answers to the questions.

   You will find a review of some of these spelling changes at the back of this book on page 230.

5. Speakers often use contractions with this tense.

I am	**I'm** talking
you are	**you're** listening
she or he is	**she's or he's** studying
we are	**we're** working
they are	**they're** explaining

6. Sometimes you will find present time words such as **now/right now/at the moment/at present** with these forms.

7. These forms are not only used for actions that are happening right now. You can also use them to talk about something that is in progress or not finished over a longer period of time.

   This month I'm working on a new project.
   This semester we're studying history.

8. To make a negative sentence with these expanded verbs, put the word **not** to the right of the **am/is/are**. [For more information and practice with negative sentences, see Lesson 20.]

   Follow this pattern: am/is/are + not + verb (-ing form)

   I **am not studying** grammar now.
   The teacher **is not explaining** grammar to the class right now.
   We **are not trying** to learn the rules.

   Native speakers often use contractions with the *is/are* and the *not*.

   We **aren't trying** to learn the rules.
   The teacher **isn't explaining** grammar to the class right now.

   Do not make a contraction with *am* and *not*. The contraction with "am" is as follows:

   I'm not studying grammar now.

9. To make a question with these expanded verbs, put the **am/is/are** to the left of the subject. [For more information and practice with this kind of question, see Lesson 21.]

   Follow this pattern: am/is/are + subject + verb (-ing form)

   Am I studying grammar now?
   Is the teacher explaining the grammar to the class now?
   Are we trying to learn the rules?

Practice

ACTIVITY ONE

A. Fill in the blanks in the paragraph below with the correct form of the verb in parentheses using the present progressive (continuous).

Right now Scot and his friends (practice) _____ for their school play. One boy (try) _____ to memorize several sentences. Another friend (listen) _____ to instructions from the director, Mrs. Riley. Mrs. Riley (explain) _____ how the children should speak to the audience. All the students (get) _____ excited about the play.

B. Fill in the blanks in the paragraph below with the correct form of the verb in parentheses. Think about the time in each sentence and look carefully for time words. You will use either the simple past or present progressive (continuous) for each verb.

This month we (build) _____ an addition on our house. We (start) _____ this project a few weeks ago when the builders (begin) _____ to prepare the ground for a new foundation. Last week they (pour) _____ the concrete for the new room. Yesterday, the carpenters (start) _____ to work. Now they (put) _____ up the walls. Today the electricians (discuss) _____ their plans with the builder and I (plan) _____ how I can decorate the room.

ACTIVITY TWO

A. Heidi and Dennis are old friends and Heidi is visiting Dennis for the first time in a long time. They are talking about their families and friends. They are discussing what everyone is doing now.

Complete what Heidi is telling Dennis, using the verbs given below. Choose the verb that fits best in the blank and put it in the correct form (*be + base + ing*). You should use each verb only one time.

| attend | live | do | look |
| teach | take | work | rent |

My sister _____ at a new school now and her husband _____ at a pharmacy near their home. Their son _____ a small college in Michigan and he _____ very well there. Their daughter is still in high school, but she _____ some special classes for early graduation. Do you remember Sue and Eric? They _____ in Seattle now. They _____ a big apartment for now but they plan to buy a house soon. I think both of them _____ for new jobs.

LEARNING STRATEGY

Overcoming Limitations: Talking or writing about people you are familiar with can help you overcome language limitations.

B. Now write your own sentences about five people you know. You should write about people in your family or some friends. What is each one of these people doing these days?

ACTIVITY THREE

Write a sentence next to each number below using the words given. The verb in each sentence should use the present progressive (continuous) form.

1. Right now the class _____
2. Today we _____
3. This week my friend _____
4. This month I _____

ACTIVITY FOUR

WHAT AM I DOING? WHO AM I?

Think of a job that you can demonstrate to the class with your actions only (no words). Try to think of at least three actions for this job that you can show the class. Your classmates will make sentences to describe what you are doing. Then they will try to guess what kind of job you are demonstrating.

EXAMPLE Pick up a book and show it to the class. Open it and make believe you are reading from it or explaining what is on a certain page. Write something about what is in the book on the blackboard. Go to one or two students and show them what is in the book. (Do not say anything!)

While you are doing these things, your classmates will say things like:

- You are reading a book.
- You are discussing the book.
- You are explaining page 53.
- You are writing on the blackboard.
- You are helping some of the students.
- You are a teacher.

ACTIVITY FIVE

FIND THE MISTAKES

A. The pictures on the next page show people working on their jobs. In both pictures you will see some things that are unusual or wrong.

With a partner, look for these problems and then write two sentences about each problem. Write your sentences as follows:

- In your first sentence describe the action that is unusual or wrong.
- In your second sentence, describe what this person usually does or what is usually correct for this job.

EXAMPLE If the picture shows a cook or chef fixing a television set in a kitchen, you can say:

1. This cook is fixing a television set.
2. A cook usually prepares food.

IT WORKS!
Learning Strategy:
Cooperating and
Discussing Things
with Others

LESSON 6: WHAT'S
HAPPENING NOW?—
DISCUSSING THE PRESENT

LEARNING STRATEGY

Managing Your Learning: Evaluating your own work can help you focus on your learning.

B. After you write your sentences, check your work for the following:

If your sentence includes the present progressive (continuous)

❏ it includes a form of *be* and the *base + -ing*.

❏ the form of *be* agrees with your subject.

If your sentence discusses a habitual activity:

❏ The verb is the *base* or *base + -s form*.

❏ The sentence includes a frequency time word or expression. (How many different frequency words or expressions did you use?)

C. Share your answers with the class as a whole.

LESSON 7: WHAT'S IN YOUR FUTURE?—MAKING PREDICTIONS

Focus: will + base/be going to + base

Preview

Look at the following pictures and think about how people use these things today. Then try to predict how people might use them or how they might change in the future. Discuss your predictions with a partner and then share them with your class.

Presentation

A. Nostradamus was a famous doctor and writer from France in the sixteenth century. He wrote many predictions about the world. Many people believe that his predictions were correct. Read the following examples of two of his poems. Then answer the questions that follow.

1. The speeches at Lac Leman will become angry.
   The days will drag out into weeks, then months, then years.
   Then everything will fail.
   The *authorities* will be angry about their useless powers.
   (Is this about the League of Nations? Its first meeting was in Geneva, Switzerland on Nov. 15, 1920.)

   rulers/people in charge

2. *Pestilences* passed, the world becomes smaller.
   For a long time lands will be *inhabited* peacefully.
   People will cross through the skies, safely, over land and seas.
   Then wars will start up again.
   (Could this be about the twentieth century with air travel popular and several wars?)

   plague/disease that spreads widely and kills quickly
   lived in/settled

QUESTIONS

1. Look at poem #1 above. What is the time in each sentence? How do you know this? What word tells you the time?
2. What form of the verb follows the word "will" each time it appears in both poems?

B. Now look at the cartoon. What is the prediction in this cartoon? What is the time in this prediction? How do you know this?

MOTHER GOOSE & GRIMM *by MIKE PETERS*

Explanation

1. Predicting is announcing a future event before it happens. There are two forms that we often use to make predictions in English.
   - **will + base**
   - **be going to + base**

2. will + base
   The base form of the verb follows **will**. Do not add any endings (such as *s* or *ing*) on a verb that follows **will**.

   The speeches at Lac Leman **will become** angry.
   Then everything **will fail**.

3. be going to + base
   When you use **be going to,** you must change the *be* to agree with the subject of the sentence. The base form of a verb follows the **to**.

   You **are going to live** three days.
   She **is going to be** a doctor someday.

4. Speakers often use contractions (short forms) with *will* and *be going to*.

   You**'re going to have** 1400 kids.
   She**'ll** be a doctor someday.
   He**'s** going to lose all of his money in Las Vegas.

5. The **be going to** is more informal than the **will**. You will probably hear **be going to** most often in conversation or other informal situations. When you hear these words in conversation, the **going to** might sound like **gonna.**

6. There are several time words or expressions that you may find with predictions. Some of these words and expressions are:
   - tomorrow
   - next week/month/year
   - in two hours/days/weeks/months/years
   - five hours/days/weeks/months/years from now

7. To make a negative sentence with will + verb, put the word **not** to the right of **will.**

   Follow this pattern: will + not + verb (base form)

   The speeches at Lac Leman **will not become** angry.
   Then everything **will not fail.**

Native speakers often use a contraction of *will* and *not*. The contraction is **won't**.

The speeches at Lac Leman **won't** become angry.
Then everything **won't** fail.

To make a negative sentence with *be going to,* follow the rules in Lesson 6. (For example: You are not going to have 1400 kids.) [For more information and practice with negative sentences, see Lesson 20.]

8. To make a question with will + verb, put the **will** to the left of the subject. Follow this pattern: will + subject + verb (base form)

   Will the speeches become angry?
   Will everything fail?

   To make questions with *be going to,* follow the rules in Lesson 6. (For example: Are you going to have 1400 kids?) [For more information and practice with this kind of question, see Lesson 21.]

Practice

ACTIVITY ONE

Below you will find several predictions about the future. In each prediction you will see a blank. Fill in each blank with one of the verbs below. Use a different verb for each sentence. Be sure to use the *will + base* in some of your answers and the *be going to + base* in other answers.

   take   live   learn   explore   find   discover

The following predictions are for 100 years from now:

A. Astronauts _____ other galaxies.

B. Someone _____ a cure for cancer on another planet.

C. Many people _____ vacations on the moon.

D. A space explorer _____ life on a distant star.

E. Some people _____ on Mars.

F. Scientists _____ more about Earth by visiting other planets.

ACTIVITY TWO

Nancy asked some of her friends and family to make predictions about their futures. Listen carefully as your teacher reads these predictions to you. Then write the sentences. If you hear contractions, write the contractions. If you hear the short form **gonna,** write the long form **going to.**

Now compare and discuss your sentences with a partner. Were your answers the same? If necessary, ask your teacher to read the sentences again.

LEARNING STRATEGY

Personalizing: Thinking of examples from your own life helps you understand more effectively.

ACTIVITY THREE

A. What can you predict about your life? Answer the two questions below. In one answer use *will* and in the other answer use *be going to.*

1. What can you say about your life in five years?

   In five years _____

2. What can you say about your life ten years from now?

   Ten years from now _____

B. On a separate piece of paper write your sentences from A above. Don't tell anyone your predictions, fold your paper and give it to your teacher. Your teacher will read each person's predictions and the class will guess who wrote each one.

ACTIVITY FOUR

A. Look back at the pictures in the Preview of this lesson. Write a sentence for your predictions about each of the things in these pictures. Use *will* in some sentences and *be going to* in others.

computers _____

telephones _____

televisions _____

watches _____

B. Share your sentences from Part A with a partner. Then, with your partner, think of other common things that we use in our everyday lives today.

EXAMPLES   fax machines   video games

Make a list of these things.

Now predict how you think the things on your list will be different in the future. Use *will* and *be going to* in your predictions. Share these predictions with the class.

LEARNING STRATEGY

Managing Your Learning: Expressing your ideas and opinions gives you a chance to practice your English.

ACTIVITY FIVE

A. Work in small groups. Tell the other people in your group about the city you are from or the city you are living in now (or a city you know well). Give the others in your group information about the following: (If you don't know about all of these things, just tell them about the ones you know.)

- population (How many people live in this city?)
- industry (What kind of industry can you find there?)
- transportation (What kind of public transportation can you find there?)
- buildings (Are there any old or famous buildings in this city?)
- other information

LESSON 7: WHAT'S IN YOUR FUTURE?— MAKING PREDICTIONS

B. Now give the group predictions about this same city in the year 2100. Talk about the same things you discussed above.

C. Write a paragraph discussing your predictions. After you write your paragraph, check your work for the following:

❏ You have several predictions about this city in the future.

❏ You used *will* + *base* in some of your predictions.

❏ You used *be going to* + *base* in some of your predictions.

LESSON 8: WHAT'S ON THE PROGRAM?—PLANNING AND SCHEDULING

Focus: be + base + -ing/be going to + base/base + -s

Preview

Answer the following questions about your future plans. Then discuss your answers with a partner.

1. Do you have any plans for tonight? What are they?
2. What are your plans for next weekend?
3. What are your plans for your next vacation?

Presentation

Below is an e-mail message that Jack received from his sister, Dottie. Read the message and then answer the questions that follow.

(1) How are you all? (2) Everything here is fine. (3) We're going to take a camping trip to Death Valley the weekend of the 25th with our friends. (4) We're spending a three-day weekend there. (5) What are you doing that weekend?

(6) I hear you are going to be in Tucson on April 2, but you probably aren't staying there very long. (7) We're going there that weekend too! (8) We're flying in from Los Angeles and we arrive around 12:30 at the Tucson airport. (9) I figure we'll arrive at our hotel around 1 or 1:30. (10) Do you want to try to get together there?

QUESTIONS

1. Look at sentence #3.
   - What are Dottie's plans about Death Valley?
   - What words does she use to tell you her plans in this sentence?
   - What is the time in this sentence? How do you know?
2. Look at sentence #4.
   - What words does Dottie use to tell you her plans in this sentence?
   - What is the time in this sentence? How do you know?
3. Look at sentence #8.
   - How does Dottie plan to go from Los Angeles to Tucson? What form of the verb does she use to tell you this?
   - When does Dottie plan to arrive at the Tucson airport? What form of the verb does she use to tell you this?
   - What is the time in this sentence? How do you know?

Explanation

1. When talking about making plans in English, you will often find two different forms:
   - **be going to + base**
   - **be + base + -ing**
2. Here is an example of using **be going to + base** to talk about a future plan.

   We**'re going to take** a camping trip to Death Valley the weekend of the 25th with our friends. [For more information about using this form, see the explanation in Lesson 7.]

3. You can also use **be + base + -ing** to talk about plans for the future. In this case, you are using the same forms you learned in Lesson 6 (present actions).
   - If you use these forms for future plans, be sure to use a future time word or expression in the sentence. (See Lesson 7, explanation #6, for examples of these words/expressions.)
   - We use these forms most often in conversation or informal writing. If the speaker or writer makes it clear that the time is future, you do not have to use the time words or expressions in every sentence.

     EXAMPLE We're going to take a camping trip to Death Valley the weekend of the 25th with our friends. We're spending a three-day weekend there.

     (We learn about the future time in the first sentence, so we do not have to say anything about the time in the second sentence.)

4. When we want to discuss future schedules, we often use two forms as well:
   - **be + base + -ing**
   - **base or base + -s**

   We **arrive** around 12:30 at the Tucson airport.
   Our plane **departs** at 6 P.M. tomorrow night.
   The party **is starting** at 8 P.M. Don't be late!

   When you use these forms for future schedules, use the same information about time words discussed in #3 above.

LESSON 8: WHAT'S ON THE PROGRAM?—PLANNING AND SCHEDULING

5. To make a negative sentence with the expanded forms *be going to + base* or *be + base + ing,* follow the rules in Lesson 6 and Lesson 7. (For example: We aren't going to take a camping. trip. The party isn't starting at 8 P.M.)

    To make a negative sentence with the simple forms *base* or *base + s,* follow the rules in Lesson 5. (For example: We don't arrive around 12:30. Our plane doesn't depart at 6 P.M.) [For more information and practice with negative sentences, see Lesson 20.]

6. To make a question with the expanded form *be going to + base* or *be + base + ing,* follow the rules in Lesson 6 and Lesson 7. (For example: Are we going to take a camping trip? Is the party starting at 8 P.M.?) [For more information and practice with this kind of question, see Lesson 21.]

    To make a question with the simple form *base* or *base + s,* follow the rules in Lesson 5. (For example: Do we arrive around 12:30? Does our plane depart at 6 P.M.?) [For more information and practice with this kind of question, see Lesson 21.]

Practice

LEARNING STRATEGY

Forming Concepts: Analyzing the context of grammatical forms helps you understand when to use them.

ACTIVITY ONE

Look back at the e-mail message from Dottie. You will see examples of predictions, plans, and scheduled events, using several of the following forms:

predictions:	• **will + base** (or a contraction)
	• **be going to + base** (or a contraction)
plans:	• **be + base + -ing** (or a contraction)
	• **be going to + base** (or a contraction)
scheduled events:	• **be + base + -ing** (or a contraction)
	• **base** or **base + -s.**

Look at the sentence numbers from the e-mail message on page 44. Find one of the forms listed above in these sentences. Then decide if it is a prediction, a plan, or a scheduled event. Write the form in the correct column for the meaning. Add any time words you find in these sentences as well.

Fill in this information for only the sentence numbers given in the chart. One example is done for you.

SENTENCE #	PREDICTION	PLAN	SCHEDULED EVENT
3		*we're going to take the weekend of the 25th*	
4			
5			
6			
7			
8			
9			

ACTIVITY TWO

A. Nancy asked some of her friends and family to make predictions about their futures in Lesson 7. She asked these same people about their future plans as well. Listen carefully as your teacher reads these plans to you. Then write each sentence after your teacher reads it. If you hear the short form **gonna,** write the long form **going to.**

Now compare and discuss your sentences with a partner. Were your answers the same? If necessary, ask your teacher to read the sentences again.

B. What plans do you have for your future? Write three sentences about your future plans. Then share your answers with another student.

- Be sure to use *be going to + base* in some of your answers and *be + base + -ing* in other answers.
- Begin each of your sentences with one of the following time words/expressions. Use a different word/expression in each sentence. (You will not use two of them.)

tonight   tomorrow   next week   in two weeks   three months from now

ACTIVITY THREE

You are a tourist in a city that you have never visited before. You want to visit different places in this city and you have one day to do this. You would like to visit as many places as possible.

A. Look below at the list of tours available. For each tour you will see the name of the place(s) you can visit, the time the tour leaves, and the time it returns to your hotel. Read the choices below. Choose the tour(s) that you would like to take.

Walking Tour of Downtown
leaves: 12 noon
returns: 1:30 P.M.

Zoo
leaves: 9 A.M.
returns: 1 P.M.

Natural History Museum/Art Museum
leaves: 10 A.M.
returns: 2:30 P.M.

Beach Areas
leaves: 2:30 P.M.
returns: 5:30 P.M.

Shopping Mall
leaves: 11 A.M.
returns: 2 P.M.

Old Town (historical area)
leaves: 3:30 P.M.
returns: 6:30 P.M.

B. Work in small groups for this part of the activity. Each person should tell the others in the group what his or her plans are, using the forms from this lesson.

C. Now together with the others in your group, imagine you must plan your day together. You must all go together as a group, so you must agree on the places to visit.

After you make your final decision as a group, write your plans. Write this information in sentences, using the *be going to + base* or *base + -ing* forms for your plans. You should also write sentences about the times for the tours using the *base + -s* or *base* form.

LESSON 8: WHAT'S ON THE PROGRAM?—PLANNING AND SCHEDULING

ACTIVITY FOUR

Today is March 2 and you are looking at the following chart of temperatures in different cities in the United States and Canada in your local newspaper. This chart includes temperatures and weather for yesterday and today and predictions for tomorrow.

You are going to take a trip to one of the cities below in a few days, on March 5. Choose one of the cities on this list as the city you will visit. Then write the following about this city and your trip:

A. Write a prediction about what kind of weather you think you will find.

B. Write some plans you have for this trip. You can include the following information in your plans:

- the kind of clothing you plan to take
- other things you plan to take with you
- places you plan to visit in this city/what you plan to do there
- other plans you may have about your trip to this city

Share your answers with the class.

NOTE Temperatures are given as two numbers: high/low and are in Fahrenheit degrees.

s=sunny   r=rain   c=cloudy   pc=partly cloudy
sn=snow   ts=thunderstorms   o=overcast

CITY	DAILY TEMPERATURES		
	March 1	March 2	March 3
Anchorage	29/15 o	33/13 pc	32/10 s
Boston	29/27 r	36/19 s	32/14 pc
Chicago	23/10 o	25/16 pc	24/17 pc
Denver	18/14 sn	24/15 sn	42/23 r
Las Vegas	61/48 r	65/49 c	63/46 pc
Miami Beach	86/69 o	82/64 ts	82/65 pc
Montreal	28/18 pc	20/8 pc	18/8 sn
New York	44/36 o	40/25 pc	38/22 c
Palm Springs	77/54 s	77/54 pc	76/53 s
Vancouver	47/31 s	51/30 s	49/30 pc
Washington D.C.	40/32 c	38/29 pc	34/22 s

LEARNING STRATEGY

Personalizing: Applying new knowledge about grammar to personal situations reinforces what you learned in class.

ACTIVITY FIVE

In the Presentation part of this lesson, Dottie sent an e-mail message to her brother Jack about her future plans. In this message she also included information about schedules and predictions.

Write your own message to a friend or relative about your future plans. Include as much information as possible about these plans, including schedules and predictions if possible.

After you write your message, check your work for the following:

❏ You included plans, predictions and schedules as much as possible.

❏ You included some future time words.

❏ You included several of the following forms:
  - *will + base*
  - *be going to + base*
  - *be + base + -ing*
  - *base/base + -s*

❏ When you used the *be + base + -ing* and *base/base + -s* forms, the future time was clear. (For example, you used a time word/expression in the sentence or the sentence before.)

LESSON 9: ONGOING EVENTS IN THE PAST— DESCRIBING PAST CONTINUOUS EVENTS

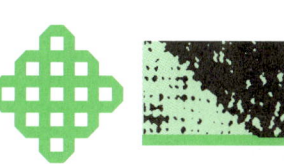

Focus: past progressive (continuous) [be (past) + base + -ing]

Preview

Last night Gerry tried to call his friend Debbi, but she did not answer the telephone. Finally, at 10 P.M. he spoke with her and asked her why she did not answer the phone before then.

The pictures below show why Debbi couldn't answer the telephone at different times. With a partner, look at each picture and explain why Debbi couldn't answer the telephone when Gerry called. Then discuss your answers with the class.

7:00 P.M.

9:00 P.M.

CHAPTER 3
EXPANDED VERBS

Presentation

An accident has just happened at a busy intersection. One of the witnesses is talking to a newspaper reporter and telling him what he saw. This is his report:

(1) I saw the truck when it was coming down College Avenue. (2) Immediately I noticed that it was traveling too fast for this busy street. (3) In fact, I heard someone yell to the driver to slow down. (4) Just as the yellow light was turning red, the driver sped up. (5) Then I saw the blue car. (6) It was turning from 89th Street onto College Avenue. (7) A few seconds later, I heard a big crash. (8) The driver of the blue car saw the truck while it was speeding up at the yellow light, but it was too late.

LEARNING STRATEGY

Testing Hypotheses: Repeating a story to another person can help you check your understanding of it.

Below you will see a drawing of the intersection where this accident happened. Draw the truck and the blue car in this scene and show what happened during the accident.

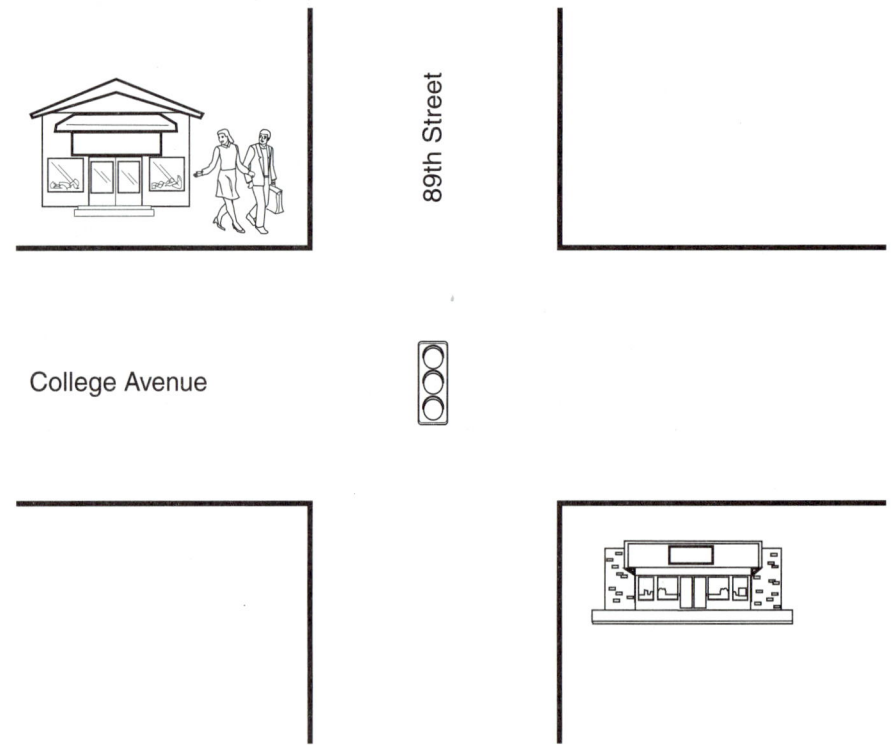

Now show your drawing to a partner and explain the accident to each other from this drawing. As you are discussing the story, write the verbs you use below. Then answer the questions on the next page.

_____
_____
_____

QUESTIONS

1. Which verbs on your list on the previous page have the **-ed** ending or are irregular verbs in the past?
2. Which verbs on your list have the **-ing** ending? Did you use any other words with these **-ing** verbs?
3. Look carefully at the sentences in the Presentation above that have the verbs with the **-ing** ending. Why do you think these verbs have this ending? What word do you see just before the verbs with **-ing**?

Explanation

1. When we want to talk about actions in the past that were not finished or are continuous, we use an expanded verb. This expanded verb is often called the "past continuous" or "past progressive" tense.

    In this case the expanded verb has two words: a past form of the auxiliary *be* (*was/were*) and the verb.

    I noticed that it **was traveling** too fast for this busy street.

    (be) + (verb) = expanded verb

2. When you use this expanded verb form, the verb must have an **-ing** ending after the base form. This ending tells you the action was not finished or was continuous.

    In addition, the past form of *be* (*was/were*) must agree with the subject of the sentence.

    It **was turning** from 89th Street onto College Avenue.
    They **were turning** from 89th Street onto College Avenue.

    (*Reminder:* Sometimes you must make a spelling change when you add the **-ing** ending to a verb. You will find a review of some of these spelling changes at the back of this book on page 230.)

3. Often you will find these forms in sentences with words such as **when, while,** and **as.** These words mean:
    - when/as = at that time
    - while = during that time

    When you use these words, you will often find two parts to the sentence. That is because in this case, these words are connecting two ideas. Each of these ideas has its own verb. Often one verb uses the past form (*-ed* or irregular ending) and the other uses the *was/were* + *base* + *-ing* form.

    EXAMPLES

    I **saw** the truck **when** it **was coming** down College Avenue.
      past   was + base + -ing

    Just **as** the yellow light **was turning** red, the driver **sped** up.
                           was + base + -ing   past

    The driver of the blue car **saw** the truck **while** it **was speeding** up at the yellow light.
                               past   was + base + -ing

    In these cases, both verbs are discussing past time events, but one verb was finished and the other was not finished (in progress/continuous). In each sentence, which verb is finished and which verb was in progress?

CHAPTER 3
EXPANDED VERBS

4. Sometimes you may find that both actions in the sentence were continuing or not finished in the past. In this case, both verbs are expanded verbs with *was/were* and the *base + -ing*.

   My friend and I **were eating** dinner **while** my son **was talking** on the telephone.

5. Other times, one action may interrupt another one that was not finished in the past.

   While I **was eating** dinner, the telephone **rang.**
      not finished eating dinner   interrupted my dinner

   The student **asked** a question while the teacher **was talking.**
      interrupted the teacher   not finished talking

6. To make a negative sentence with these expanded verbs, put the word **not** to the right of the **was/were.** [For more information and practice with negative sentences, see Lesson 20.]

   Follow this pattern: was/were + not + verb (-ing form)

   I **was not eating** dinner when the telephone rang.
   The student asked a question while the teacher **was not talking.**
   My friend and I **were not eating** dinner while my son was talking.

   Native speakers often use contractions with the *was/were* and the *not*.

   I **wasn't eating** dinner when the telephone rang.
   The student asked a question while the teacher **wasn't talking.**
   My friend and I **weren't eating** dinner while my son was talking.

7. To make a question with these expanded verbs, put the **was/were** to the left of the subject. [For more information and practice with this kind of question, see Lesson 21.]

   Follow this pattern: was/were + subject + verb (-ing form)

   Was he eating dinner when the telephone rang?
   Were my friends eating while my son was talking?

Practice

ACTIVITY ONE

You are in a courtroom because you received a speeding ticket. There are several other people there and they all have different reasons for their tickets.

Below you will find all their reasons. Fill in each blank with one of the verbs below. Be sure to use the past progressive (continuous) for each one. Use each verb only one time.

   EXAMPLE (Your reason) I _____*was speeding*_____ on College Avenue when the police officer saw me.

    drive   carry   make   pass   go   cross

1. One man _____ through a red light when the police officer saw him.

2. A woman _____ an illegal U turn at a busy intersection when the police officer stopped her.

3. Two drivers _____ a double yellow line to turn into a parking lot while the police officer was in the lot.

4. When the police officer saw her, a teenager _____ several friends in the back of her pickup truck.

5. A woman and her husband _____ in their car without the registration when the police officer stopped them.

6. Another driver _____ a car in a "no passing" zone when the police officer saw him.

ACTIVITY TWO

Last night there was a robbery in apartment B5 in a building on 37th Avenue. Today the police are asking all the neighbors where they were and what they were doing at the time of the robbery. Your teacher will read each person's answer. Listen carefully and then write down all the verbs in the past you hear. Be sure to write the simple past forms (*base +ed*) as well as past progressive (continuous) forms (*was/were + base + -ing*).

Compare answers with the person next to you. Did you write the same verbs? If necessary, ask your teacher to read the sentences again.

ACTIVITY THREE

A. Look back at the Preview section of this lesson. Complete the following sentences about the pictures.

1. (7 P.M. picture) While Debbi _____, Gerry tried to call her.

2. (9 P.M. picture) When Gerry called at 9 P.M., Debbi _____
_____.

B. Now think about your day yesterday or one busy day in the past. Write down at least three different times of that day when you were busy. Then on the line below each time, write a sentence about what you were doing at that time.

EXAMPLE TIME: *10 P.M.*
At 10 P.M. last night I was watching my favorite television program.

1. TIME: _____

2. TIME: _____

3. TIME: _____

C. Look back at your answers to B. Can you think of other things that happened during those times? Rewrite those sentences to include **when, while,** or **as.**

EXAMPLES Everyone in my family was sleeping while I was watching my favorite television program.

When I was watching my favorite television program, my friend called me.

LESSON 9: ONGOING EVENTS IN THE PAST—DESCRIBING PAST CONTINUOUS EVENTS

ACTIVITY FOUR

People often remember where they were and what they were doing when something important or special happened. Think of some important or special things that happened during your lifetime and try to remember where you were and what you were doing at that time. They could be world or national events or things that happened in your town, your school, or even your family. Write some of the events you remember.

EXAMPLES *John F. Kennedy assassination*

Challenger disaster

Now write a sentence about what you were doing when each of these happened.

Try to include the following in your sentences:

- some simple past verb forms
- some past progressive (continuous) forms
- some sentences using *when/while/as*

EXAMPLES *I was walking in the hallway at school when I heard about the John F. Kennedy assassination.*

While I was talking with a friend at work, another friend told me about the Challenger disaster.

ACTIVITY FIVE

A. Look at the following timeline and think about your life during any of these years. Write an X on four or five times on this line. Under each X write where you were or what you were doing at that time. (You should write only a word or two for each one.) You will find one example on the timeline.

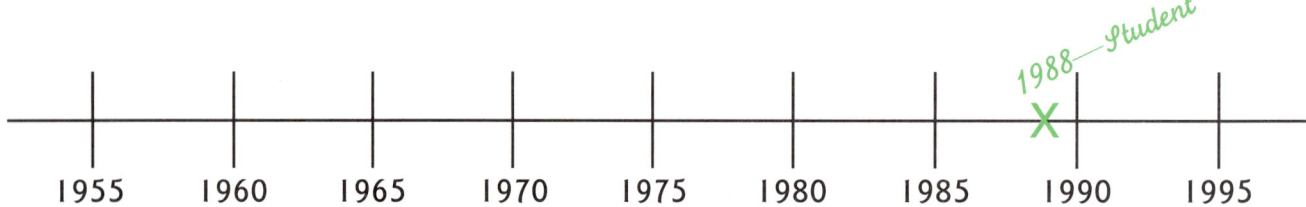

1955   1960   1965   1970   1975   1980   1985   1990   1995

B. Now write a sentence or two about what you did or were doing at that time. Use a simple past form or past progressive (continuous) form in each sentence.

EXAMPLES *In 1988 I was a student.*

I was studying for my Master's Degree.

C. Work in small groups. Discuss your answers with the others in your group. Together, write as many sentences as you can discussing what some people in your group were doing at the same time on the timeline. Use *when/while/as* in your sentences as much as possible.

EXAMPLE *When I was taking classes at the university, Claudia was working at a bank.*

ACTIVITY SIX

Look back at the timeline in Activity 5 and choose one of the times you picked on this line. Write a paragraph or two about what you can remember about your life at that time.

After you write your paragraphs, check your work for the following:

❏ Some of your sentences included the past progressive/continuous form of the verb (*was/were + base + -ing*).

❏ You included *when/while/as* in some of your sentences.

LESSON 10: ACCOMPLISHMENTS—DESCRIBING EXPERIENCES—UNSPECIFIED TIME

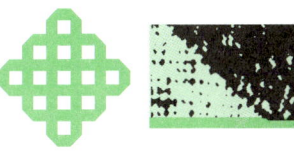

Focus: present perfect (have/has + past participle)

Preview

Look at the following photographs of some well-known people. Do you know anything about these people? Why are they famous?

Presentation

A. Often when someone fills out an application for a new school or job, she or he must write about her or his past work, including accomplishments. Below you will find parts of an application from a high school student in the United States. Read some of his answers. Then answer the questions that follow.

1. *What special interest projects have you completed this year?*

   My most important project was a computer science project that went into the County Science and Engineering Fair in April. Its title was "Creation of Virtual Scientific Laboratory *Software*" and the project earned a second place and a society *award* at the fair.

   I have also designed several multimedia book reports over the course of the year. I completed the first report last semester and it was about "David Copperfield" by Charles Dickens. The second report was about "The Invisible Man" by H. G. Wells. Last month I did a third report on several short stories as well.

computer program

prize

outside or after school

2. *What extracurricular activities are you currently involved in?*

One of my favorite *extracurricular* activities is art. During the past year, I have created three stained glass pieces. I have also entered some computer art into WIRED magazine's contest for electronic art. Presently I am continuing to take an art class at a local recreation center.

QUESTIONS

1. Look at the first paragraph answer to question #1.
   - What was the most important project?
   - When was this project at the County Science and Engineering Fair?
   - Write down all the verbs and any time words you can find in this paragraph.
   - What is the time in this paragraph? How do you know this?
2. Look at the second paragraph in the answer to question #1.
   - In the first sentence of this paragraph, what information can you find about the time?
   - Can you find any exact (specific) time in this paragraph?
   - Look at the other sentences in this paragraph. What information can you find about the time in these sentences? What time words or expressions can you find in these sentences?
   - Why do you think the writer used "have designed" in the first sentence but then used simple past forms of the verbs in the other sentences?
3. Look at the answer to question #2.
   - When did this person create the stained glass art?
   - When did he enter his artwork in the electronic art contest?
   - Why did the writer use the verb forms "have created" and "have entered?"

B. Now read one more question and answer from this application. Then answer the questions that follow.

What projects do you propose for next year?

Next year, I'd like to enter a journalistic writing contest, such as the editorial contest of the local newspaper. I enjoy these contests very much as I have entered them several times in the last few years and I have received some awards (second place and honorable mention).

QUESTIONS

1. When did the writer enter the journalistic writing contests in the past? How many times did he enter these contests?
2. When did the writer receive the awards for these contests?
3. Why did the writer use the verb forms "have entered" and "have received" in this paragraph?

Explanation

1. In Lesson 4 you learned about past events. The form of the verb we use to describe these events is a simple verb (*base + -ed*).
2. Sometimes we want to talk about events in the past, but we do not know or want to discuss the specific time. In these cases, we use an expanded verb. This expanded verb is often called the "present perfect tense."

LESSON 10:
ACCOMPLISHMENTS—
DESCRIBING
EXPERIENCES—
UNSPECIFIED TIME

3. When you use this expanded verb form, the verb must be the past participle form. The past participle of regular verbs is the same as the simple past form (base + -ed). Regular verbs use the **-ed** ending, but irregular verbs have different forms. Many irregular verbs have a **-d,** a **-t** or an **-n** ending.

   You must memorize the irregular forms. You will find a list of irregular verbs at the back of this book on page 228. This chart shows the verbs in groups according to the kind of change the verb makes.

   EXAMPLES
blow	blew	blown
draw	drew	drawn
fly	flew	flown
grow	grew	grown
know	knew	known
throw	threw	thrown

*IT WORKS!
Learning Strategy:
Grouping Words
with Similar
Endings*

4. In addition, a form of **have** (*has/have*) must come before the main verb. This form must agree with the subject of the sentence.

   I **have designed** several multimedia book reports.
   He **has created** three stained glass pieces.

5. Speakers often use **contractions** with these expanded verbs.

   I'**ve designed** several multimedia book reports.
   He'**s created** three stained glass pieces.

6. You will not find specific time words in sentences with these forms. This is one difference between using simple past forms of the verb and these expanded forms. Note this difference in the examples below.

   My computer science project **went** into the fair **in April.**
   I **completed** the first report **last semester.**
   I **have entered** some computer art into a magazine's contest for electronic art.
   I **have received** some awards for my writing.

7. These expanded forms are also used for repeated actions in the past.

   I **have entered** these contests **several times** in the last few years.

8. Sometimes you will find that a writer or speaker introduces a topic in a general way with the present perfect (*has/have* + *verb*). Then the details follow. The details often use the simple past form and time words in order to give more specific information.

   EXAMPLE   I'**ve entered** another writing contest. Last month I **wrote** a short story about my trip to the mountains. I **showed** it to my teacher last week and I **revised** it for the contest. We **sent** it in yesterday.

9. As discussed above, these expanded verb forms describe past events (with no specific time words) or repeated actions. In addition, these forms tell us a relationship with the present. For this reason, we use these forms for accomplishments of living people. This is because we feel they made these accomplishments in the past and may continue to make them again.

   The student **has entered** some writing contests. (He may enter again.)
   He **has received** some awards for his work. (He may receive more awards.)

   However, we do not use present perfect forms to discuss accomplishments of dead people. We describe these accomplishments with simple past verb forms.

   Ernest Hemingway **wrote** many famous stories.
   Charlie Chaplin **performed** in many silent films.

10. To make a negative sentence with these expanded verbs, put the word **not** to the right of the **has/have**. [For more information and practice with negative sentences, see Lesson 20.]

    Follow this pattern: has/have + not + verb (past participle form)

    I **have not received** some awards for my writing.
    He **has not received** awards for his writing.

    Native speakers often use contractions with the *has/have* and the *not*.

    I **haven't received** some awards for my writing.
    He **hasn't received** awards for his writing.

11. To make a question with these expanded verbs, put the **has/have** to the left of the subject. [For more information and practice with this kind of question, see Lesson 21.]

    Follow this pattern: has/have + subject + verb (past participle form)

    Has he received awards for his writing?
    Have they received awards for their writing?

Practice

ACTIVITY ONE

Complete the following sentences about different people's accomplishments using the verbs given below. Choose the verb that fits best in each blank and put it in the correct expanded form, using the present perfect. You should use each verb only one time. (Some sentences may have more than one possible answer.)

NOTE Some of these sentences may also be grammatically correct with simple past verb forms. For this exercise, practice using the expanded verbs from this lesson. Do not use simple past forms in your answers.

enter   write   start   take   act   complete   build   make

A. He _____ some writing contests with the local newspaper.

B. My brother _____ several business trips to Bali, Indonesia.

C. I _____ a new textbook for language learners.

D. My sister and brother-in-law _____ a new house just outside Tucson.

E. A friend of mine _____ a new children's toy business.

F. You _____ your first year at a new school.

G. We _____ several repairs to our house, both on the inside and outside.

H. Those children _____ in several school plays.

ACTIVITY TWO

Listen to some of the answers from Activity 1 with contractions. You will also hear other sentences about accomplishments in the past. Listen carefully as your teacher reads these sentences to you. As you listen, decide if the verb in the sentence is simple past or present perfect. Write the verbs in the correct column below. You should also listen for any time words and write them on the chart.

SIMPLE PAST	PRESENT PERFECT
1.	1.
2.	2.
3.	3.
4.	4.
5.	5.
6.	6.
7.	7.
8.	8.

Now compare and discuss your sentences with a partner. Make any changes that you think are necessary. Ask your teacher to repeat the sentences if necessary.

ACTIVITY THREE

A. In the spaces below write two sentences about things you have done in the past year or two. (Think about any part of your life, such as school, family, job, etc.) Be sure to use the present perfect in your sentences.

1. _____

2. _____

B. Turn to the person next to you and discuss your answers. Write your classmate's answers on the lines below.

1. My classmate (_____) _____.
              (name)
   _____

2. My classmate (_____) _____.
              (name)
   _____

Share your answers with the rest of the class. After a class discussion of these answers, try to complete as many of the sentences below as possible. Be sure to use the present perfect in your answers.

3. My classmates (_____ and _____) _____
               (name)   (name)
   _____

CHAPTER 3
EXPANDED VERBS

4. My classmates (_____(name)_____ and _____(name)_____) _____

_____

5. We (my classmate _____(name)_____ and I) _____

_____

6. We (my classmate _____(name)_____ and I) _____

_____

LEARNING STRATEGY

Overcoming Limitations: Guessing intelligently, whether right or wrong, promotes your language learning.

ACTIVITY FOUR

As discussed in the explanations on page 57 (see #8), people sometimes introduce a subject using the present perfect and then follow with specific details using simple past forms. This is often the case in newspaper articles.

All of the following short paragraphs come from newspaper articles. In each paragraph you will find verbs in parentheses and blanks. Use the verb in parentheses to fill in the blank in each sentence. Follow the information above about using present perfect *(have/has + past participle)* for general statements and simple past forms *(base + -ed)* for details. In some cases, more than one answer may be possible.

medication given to people to prevent disease
endorsement/support
a doctor for children

A. A new chickenpox *vaccine* (win) _____ *approval* from the nation's largest group of *pediatricians*. The American Academy of Pediatricians (recommend) _____ last week that all children ages 12 months to 18 months should get this vaccination. They also (recommend) _____ that it should be given to children under 13 who (have) _____ not _____ the disease.

save/free from danger
a disease causing problems with breathing
the state of being awake and aware

B. Lucky Fugnetti, 14, is lucky he has little sister Katie. Katie, 12, twice (come) _____ to the *rescue* of her brother during a violent *asthma* attack, possibly saving his life. On Sunday, Lucky (lose) _____ *consciousness* when he (stop) _____ breathing. Three months ago, she (be) _____ with her brother when another asthma attack (make) _____ him helpless. She (save) _____ him then too.

C. A federal *jury* (award) _____ $19 million to the widow of an executive killed in the 1988 bombing of Pan Am Flight 103 over Lockerbie, Scotland. The woman, Faith Pescatore, (cry) _____ when she heard the *verdict*. Her husband of 2 1/2 years (be) _____ one of the 259 people killed aboard that flight.

group of people making a decision in a court of law

judgment/decision of guilty or not guilty

D. An aluminum jet boat from Australia (wash) _____ up on a beach in Mozambique, 5,000 miles away. Last August the boat (slip) _____ its *moorings* on the coast of Western Australia. An Australian tourist, who, by enormous *coincidence*, (know) _____ the owner of the boat, (recognize) _____ the boat in Mozambique.

place for a boat to be tied to a dock

the happening of events at the same time by chance

LEARNING STRATEGY

Remembering New Material: Applying new materials immediately makes them easier to remember.

ACTIVITY FIVE

A. Look back at the pictures in the Preview part of this lesson. What have these people done to become famous? Write down one or two accomplishments for each of these people. Be sure to use the present perfect of your verbs in these sentences. If you know any details or specific information about what these people did, write that information also. Be sure to use simple past forms when necessary for these details.

B. Work in small groups. Think of two or three famous people who are still alive. With the others in your group write some sentences about these people's accomplishments. (Write your sentences in the same way as above.) Then share your sentences with the class so that they can guess the name of each famous person.

ACTIVITY SIX

In the Presentation part of this lesson you read some questions and answers from an application form. Imagine that you are filling out a similar application. Answer the following question by writing about your accomplishments. Give both general and more detailed information (with specific information and dates) in your answer.

What projects have you completed this year at school or on your job?

After you write, check your work for the following:

❑ You used present perfect forms in some of your sentences.
❑ In sentences with the present perfect, you did not use specific time words.
❑ In sentences with specific time words, you used simple past verb forms.

LESSON 11: MORE ACCOMPLISHMENTS—EXPERIENCES—PAST RELATED TO PRESENT

> Focus: present perfect (have/has + past participle)

Preview

Look at the following list of activities. Which ones have you done? Then look at the chart below. Put some of the activities on the list in the column of the chart that fits for you. Try to put at least one activity in each column. Do not write whole sentences on the chart. Just use the words you see below.

saw a funny movie
read a book about history
talked to a good friend
flew in an airplane
visited the downtown area
   of the city I am in
swam in the Indian Ocean

saw a sad movie
read an exciting book
talked to someone from my
   native country
flew in a rocket ship
visited a museum
swam in a lake

NEVER (at no time)	RECENTLY (in the near past)	ALREADY (at some time in the past)	JUST (very near past)

Presentation

The same student that made out the application in Lesson 10 is now talking to his school counselor. They are discussing some details about classes he has taken and what he plans to take next year. Read the interview and look for expanded verb forms that include the following words: *never/recently/already/just* and *ever*. Then follow the instructions for the chart below the conversation.

    Counselor: We offer several science classes. Are you interested in Biology or Chemistry?

    Student: I've already taken Biology, so I guess I'd like to take Chemistry next year.

LESSON 11: MORE ACCOMPLISHMENTS—EXPERIENCES—PAST RELATED TO PRESENT

Counselor: Okay. Now, how about your English class? We have several literature courses, including one about the works of Shakespeare, one about British literature and another on American literature of the 20th century.

Student: Well, I've just read one of Shakespeare's plays, *Hamlet,* and I'd like to study more works by him. Do you know which plays they study in that class?

Counselor: That information is in the catalogue. Here it is. Let's see . . . They read *Romeo and Juliet, Twelfth Night* and *A Midsummer's Night's Dream.* Have you ever studied those?

Student: I read *Romeo and Juliet* a few years ago, but I don't mind studying it again. I've never read the others, so I think that class will be a good one for me.

Counselor: Very good. I think that takes care of everything for now. I'll get back to you with your exact schedule in a few days. We've recently changed our computer system, so it might take a day or two to finalize everything. Thanks for coming in today and you'll hear from me soon.

Fill in the chart below by writing the expanded verb forms you found in the conversation in the appropriate column.

NEVER	RECENTLY	ALREADY	JUST	EVER

QUESTIONS

1. Look at the expanded verbs you wrote in the chart after the conversation. What words do you find in each one?
2. Look at the words at the top of each column in the chart. Where do you find the **never, recently, already,** and **just** in relation to the expanded verb?
3. How is the **ever** different from the words you found in question #2 above? Where do you find it in the sentence?
4. What can you say about the time in all of the sentences with these words? Is the speaker talking about only one time or is the speaker making a kind of relationship between two times? When did these things happen in relation to the time that the speaker is discussing them?

Explanation

1. In Lesson 10 you learned about another expanded verb form: present perfect. [See Lesson 10 for a review of this.] In this lesson you are going to practice using these forms in another way.
2. Often we use these forms to make a relationship between the past and the present. In some cases when we do this, we use other words in the sentence, such as **already, just, recently, never** and **ever.** These words give more information about the relationship between these two times (past to present).
3. Below you will find a list of words that you may sometimes find with present perfect forms. Next to each word you will find its meaning. Below each one you will find an example of how to use it in a sentence for that meaning. Notice that in each of these cases you find the word in between the two parts of the expanded verb.

   already   previously/by now
   I'**ve already taken** Biology, so I guess I'd like to take Chemistry next year.

   just   very near past/very short time ago
   I'**ve just read** one of Shakespeare's plays, Hamlet, and I'd like to study more works by him.

   recently   not long ago/in the near past
   We'**ve recently changed** our computer system, so it might take a day or two to finalize everything.

   never   at no time/not ever
   I'**ve never read** the others, so I think that class will be a good one for me.

       NOTE   The word **never** makes this sentence negative. Do not use **not** in addition to the word **never.**

   finally   at long last/after a while
   We **have finally replaced** our computer system.

       NOTE   Although you will often find these words with present perfect forms, sometimes you will find them with simple past forms as well.

4. To make a negative sentence with the present perfect and **already, just, recently** and **finally,** follow the rules in Lesson 10. (For example: I haven't recently changed the computer system. She hasn't just read that play.) [For more information and practice with negative sentences, see Lesson 20.]

       DO NOT make negative sentences with these verb forms and **never.** (This will make two negatives in the sentence and this is not acceptable.) See #6 for information about making negative sentences with **ever.**

5. To make questions with the present perfect and **already, just, recently,** and **finally,** follow the rules in Lesson 10. (For example: Have you recently changed the computer system? Has he just read that play?) [For more information and practice with this kind of question, see Lesson 21.]

   DO NOT make questions with these verb forms and **never.** See #6 below for information about making questions with **ever.**

6. Sometimes you will find the words **ever** and **yet** with these expanded verb forms. We do not usually use these words in exactly the same way as the words in #3 above. We often use them in negative sentences or questions.

   ever   at any time
   Have you **ever studied** those?
   I **haven't ever studied** those.

   yet   until now
   Note that the **yet** comes at the end of the sentence or question.
   Have you **read** those books **yet?**
   No, I **haven't read** them **yet.**.

Practice

ACTIVITY ONE

Read the following sentences and fill in the blanks with the words given in parentheses. Use the present perfect form of the verb in each one.

Professor Lustig (return-just) _____ from his trip to Rome for an international conference on intercultural communication. He said his trip was a great success and he (make-already) _____ plans to attend another conference in Tokyo with a colleague. They (complete-recently) _____ a new study and are anxious to present the results at the conference. They are looking forward to that trip, especially because they (be-never) _____ to Japan before.

CHAPTER 3
EXPANDED VERBS

ACTIVITY TWO

Below are several short letters. Read each letter and find the mistakes. The mistakes will be about using the present perfect forms discussed in this lesson as well as simple past verb forms. Correct each mistake you find.

Dear Mom & Dad,
  I've arrived here just and I'm writing to tell you that everything is fine. I've already meet someone at my new school. She is also studying Business Administration and I think we will be in some of the same classes. A few minutes ago she has asked me to take a walk around campus with her. I'll find a mailbox and mail this to you immediately.
  I'll try to call you soon.

                                        Love,
                                        Gabriela

Dear Mom & Dad,
  I have just receive your telephone message. I don't understand why you haven't received my first letter. I have mailed it a week ago! Already I has tried to call you three times, but you haven't never been home.
  I will try to call you again. Please don't worry about me. I am fine.
                                        Love,
                                        Gabriela

Dear Gabriela,
  We have received finally your two letters. They both have arrived this morning at the same time!
  We hope you are enjoying your classes and having a good time there. We will try to call you again soon, so maybe we will speak to you before you get this note.
                                        Love,
                                        Mom & Dad

LEARNING STRATEGY

Testing Hypotheses: Checking with a native speaker can help you make sure you understand differences in meaning.

ACTIVITY THREE

Look back at the chart in the Preview section of this lesson. Write a sentence using the present perfect form of the verb for each activity you wrote in each column. Be sure to include the word at the top of the column in each sentence as well. Write your sentences on the first line under each word below.

Then share your answers with a partner by reading your sentences to each other. Write your partner's answers, using s/he for the subject. Write these sentences on the second line under each word below.

NEVER

_____
(your answer)

_____
(your partner's answer)

RECENTLY

_____
(your answer)

_____
(your partner's answer)

ALREADY

_____
(your answer)

_____
(your partner's answer)

JUST

_____
(your answer)

_____
(your partner's answer)

ACTIVITY FOUR

A. Read the following questions and answer them truthfully. If the answer is no, write a sentence using the present perfect and **never** or **ever**. If the answer is yes, do two things:
- Write a sentence using the present perfect.
- Then write another sentence that gives a specific detail (such as the exact time), using a simple past form of the verb.

EXAMPLE Have you ever climbed to the top of Mt. Everest?

No, I have never climbed to the top of Mt. Everest.

OR *No, I haven't ever climbed to the top of Mt. Everest.*

Yes, I have climbed Mt. Everest. I climbed to the top in 1992.

1. Have you ever gone scuba diving?
2. Have you ever eaten steak tartar?
3. Have you ever gone horseback riding?
4. Have you ever ridden in a helicopter?
5. Have you ever seen a UFO?
6. Have you ever tried bungee jumping?

LESSON 11: MORE ACCOMPLISHMENTS— EXPERIENCES—PAST RELATED TO PRESENT

IT WORKS!
Learning Strategy:
Having a Good Time

B. Now write a few *Have you ever . . .* questions of your own. Try to think of unusual things to ask your classmates. Then read your questions to the class and see if anyone has ever done those things.

ACTIVITY FIVE

A. Below you will find some statements about various human accomplishments. Some of these statements are true, but some of them are not. Decide which statements are true and which ones are false. Write a **T** for true and an **F** for false in the space next to each number. (Answers are at the end of this lesson.)

_____ 1. The fastest runners have already run the mile in less than four minutes.

_____ 2. Scientists have never found skeletons of dinosaurs as small as dogs.

_____ 3. Astronauts have recently gone to the moon to explore it.

_____ 4. Researchers haven't found a vaccine to prevent cancer yet.

_____ 5. Scientists have finally found a sure way to predict earthquakes.

_____ 6. Nobody has ever swum the English Channel.

_____ 7. Archaeologists have just discovered a new pyramid in Mexico.

B. In small groups, compare your answers and decide which statements are true and which ones are false. Then with your group make up some of your own statements about accomplishments using the present perfect. Some of your statements should be true and some should be false. (Make sure someone in your group knows the correct answer.) You should have at least five sentences. Try to use the following words in your sentences as much as possible:

already   just   never   ever   yet   finally   recently.

Write your sentences on a piece of paper. Then exchange papers with another group. Each group should try to answer the other group's questions.

ACTIVITY SIX

Write a letter to a friend or relative and tell them about some things you have done (or haven't done) in the past few weeks. You can tell them about what you have done at work, at school, or for fun. Be sure to use some simple past forms of the verb and some present perfect forms.

After you write your letter, check your work for the following:

❑ You used some present perfect forms *(have/has + past participle)*.

❑ You used some of the following with the present perfect forms: *already / just / recently / never / yet*.

❑ If your sentence has a specific time word, you used the simple past form of the verb.

Answers to Activity Five:
Only **1** and **4** are true. All other statements are false.

LESSON 12: ACCOMPLISHMENTS—DESCRIBING EXPERIENCES FROM PAST TO PRESENT—PART ONE

Focus: present perfect (have/has + past participle with for/since)

Preview

Answer the following questions "yes" or "no." If your answer is "no," go to the next question. If your answer is "yes," write how long this has been true for you.

1. Are you a full-time student?
   ❑ no   ❑ yes   how long? _____
   Are you a part-time student?
   ❑ no   ❑ yes   how long? _____
2. Do you work at a full-time job?
   ❑ no   ❑ yes   how long? _____
   Do you work at a part-time job?
   ❑ no   ❑ yes   how long? _____
3. Do you know how to use a computer?
   ❑ no   ❑ yes   how long? _____
   Do you know how to use the Internet?
   ❑ no   ❑ yes   how long? _____
4. Do you own a car?
   ❑ no   ❑ yes   how long? _____
   Do you own a bicycle?
   ❑ no   ❑ yes   how long? _____

Presentation

A. Look at the drawings below and read all the sentences.

This is Janet. She moved here in 1984. She has lived in this house since 1984.

This is Barbara. She moved here in 1985. Barbara has lived in this house for more than 10 years.

They became friends immediately after Barbara moved in.
They are still friends today. Barbara and Janet have known each other since 1985.
They have been friends for more than ten years.

CHAPTER 3
EXPANDED VERBS

B. Do this part with a partner. Below are pictures of Janet and Barbara. Next to each picture you will find a timeline and some words from the sentences on page 69. In the example below (#1) these words are also on the timeline.

For #2 and #3 put the words on the timeline for the time you think they fit best. In some cases you will put them at one exact time and in other cases you will need to use an arrow or line to show longer periods of time (as in the example).

moved   has lived here

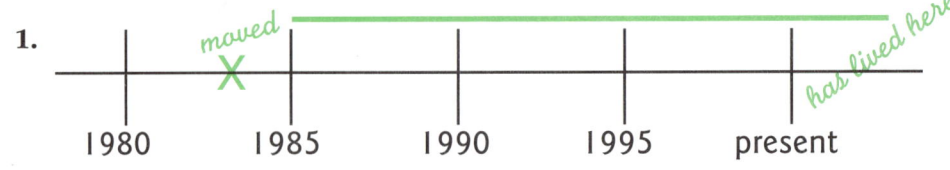

moved   has lived here

became friends
have known each other
have been friends

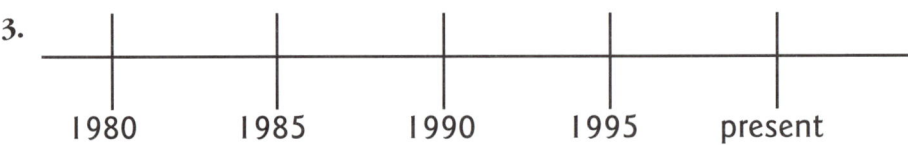

QUESTIONS

1. Look at the sentences and the timeline beside Janet. When did Janet move to her house? Is this an exact time? Why do you think the simple verb **moved** is in the second sentence in Part A?

    How long has Janet lived in this house? How do you know this? Why do you think the expanded verb **has lived** is in the third sentence in Part A?

    Answer the same questions as above about Barbara.

2. Look at the timeline beside the picture of Janet and Barbara together. Where did you put **became friends**? Why? Is this a specific time?

    Where did you put **have known** and **have been friends** on this timeline? Why?

Explanation

1. In Lessons 10 and 11 you learned about using present perfect (*have/has + past participle*) for three things:
   • unspecified past
   • repeated past
   • past with a relationship to the present

    In addition, sometimes these forms give information about actions or states that started in the past and continue to the present. In this lesson you will study and practice using these expanded verb forms to show this relationship between the past and the present.

2. As discussed in Lessons 10 and 11, these expanded verb forms need two parts: *have/has* + *verb* (past participle form). Sometimes you may find contractions with these forms. [See Lessons 10 and 11 for a review of this.]
3. Sometimes you will find these forms with the words **for** and **since**. The **for** and **since** show that something started in the past and continues until now.
    Use these words as follows:
   - for = amount of time (how long/duration)

     Barbara **has lived** in this house **for over ten years.**
               how long
     They **have been** friends **for more than ten years.**
   - since = starting time (when this action or state started)

     Janet **has lived** in this house **since 1984.**
             starting time
     Barbara and Janet **have known** each other **since 1985.**
4. To make a negative sentence with these expanded forms follow the rules in Lesson 10. (For example: They haven't known each other since 1985. She hasn't lived here for ten years.) [For more information and practice with negative sentences, see Lesson 20.]
5. To make questions with these expanded forms follow the rules in Lesson 10. (For example: Have they known each other since 1985? Has she lived here for ten years?) [For more information and practice with this kind of question, see Lesson 21.]

LESSON 12:
ACCOMPLISHMENTS—
DESCRIBING EXPERIENCES
FROM PAST TO
PRESENT—PART ONE

Practice

ACTIVITY ONE

Complete the following paragraph by doing two things:
- Choose the verb that best fits each blank and put it in the present perfect. You should not use any verb more than one time. (You will not use all of the verbs.) Add any words in parentheses as well.
- Choose the **for** or **since** in parentheses by circling the correct one for the sentence.

be live know return watch

My friend _____ in Toronto (since / for) 1974. She moved there from New York and she (never) _____ to her hometown. She met her husband in Toronto very soon after she arrived there. They _____ each other (since / for) more than twenty years now. They _____ married (since / for) 1976 and they have two children.

ACTIVITY TWO

Read the following paragraphs and choose the correct words in parentheses. Think carefully about the time of each sentence before you circle your answers.

A. Two weeks ago Jordan (has taken / took) a vacation to Banff, Canada. The first day there he (had / has had) a skiing accident and (broke / has broken) his leg. (For / Since) the accident he (wore / has worn / wears) a cast from his ankle to his knee. He (is / was / has been) uncomfortable (for / since) the last few weeks.

B. Mr. Russo (is / has been / was) a high school Physics teacher (since / for) 1972. In that year he (began / begins / has begun) his teaching career at Patrick Henry High School. Then he (has changed / changed) schools in 1980 and again a few years ago. He (taught / has taught / teaches) at the same school (since / for) five years now. He is a very dedicated teacher and (has been / is / was) active in several areas of teaching (since / for) many years. He (belongs / belonged / has belonged) to a teacher's union (for / since) his first year of teaching and next year he will become the President of his school's chapter.

ACTIVITY THREE

You are going to listen to a short paragraph about Jordan and his life since the skiing accident (from Activity Two above). Your teacher will read this paragraph one time and you will listen only. Then your teacher will read it again and you will write it. Your teacher will use some contractions when she or he reads it. When you hear these contractions, write the long forms.

Work with a partner and compare answers. Discuss any differences you may have about the paragraph. Make any changes to your work you think are necessary.

ACTIVITY FOUR

Next to each number below you will find some words. Choose three of these and write sentences using the words given. You should also use a verb from the list below for each of these sentences. Choose a different verb for each sentence and use the present perfect (*have/has + past participle*).

study   want   own   need   be   work

1. my parents   for

_____

2. my friend   since

_____

3. some of my classmates   since

_____

4. my car/bicycle   for

_____

ACTIVITY FIVE

Look back at the Preview part of this lesson. Use your answers to these questions to write some sentences using the present perfect and **for** or **since**. You should write at least four sentences and be sure to use **for** in some and **since** in others.

> ### LEARNING STRATEGY
>
> **Managing Your Learning: Working with other language learners helps you improve your language skills.**

ACTIVITY SIX

A. Fill in this timeline about your life, using the verbs below. Add specific years to the line. Think of things that started in the past and continue until today. Put any of the verbs below that fit your life in the appropriate places on the line. If you can think of other verbs, put those on the line as well.

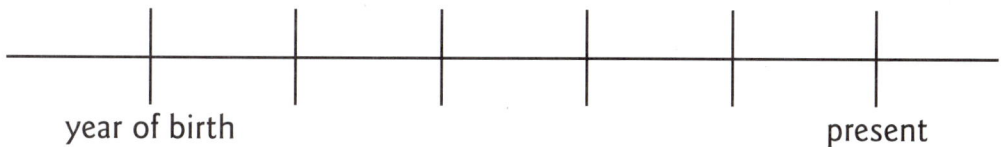

IT WORKS!
Learning Strategy:
Taking Good Notes

live   know   be   want   own   belong   have   work   study   move

Now write sentences about your life using the information from the timeline. Be sure to use present perfect forms and **for** and **since** in your sentences. Discuss this information with a partner.

B. Write some of the information you learned about your partner.

> ### LEARNING STRATEGY
>
> **Remembering New Material: Practicing grammatical structures in your writing helps you learn them.**

C. Write a paragraph about what you learned about your partner's life. Be sure to use the present perfect as well as **for** and **since** in some of your sentences. After you write about your partner, check your work for the following:

- ❏ You included things about your partner's life that started in the past and continue until now.
- ❏ Some of your sentences have present perfect verb forms (*have/has + past participle*)
- ❏ Some of your sentences have *for* or *since* in them.
- ❏ When you use *for,* the information that follows is the amount of time.
- ❏ When you use *since,* the information that follows is the starting time.

LESSON 12:
ACCOMPLISHMENTS—
DESCRIBING EXPERIENCES
FROM PAST TO
PRESENT—PART ONE

LESSON 13: THE ENVIRONMENT—DESCRIBING EXPERIENCES FROM PAST TO PRESENT—PART TWO

Focus: present perfect progressive (continuous) (has/have + been + base + -ing)

Preview

LEARNING STRATEGY

Understanding and Using Emotions: Listening to other people's thoughts and feelings helps you understand your own feelings.

What does the term "environmental problems" mean to you? With a partner, name some of these problems. List them below and discuss with your partner which ones you think are most serious or most important today. Then share your answers with the class.

_____

_____

_____

Presentation

Look at photo #2. Then read all the sentences.

make unclean/ unhealthy/impure   (1) This factory has been *polluting* the environment for more than five years now.

(2) The smoke has been filling the air with chemicals.

unusable material/garbage   (3) Factory *waste* has also been *contaminating* a nearby river.

(4) A few months ago some people in a nearby town got very sick.

make dirty or unfit for use   (5) Many people have been talking about this situation since then.

QUESTIONS

1. In which sentence do you find a specific time? What form of the verb do you find? What is the time in this sentence? How do you know this?
2. Look at the verb forms in the other sentences. Are these simple verb forms or expanded forms? Write some specific examples from the sentences in the space below.

   _____

   _____

3. What is the time in the following sentences? How do you know this?

   #1   #2   #3   #5

4. Do you see any similarities between the verb forms and time in the sentences from #3 above and the forms and time discussed in Lesson 12? Do you see any differences?

   Similarities:

   _____

   _____

   Differences:

   _____

   _____

Explanation

1. In Lesson 12 you learned about using present perfect forms with (*have/has + past participle*) for actions or states that started in the past and continue to the present. In this lesson you will learn and practice another way to show this relationship between the past and the present.
2. These expanded verb forms require several parts as follows:

   has/have + been + base + -ing

   These verb forms often have the name "present perfect progressive" or "present perfect continuous."

   Factory waste **has been contaminating** a nearby river.
   Many people **have been talking** about this situation since then.

3. We often use these expanded verb forms with **for** and **since**. [See Lesson 12 for more information about using these words.]

   This factory **has been polluting** the environment **for more than five years now.**
   Many people **have been talking** about this situation **since then.**

4. Some verbs can be used either as discussed in Lesson 12 or with the *-ing* form of the verb without any difference in meaning. These verbs include:

   live   work   teach   study   stay   wear

   I **have lived** here for five years.
   I **have been living** here for five years.

LESSON 13:
THE ENVIRONMENT—
DESCRIBING EXPERIENCES
FROM PAST TO PRESENT—
PART TWO

CHAPTER 3 EXPANDED VERBS

5. To make a negative sentence with these expanded verbs, put the word **not** to the right of the **has/have**. [For more information and practice with negative sentences, see Lesson 20.]

    Follow this pattern: has/have + not + been + verb (-ing form)

    I **have not been living** here for five years.
    This factory **has not been polluting** the environment for more than five years.

    Native speakers often use contractions with the *has/have* and the *not*.

    I **haven't been living** here for five years.
    This factory **hasn't been polluting** the environment for more than five years

6. To make a question with these expanded verbs, put the **has/have** to the left of the subject. [For more information and practice with this kind of question, see Lesson 21.]

    Follow this pattern: has/have + subject + been + verb (-ing form)

    Have they been living here for five years?
    Has this factory been polluting the environment for more than five years?

Practice

ACTIVITY ONE

A. Below are some problems about the environment and some sentences about them. Fill in the blanks with verbs in parentheses using the present perfect progressive (continuous) for each verb. Then choose the problem that best fits the other blanks in the sentences. (Use each problem only one time.)

Problems: ozone layer   acid rain   greenhouse effect

Power plants, cars, etc. (release) _____ many gases. Some of these gases in the air (mix) _____ with water to make _____. This (fall) _____ back to earth and getting into

catch   rivers and lakes, etc. Some of the gases (trap) _____ the sun's heat. This (cause) _____ the _____. Other gases (such as

hurt/harm/injure   CFC's and halons) (damage) _____ an important layer of gas that protects us from the strong rays of the sun. These particular gases (eat) _____ up the _____ and making a hole in it. This (allow)

causing hurt or damage   _____ more *harmful* rays of the sun to reach people.

LESSON 13:
THE ENVIRONMENT—
DESCRIBING EXPERIENCES
FROM PAST TO PRESENT—
PART TWO

B. Fill in the blanks in each sentence with one of the verbs listed below. Use an expanded form of the verb as you did above. (Use each verb only one time. Some spaces may have more than one possible answer.) Then choose **for** or **since** in parentheses wherever necessary.

add   turn   put   announce   develop

Some air pollution problems _____ (for/since) the start of the Industrial Revolution. This means that (for/since) over 150 years factories _____ harmful gases in the air. Sometimes these factories make products that also hurt the environment. For example, cars _____ harmful gases to the air. In many cities around the world, the air _____ brown because there is so much smog. In some places, it is not always safe to breathe. Some cities _____ smog information to the public (for/since) several years now.

LEARNING STRATEGY

Forming Concepts: Using charts and other visuals can improve your understanding.

ACTIVITY TWO

You are going to listen to some information about the movement to help the environment. Your teacher will read it two times. The first time just listen carefully. The second time your teacher will read the information sentence by sentence and you should complete the chart below.

To complete the chart:

- Listen specifically for verbs with the forms at the top of each column on the chart.
- Put the verbs you hear in the correct columns. If you hear contractions, write the complete forms (without contractions).
- Add any words that tell you about time as well.

simple past forms	present perfect forms	present perfect progressive (continuous) forms
_____	_____	_____
_____	_____	_____
_____	_____	_____
_____	_____	_____
_____	_____	_____
_____	_____	_____

Compare answers with a partner. Ask your teacher to repeat the paragraph if necessary.

ACTIVITY THREE

Work with a partner for this activity. Read the paragraphs below and discuss any vocabulary words. Then read each one again and answer the questions that follow.

A. People have been making glass for more than 3,000 years. For a long time people thought it was precious. Then people got so good at making it that they started thinking of it as garbage. Now we throw out billions of glass bottles and jars every year. Some people have decided to reuse bottles and jars by recycling them. Factories have been recycling glass for quite a few years now.

Answer the following questions as true or false according to the information in the paragraph above. Put a T for true or an F for false in the blank next to each number. Be prepared to explain your answers.

_____ 1. Glass is a fairly new invention.

_____ 2. People thought glass was precious in the past and continue to think this today.

_____ 3. Today we think of glass as garbage and throw much of it away.

_____ 4. People decided to reuse glass by recycling it twenty five years ago.

_____ 5. Factories started recycling glass years ago and continue to recycle it today.

B. Many years ago people used things again and again. Most people never threw something away after using it just once. For example, people used cloth instead of paper products because there were no paper napkins or towels back then.
Over the years, people have developed many disposable products, including paper goods, aluminum foil and plastic bags and wraps. Many people have been throwing away these items for years. They have not been thinking about how much waste they have been making. Many landfills have become full. For several years now we have been looking for new places to put all this disposable garbage.

Answer the following questions as true or false according to the information in the paragraphs above. Put a T for true or an F for false in the blank next to each number. Be prepared to explain your answers.

_____ 1. In the past, people used things once and then threw them away.

_____ 2. In the past, people used things many times because they did not have many disposable things.

_____ 3. People developed disposable products such as plastic wrap and paper napkins less than fifty years ago.

_____ 4. People started throwing away disposable items in the past and continue to do this today.

_____ 5. According to the information above, we know exactly when many landfills became full.

_____ 6. People have just started to look for new places to put garbage.

ACTIVITY FOUR

Below you will find a list of some environmental problems. Choose two of these problems and do two things:

- Write a sentence or two about what people have been doing to cause each of the problems you chose. Be sure to use the present perfect progressive (continuous) in each sentence you write.
- Write a sentence or two about what people have been doing to solve each of the problems you chose. Be sure to use the present perfect progressive (continuous) in each sentence you write.

Choose Two:
air pollution   water pollution   disappearing rain forests   too much garbage

ACTIVITY FIVE

A. Below is a paragraph in which an environmental problem is describing itself to you. What is this problem?

PROBLEM
More and more people have been populating the Earth. All these people need room to live. Some people have been cutting down forests and wild areas. These are places where many of us have been living for thousands of years. Too many people have been moving into places that are already homes for plants and other living creatures like me. These people have been filling my habitat with stores and houses. All this has made my problem.

B. Now work in groups of three or four people. With the others in your group think of an environmental problem. Make believe you are this problem and describe yourself in a paragraph. Then have the other groups guess the problem. Try to use the present perfect progressive (continuous) as much as possible.

ACTIVITY SIX

Look back at your answers to the Preview part of this lesson. Were some of the problems you listed discussed in this lesson? Which problems have been the worst in your native country? What solutions have people in your country been trying? Have you personally been involved in any of these solutions?

Write a paragraph or two about what has been happening to the environment in a country you know well. (It can be your native country or the country where you are now living.) Include information about what people/you have been doing to help with some of the problems. Use the present perfect progressive (continuous) as much as possible in your writing. If possible, also use **for** and **since** in some of your sentences.

After you write, check your work for the following:

❏ You discussed at least one environmental problem and solution.

❏ You used the present perfect progressive (continuous) where possible.

❏ You used *for* and *ß∑* where possible.

LESSON 13:
THE ENVIRONMENT—
DESCRIBING EXPERIENCES
FROM PAST TO PRESENT—
PART TWO

Modals and Semi-modals

CHAPTER 4

LESSON 14: EVERYDAY ACTIVITIES— DISCUSSING POSSIBILITIES

Focus: might/may/could

Preview

Think about what you would like to do this weekend. Look at the list of possibilities below.

- Put a check next to the ones you think are possible for you for this weekend.
- Put a line through the choices that you think are impossible for you.

_____ see a movie

_____ eat out at a restaurant

_____ have a picnic in the park

_____ visit friends

_____ go skiing in the mountains

_____ stay home and relax

_____ attend a sporting event (soccer/baseball, etc.)

Share your answers with other students in the class. Discuss why some of these activities are possible and some are impossible. Discuss why you are sure or not sure about doing some of these activities.

Presentation

The following are some students' answers to the Preview activity above:

1. One student **may** attend a baseball game. She is not sure about this because her friend invited her, but hasn't called her back to confirm the date.
2. Another student **might** go skiing in the mountains. He'll only go if he can find someone to drive him there because his car is not running.
3. Some students **could** see a movie. They are not sure because they need to see the list of movies in their neighborhood in the newspaper.

QUESTIONS

1. Look at the first sentence in each of the answers above. Is there a word in each that tells you something is possible, but not definite?
2. Look at the words **may, might,** and **could** in each of the answers. Do these words have any endings? Do the verbs that follow these words have any endings?

Explanation

1. As discussed in Chapters 2 and 3, there are simple verbs and expanded verbs in English. Expanded verbs include a verb and one or more other words that work with the verb.
   - **Modal auxiliaries** work with verbs.
     MODAL AUXILIARY + VERB = EXPANDED VERB
   - Modal auxiliaries also add meaning to a sentence.
        In Lessons 14–19 you will learn about and practice how to use some **modals** in English.
2. **Could, might,** and **may** are modals. They add meaning to a sentence.
        As discussed in Lesson 7, when you are predicting something or have a definite intention, you should use **will + verb**. [See Lesson 7 to review this.]
        Sometimes you are *not sure* about something because it is only a possibility. When you are not sure, you can use **could, might,** or **may.** When you use these words, you are saying *maybe* or *perhaps*.

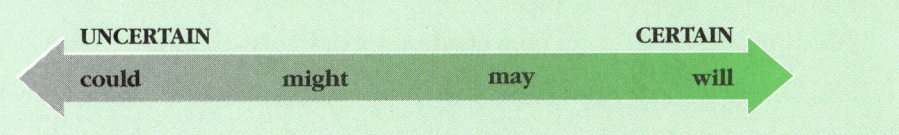

3. There are several grammatical rules about modals that never change.
   - Modals always come before the verb.
   - These words never change form. Never add an ending *(-ed/-s/-ing)* to them.
   - The verb that follows a modal also will not add any endings.
   - Never add **to** between a modal and the word that follows it.

   One student **may attend** a baseball game.
   Another student **might go** skiing in the mountains.

4. We can also use these modals for possibility about something that is possibly happening now or in the future. In this case we use the following pattern:

   modal + be + verb (base) + -ing

   Where is Jack studying now?
   Where is Jack studying next year?
   I'm not sure. He **might be attending** a state university.

   Where is Barbara? I called her and got her answering machine.
   She **may be visiting** her aunt in the hospital. She had a baby yesterday.
   Where is Barbara taking her vacation next summer?
   She **may be traveling** to New York to see her family.

   > NOTE Do not confuse the word **maybe** (one word) with **may be** (two words).
   >   Maybe is not a verb. (Maybe he is sick today.)
   >   May + be = modal auxiliary + verb (He may be sick today.)

5. To make a negative sentence with expanded verbs with a modal, add the word **not** after the modal. [For more information and practice with negative sentences, see Lesson 20.]
        Follow this pattern: modal + not + verb (no ending)

   He **may not attend** a baseball game.
   She **might not go** skiing in the mountains.

6. To make a question with expanded verbs with a modal, you must change the word order. Put the modal to the left of the subject. [For more information and practice with this kind of question, see Lesson 21.]

Follow this pattern: modal + subject + verb (no ending)

Might they go skiing in the mountains?
Could that team win the game tonight?

Be careful using **may** in questions. In this case, the meaning is usually permission, not possibility. [See Lesson 19 for more information and practice with permission and requests.]

Practice

ACTIVITY ONE

Complete the following conversation by doing two things:

A. Choose a verb from the list that best fits each blank. Use each verb only one time.

B. Add **might, may,** or **could** before each verb. Be sure to use each of these modals at least once.

NOTE In most of these sentences the different modals will not make a difference in meaning. Use the different modals in the activity for practice.

be   give   forget   ask   invite   have

Rio: I hear you're thinking about having a Halloween party this year. Will you tell everyone to wear a costume?

Seth: Yeah. That's what makes Halloween parties so much fun. I also _____ a contest. I _____ prizes for the funniest and scariest costumes.

Rio: How many people are you expecting?

Seth: I'm not sure because I haven't sent out the invitations yet. I _____ as many as fifty people. Halloween parties are more fun when you have a large group.

Rio: Will you make it potluck?

Seth: I'm not sure about that either. First I have to see how many people are coming. I _____ everyone to bring some desserts.

Rio: You know, it's October 10 and Halloween isn't very far away. Soon it _____ too late to make this party.

Seth: That's true. It sounds like a good idea, but it also sounds like a lot of work. I _____ the whole thing!

ACTIVITY TWO

Each statement below is a positive statement. Add the idea of maybe or perhaps by adding **may, could,** or **might** to each sentence. Rewrite each sentence including the modal in the space provided. Be sure to use all three modals at least once.

   EXAMPLE   He stays home to relax on Saturdays.
   He may stay home to relax on Saturdays.
   OR
   He might stay home to relax on Saturdays.
   OR
   He could stay home to relax on Saturdays.

1. I want to eat at that new restaurant downtown.

2. That man is the manager of this movie theater.

3. I'm taking a vacation to Tahiti next summer.

4. She visits her grandmother every week.

5. We plan to take a vacation in Europe.

6. The children are having a picnic in the park.

7. You are graduating from that school next June.

ACTIVITY THREE

A few people are on their way to a shopping mall. Each person is talking about what she or he plans to do there. Some people are sure about where they will go and what they will do. Other people are not sure. Listen to each person and then:

- Decide if this person is sure or not sure about what she or he will do at the mall.
- Next to each number below write **possibly** or **sure**. (Write *possibly* if you think the speaker is not sure about where she or he will go. Write *sure* if you think the speaker is sure about where she or he will go.)

1. _____
2. _____
3. _____
4. _____
5. _____

Compare answers with a partner. Did you have the same answers? If necessary, ask your teacher to read the information again.

LEARNING STRATEGY

Remembering New Material: Using words in meaningful sentences helps you remember them.

ACTIVITY FOUR

A. Steve, Sharon, and Jim are buying sandwiches for lunch. Below you will find a menu of their sandwich choices and the prices.

1. Read the information about each person's situation.
2. Decide what each person may, might, or could eat based on the menu and the information about the person. Then write two to three sentences about the different possibilities for each person.

   Try to use different verbs in your sentences as much as possible and be sure to use all three modals. Choose some of your verbs from the list below.

VERBS: buy   order   eat   have   choose   get   decide on

MENU:

Tom's "Back East" Sub Shop

Our Sandwich Menu

All subs made to your special request and served with our vegetables: lettuce, onion, tomato and pickle, plus cheese. Italian dressing is also included except as noted by*
Choice of french or wheat roll.

Cold Sandwiches

American . . . . 5" $2.19   12" $4.29   16" $5.79
Bologna, ham, spiced luncheon meat and American cheese

Combination . . . . 5" $2.19   12" $4.29   16" $5.79
Ham, bologna, spiced luncheon meat, salami, pepper loaf, pepperoni, provolone and American cheese

Seafood* . . . . 5" $2.39   12" $4.99   16" $5.99
A delicate blend of crabmeat and white fish salad with American cheese

Cheese . . . . 5" $2.19   12" $4.29   16" $5.79
American and provolone cheeses

Hot Sandwiches

Steak* . . . . 5" $2.39   12" $4.99   16" $5.99
Tender steak sliced thin with tomato sauce and American cheese

BLT* . . . . 5" $2.39   12" $4.99   16" $5.99
Old favorite of bacon, lettuce and tomato with American cheese

Meatball and Sausage* . . 5" $2.39   12" $4.79   16" $5.89
A combination of these two favorites topped with provolone cheese

Vegetarian . . . . 5" $2.19   12" $4.29   16" $5.79
American and provolone cheese melted and garnished with green peppers and mushrooms

INFORMATION:

Steve: He is a vegetarian. He doesn't eat meat, chicken or fish.

Sharon: She doesn't have much money today. She doesn't want to spend more than $4.00 on a sandwich.

Jim: He wants to have something hot for lunch. He doesn't like peppers or mushrooms.

EXAMPLE   John (another friend) loves bologna.
He might have an American sandwich.
OR
He could eat a Combination sandwich.

B. What kind of sandwich do you like to eat? Imagine you are having lunch with Steve, Sharon, and Jim. Write two to three sentences about different possibilities for your lunch. Use a different modal in each of your answers. Share your answers with the class and explain why these are possible choices for you.

ACTIVITY FIVE

Work in groups of three or four for this activity.

A. Look at the following photographs. Discuss what you think could, may, or might be happening in these pictures. Think about the following questions and discuss your ideas with the others in your group.

- Who are the people in these pictures?
- Where are they?
- Why are they there?
- What are they doing?

B. Choose one picture and create a short story or explanation about what you think is taking place. Be sure to use the modals from this lesson in your story (*can/might/could*). Share your story with the rest of the class.

LEARNING STRATEGY

Personalizing: Discussing your own personal interests helps you communicate more effectively.

ACTIVITY SIX

Look back at the Preview at the beginning of this lesson and think again about your plans for this weekend (or possibly your next vacation). What are some of the possibilities? Write a paragraph describing them. Be sure to use the modals from this lesson (*may/could/might*) in your paragraph.

Look back at your paragraph and check your work for the following.

- ❏ You have discussed the possibilities for your weekend or vacation using the modals from this lesson (*may/could/might*).
- ❏ The modals come before the verbs and do not have any endings added (*-s/-ed/-ing*).
- ❏ The verbs that follow the modals are in the simple form.

LESSON 14: EVERYDAY ACTIVITIES—DISCUSSING POSSIBILITIES

LESSON 15: SKILLS/TALENTS/CAPABILITIES— DISCUSSING ABILITIES

Focus: can/could/be able to

Preview

What specific things in the following areas do you have the ability to do? Do you have any special abilities in these areas? Discuss this with other people in your class.

- sports in general OR a specific sport
- on your job
- something you do in your free time (such as a hobby or special interest)

Presentation

Read the following facts and then answer the questions that follow.

1. Pumice is the only rock that can float. This is because it has so many holes.
2. A batted baseball can travel as fast as 120 miles per hour.
3. The Andromeda Galaxy is the farthest object you can see without a telescope.
4. The longest bicycle ever built was more than 66 feet long and could seat 35 people.
5. Seals are able to stay underwater for as long as seventy minutes.
6. A California condor is able to fly ten miles without flapping its wings.
7. The dinosaur Tyrannosaurus rex was able to eat enough meat to make 877 quarter-pound hamburgers each day.

QUESTIONS

1. Look at sentences 1–3. What word tells you this information is about ability?
   _____

   Look at sentence 4. What word tells you this information is about ability? What is the time in this sentence?
   _____

   Look at the verb in each of these sentences. What form of the verb do you see? (Does the verb have any endings on it? Does the verb change with the subject of the sentence?)
   _____

2. Look at sentences 5–7. What words tell you this information is about ability? What is the time in each of these sentences?
   _____

Explanation

1. As discussed in Lesson 14, **modals** work with verbs and form expanded verbs. They also add meaning to a sentence.

    Semimodals are special expressions that we use in place of modals. They also add meaning to a sentence.

    In some of the following lessons you will learn about several semimodals that have the same meaning as some modals.

2. Two modals and a semimodal often express **ability** in English:

    Modals: can   could
    Semimodal: be able to

3. As discussed in Lesson 14, modals:
    - always come before the verb.
    - never change form. (Never add an ending such as *-ed/-s/-ing* to modals.)
    In addition:
    - The verb that follows the modal also will not add any endings.
    - Never add **to** between the modal and the verb.

    A batted baseball **can travel** as fast as 120 miles per hour.
    The longest bicycle ever built was more than 66 feet long and **could seat** 35 people.

4. **Semimodals** also come before the verb.
    - These expressions change to fit the sentence.
    - The verb that follows the semimodal does not add any endings.

        The semimodal **be able to** changes to fit the subject.

    Seals **are able to stay** underwater for as long as 70 minutes.
    A California condor **is able to fly** 10 miles without flapping its wings.

    Be able to also changes for the time.
    The dinosaur Tyrannosaurus rex **was able to** eat enough meat to make 877 quarter-pound hamburgers. (past time)

5. Sometimes people use contractions with **be able to.**

    They**'re** able to stay under water for a long time.
    A condor**'s** able to fly for 10 miles without flapping its wings.

    NOTE   You will **not** find these contractions with **be able to** when it is used for past time.

6. Some **modals** are used for more than one time frame.
    Some modals are **not** used in the past.

    Can is not used in the past.
    Could is used to express past ability.
    I **can** speak French fairly well.
    Twenty years ago, I **could** speak French very fluently.

    We use **could** for past ability when we are talking about something that was true in general in the past. We do not use it for something that was true for one time only.

    When I was younger, I **could** visit my relatives every Thanksgiving.
    DO NOT SAY: Yesterday I could see my relatives at the airport.

LESSON 15: SKILLS/
TALENTS/CAPABILITIES—
DISCUSSING ABILITIES

7. To make a negative sentence with expanded verbs with the modals **can** and **could,** follow the rules in Lesson 14. (For example: I can't speak French fluently. Twenty years ago I couldn't speak French fluently.) [For more information and practice with negative sentences, see Lesson 20.]

   To make a negative sentence with the expanded form **be able to,** follow the rules in Lesson 6. (For example: Seals are not [aren't] able to fly. A condor is not [isn't] able to stay under the water for a long time.) [For more information and practice with negative sentences, see Lesson 20.]

8. To make a question with expanded verbs with the modals **can** and **could,** follow the rules in Lesson 14. (For example: Can he speak French fluently? Twenty years ago could you speak French fluently?) [For more information and practice with this type of question, see Lesson 21.]

   To make a question with the expanded form **be able to,** follow the rules in Lesson 6. (For example: Are seals able to fly? Is a condor able to stay under the water for a long time?) [For more information and practice with this type of question, see Lesson 21.]

Practice

ACTIVITY ONE

A. Complete the following sentences by doing two things:
   - Choose the verb from the list below that best fits each blank. You may use some verbs more than once, but try to use as many different verbs as possible.
   - Add **can** or **could** before each verb.

   fly   eat   wear   take   have   dress   attend   come

1. The Concorde supersonic jet _____ travelers from New York to Europe in less than four hours. Before the Concorde was available, people _____ from New York to Paris in no less than 7 hours.

2. Years ago I _____ lots of sweets without gaining any weight. These days I _____ a few sweets but I have to be very careful because I gain weight more easily now. Some people _____ many kinds of food without gaining weight, even as they get older. They are lucky people!

3. When we were in high school, girls _____ only _____ dresses, skirts, blouses and nicer clothes to school. A few years later, the school said female students _____ in more casual clothing such as slacks. Today, all the kids in high school _____ to classes wearing jeans and T-shirts.

LEARNING STRATEGY

Managing Your Learning: Focusing on one or two forms at a time will help you learn and use them correctly.

B. Complete the following sentences about abilities by doing two things:

- Choose the verb from the list below that best fits each blank. You should use each verb only one time.
- Add a form of **be able to** to each sentence. Be sure to change this expression to fit the subject and time.

(Some sentences may have more than one possible answer.)

run   pay   make   say   hold   get   speak

1. Usually a two-year-old child _____ at least a few words. Of course there are exceptions to this. My friend's child _____ in complete sentences when he was 18 months old.

2. Different people have different athletic abilities. Some people _____ their breath and swim under water for long periods of time. Other people _____ long races, such as marathons.

3. Often travel agents _____ arrangements for airplane travel at cheaper prices under certain conditions. For example, last month I _____ my flights for my vacation at a big discount. This was because I _____ for the flights more than a month in advance.

ACTIVITY TWO

Often as people grow older, their abilities change. Listen to the following statements made by some retired people about their abilities in the past and their abilities now. After you hear their statements, write the modal or semimodal used to express ability and the verb in the correct column below. You may hear contractions. In these cases, write out the words.

You will have more than one answer for each number below. (You will hear several sentences for each one.)

THEN	NOW
1. _____	_____
2. _____	_____
3. _____	_____
4. _____	_____

CHAPTER 4
MODALS AND
SEMI-MODALS

ACTIVITY THREE

Work in groups of three or four people. Look at the following cartoon about camping. Each person is thinking about things that she or he can do at home, but not while camping. Discuss these things.

With the others in your group, write a sentence about what each person is thinking. Use **can** or **be able to** in each of your sentences. Write your sentences in the spaces below.

Reprinted with special permission of King Features Syndicate

EXAMPLE (the baby) At home the baby can sleep in a crib.
At home the baby is able to sleep on a nice mattress in a crib.

the father _____
_____

the mother _____
_____

the little girl _____
_____

the boy with the truck _____
_____

the boy at the cooler _____
_____

Can you think of any other things that someone can do at home but not while camping outdoors? Share all of your answers with the others in the class.

ACTIVITY FOUR

Some people are happy in our modern world with all our technology and advances in many fields. Other people like to think about the past and how simple life was then. Think about life 100 years ago and life today. Think about your life in the past and your life today.

A. With a partner talk about changes between the past and today. Think about different areas such as city living, travel, communication, environment, personal lifestyle, etc.

B. Write some sentences about what could be done in the past, using **could** and **be able to (past)**.

In the past, people were able to breathe clean air.
In the past I could buy a good dinner at a restaurant for less than $5.

After you write your sentences, make some of them negative and change them to present time.

Today many people are not (aren't) able to breathe clean air.
Today I can't buy a good dinner at a restaurant for less than $5.

C. Write some sentences about what can be done today, using **can** and **be able to**.

Today we are able to use computers in our homes.
I can communicate with people in other countries very quickly with faxes
    and e-mail messages.

After you write your sentences, make some of them negative and change them to the past.

In the past we were not (weren't) able to use computers in our homes.
In the past I could not (couldn't) communicate with people in other
    countries very quickly with faxes and e-mail messages.

Share all of your answers with the other students in the class. Which do you think is better: life today or life in "the good old days"?

LEARNING STRATEGY

Overcoming Limitations: Getting and giving information in class helps prepare you for conversations in the outside world.

LESSON 15: SKILLS/
TALENTS/CAPABILITIES—
DISCUSSING ABILITIES

CHAPTER 4
MODALS AND
SEMI-MODALS

ACTIVITY FIVE

A. You are going to take a poll (survey) of your classmates and their abilities, both now and in the past.

- First, answer the following questions about your own abilities (yes or no).
- Share your "yes" answers with your classmates. Who has or had the most abilities in these areas?

YES	NO	LANGUAGE ABILITY
_____	_____	I can speak more than one language fluently.
_____	_____	I am able to say greetings (such as "hello") in three languages or more.
_____	_____	I could say words in more than one language when I was five years old.
_____	_____	I was able to speak more than one language fairly well when I was under 10.
		SPORTS ABILITY
_____	_____	I could run a marathon in the past.
_____	_____	I can run a marathon today.
_____	_____	I was able to swim when I was younger than 8 years old.
_____	_____	I am able to play goalie in soccer.
		COMPUTER ABILITY
_____	_____	I can program computer software in a specific language (i.e., C++/Pascal/Basic).
_____	_____	I could use a computer when I was in high school or younger.
_____	_____	I am able to use the Internet.
_____	_____	I was able to use a computer for my school work when I was younger.

B. Now write some more sentences about your abilities in the past and your abilities now. You can think of some other abilities in the areas above or in some different areas. Try to use the different forms for discussing abilities (*can/could/be able to*) as much as possible.

After you write your sentences, check your work for the following.

❏ Each of your sentences is about an ability and uses one of the forms from this lesson (*can/could/be able to*).

❏ The modals do not have any endings added (*-s/-ed/-ing*).

❏ The verbs that follow *can/could/be able to* are in the simple form.

❏ Sentences that use *could* are about past abilities.

In sentences that use *be able to:*

❏ the semimodal changes to fit the subject.

❏ the semimodal changes for the time.

C. Share your sentences with a partner. Tell the class one of your abilities and one of your partner's abilities.

LESSON 16: TRAVEL IDEAS—GIVING SUGGESTIONS, RECOMMENDATIONS, ADVICE

Focus: should/ought to/had better/could/might

Preview

Work with a partner for this activity. Find out what city your partner is from (or ask your partner to talk about a city she or he knows very well).

- Tell your partner you want to visit this city. Ask him or her to give you some recommendations (advice) about visiting this city.
- Find out how to prepare for your visit there.
- Get some advice about what to see and do there as well.

Presentation I

Following is some information about visiting San Diego, California.

WEATHER AND WHAT TO BRING

(1) The average daily temperature in San Diego is 70 degrees F and there are many days of warm sunshine. (2) Still, you should bring some warm clothes in the winter. (3) At night the temperature can drop about 20 degrees so you had better have some sweaters or jackets and coats for these colder nights. (4) Many people think it never rains in San Diego, but they are mistaken. (5) Most of this rain falls during the winter months (especially from December through February). (6) During these months, you ought to have an umbrella or raincoat if you plan to go sightseeing.

GETTING AROUND

(7) The most convenient way to get around San Diego is by car. (8) If you do not have a car, you should rent one, especially if you plan to visit many places in a short amount of time. (9) Most of the main attractions and shopping areas are near the freeways. (10) During rush hours you ought to check the traffic reports because sometimes there are delays on the freeways. (11) If this is your first visit to California, you had better check the laws about driving and car safety. (12) For example, you can get a ticket when you do not wear your seat belt or a young child is not in a car seat.

95

QUESTIONS

1. Find the word **should** in sentence #2 and sentence #8. Look at the form of this word and the verb that follows it in each case. Are there any endings on these words?
2. Find the words **ought to** in sentence #6 and sentence #10. Are there any endings on the verbs that follow this expression?
3. Find the expression **had better** in sentence #3 and sentence #11. Do any words come between this expression and the verb that follows it? Are there any endings on the verb that follows it in each case?
4. Do you find any difference in meaning between these words and expressions (should/ought to/had better)? Are they all of equal strength? (Does one seem stronger than the others?)

Explanation

1. There are several modals and semimodals you can use to make recommendations or give advice. Three of them are:

    MODAL: should   SEMIMODALS: ought to
                                                   had better

2. The modal **should** and the semimodals **ought to** and **had better** all come before the verb. These words never change form. In other words, you will never add an ending *(-ed/-s/-ing)* to any of them. The verb that follows **should/ought to/had better** also will not add any endings.

    You **should bring** some warm clothes in the winter.
    During these months, you **ought to** have an umbrella or raincoat if you plan to go sightseeing.
    You **had better** have some sweaters or jackets and coats for these colder nights

3. Do not add **to** between **should** and **had better** and the verb.

    You **should rent** a car, if you want to visit many places in a short amount of time.
    You **had better check** the laws about driving and car safety.

4. Sometimes people use contractions with **had better.** When you hear these contractions in everyday speech, it may be difficult to hear the "d." (It may sound like "you better . . .")

    You**'d better check** the laws.
    He**'d better take** his umbrella.

5. In conversation, **ought to** may sound like **oughtta.** You should never write this form, but you will hear native speakers use it in conversation.

6. **Should, ought to,** and **had better** are all used for recommendations or advice, but they are not always exactly the same in meaning.
    - **Ought to** is more common in British than American English. It can be a stronger way of making a recommendation than **should.**
    - **Had better** is more informal than the other two and is used mainly in speech. It is often used more strongly than **should** and can sound like a threat.

        Your boss says: You **had better** finish that report before 6 P.M.
        (If you don't, there could be a problem)

    In the examples below which one is more serious or a stronger recommendation?

    You **should bring** some warm clothes.
    You **had better** check the laws.

7. To make a negative sentence with expanded verbs with the modal **should,** follow the rules in Lesson 14. (For example: You should not [shouldn't] rent a car there. You should not [shouldn't] bring warm clothes.) [For more information and practice with negative sentences, see Lesson 20.]

   To make a negative sentence with the expanded form **had better,** add the **not** after the had better. The meaning of this is strong. It shows the situation is more serious.

   Follow this pattern: had better + not + verb (no ending)

   You **had better not drive** your car there.
   (If you drive there, you may have a serious problem.)

   NOTE   We do not usually use **ought to** in negative statements.

8. To make a question with expanded verbs with the modal **should,** follow the rules in Lesson 14. (For example: Should I bring a sweater? Should they rent a car in that city?) [For more information and practice with this type of question, see Lesson 21.]

   NOTE   We do not usually use **ought to** or **had better** in questions.

Practice

LEARNING STRATEGY

Remembering New Material: Practicing grammatical forms in context helps you understand and remember them.

ACTIVITY ONE

Read the following information. Then choose the word or expression in parentheses that fits best. Circle the correct answer.

THINGS TO DO IN SAN DIEGO

There are many interesting and famous places to visit in San Diego. For an opportunity to see several museums, you (should/ought) go to Balboa Park. To get the most for your money, you (ought/should) to buy a "*passport*" for $13. This allows you to visit up to nine museums. Of course, you (ought/had better) plan for enough time to see several museums. Also in the park, you will find the world-famous San Diego Zoo. This is one of the largest zoos in the world, so you really (ought/should) to try to make time to visit there.

name of a special ticket

Many people come to San Diego for its year-round recreation and outdoor sports. You (should/ought) bring your bathing suit because swimming is available in the ocean, Mission Bay, and public pools. Surfing is an all-year activity. However, the ocean is usually quite cold during winter months, so you (had better/ought) have a *wet suit* for those times. To watch *hang gliders* in action over the ocean, you (ought/had better) to go to the Torrey Pines beach area.

special waterproof bodysuit worn in cold water

people who practice the sport of flying through the air attached to a large set of wings

For more information about places to see in San Diego, you (should/had better/ought) to go to one of the two Visitor's Information Centers. They are located in downtown San Diego and at Mission Bay.

ACTIVITY TWO

Listen to the following pieces of advice about traveling, using **should, ought to,** and **had better.** In some of them you may hear contractions with **had better** or the short form **oughtta.** Each time you hear one of these words or expressions of advice, write it down with the verb that follows. If you hear a contraction or short form, write out the long form.

Driving Away from Home

_____

_____

Renting a Car

_____

_____

ACTIVITY THREE

A. Read each of the following pieces of information. Then give some advice about what this person can do, using **should, ought to,** or **had better** in your answers. Your answers should be complete sentences.

EXAMPLE   I can't find my traveler's checks. Someone stole them from my backpack!

You had (You'd) better call the company to report the problem.

1. I don't have enough towels in my hotel room.
   _____

2. We want to eat dinner at 8 P.M. at that expensive restaurant downtown.
   _____

3. My friend needs to get to the airport in 20 minutes.
   _____

4. I just had an accident with the car I rented.
   _____

5. My mother wants to go shopping, but she doesn't have a car.
   _____

6. We need to get up at 5 A.M. for our flight home tomorrow.
   _____

B. Work in groups of three and share your answers to this activity. Did you all use the same modals or semimodals in your sentences? Discuss the different ways people wrote their sentences.

LESSON 16: TRAVEL IDEAS—GIVING SUGGESTIONS, RECOMMENDATIONS, ADVICE

Presentation II

Read the following suggestions about things to do in Vancouver, British Columbia in Canada.

In Vancouver you can find many sports and outdoor recreational activities. People who like to be adventurous might want to try whitewater rafting on one of the rivers in the area, including the Chilliwack, the Lillooet, the Fraser and the Thompson. Visitors could also try skiing on the challenging slopes of Grouse Mountain or Mount Seymour Park in North Vancouver. While there you might try cross-country skiing as well as downhill. In the winter, you could try an icy relative of bowling, called curling. This involves throwing heavy rounded stones down the ice, followed by using a broom to smooth the course.

*IT WORKS!
Learning Strategy:
Guessing Meanings
from Context*

QUESTIONS

1. What recommendations/suggestions for sports and activities can you find in this paragraph?
2. What specific words are used to tell you these are recommendations or suggestions? Write these words and the verbs that follow them.
3. Are there any endings on the words that make these suggestions or on the verbs that follow these words?

Explanation

1. There are two other modals that we sometimes use to make recommendations or suggestions:

    could   might

2. These modals come before the verb and follow the same grammar rules as **should**. (See #2, #3, #7 and #8 above.)

    People who like to be adventurous **might want** to try whitewater rafting on one of the rivers in the area
    In the winter, you **could try** an icy relative of bowling, called curling.

3. **Could** and **might** are not as strong as *should, ought to* and *had better*. Use **could** and **might** when you want to make a suggestion that is mild or not too important.

Practice

ACTIVITY FOUR

Read the statements or questions in the column on the left. Then find the recommendation that fits each one in the column on the right. Choose the letter of the correct answer. Write the letter in the space next to each number on the left.

_____ 1. I want to buy that souvenir, but I left my cash in the hotel.

_____ 2. Do you know of any Italian restaurants near here?

_____ 3. I just met an interesting man at the front desk. He's traveling alone.

_____ 4. My sister wants to find out about tickets for a show tonight.

_____ 5. Excuse me, do you know the best way to get to the Sports Arena?

_____ 6. Uh-oh. I lost my umbrella at the museum.

a. He could go sightseeing with us if he wants some company.

b. She might try the discount ticket outlet. They often have half-price tickets.

c. I'm not sure, but you might want to take Route 8 West.

d. You could call the lost and found. Maybe it's there.

e. You could pay with a credit card.

f. No, I don't. You might try to find one in the yellow pages of the phone book.

ACTIVITY FIVE

Below you will find names of some places you can visit in Vancouver. You will also find the names of four people and their interests. These people are planning to visit Vancouver soon.

1. Make some suggestions to each person about where to go in Vancouver.
2. Also make some suggestions about where they might go together.

Write a complete sentence for each suggestion. Use the modals **could** and **might** in your suggestions.

Dr. Sun Yat-Sen Classical Chinese Garden
Playland Amusement Park
H.R. Macmillan Planetarium
Maritime Museum
Science World
Capilano Fish Hatchery
Burnaby Village Museum

Vancouver Public Aquarium
Museum of Anthropology
M.Y. Williams Geological Museum
Vandusen Botanical Gardens
Chinatown
Lynn Canyon Park
Capilano Suspension Bridge and Park

Marc: science & technology
boating and the oceans
hiking

Stephane: flowers and gardening
fishing
hiking

George: rocks and minerals
archaeology
hiking

Urs: history
Chinese food
hiking

LESSON 16: TRAVEL IDEAS—GIVING SUGGESTIONS, RECOMMENDATIONS, ADVICE

SUGGESTIONS:

Marc _____

_____

Stephane _____

_____

George _____

_____

Urs _____

_____

Together _____

_____

LEARNING STRATEGY

Forming Concepts: Applying new information to a realistic situation helps you understand it better.

ACTIVITY SIX

Look back at the Preview section of this lesson. Think of a city you know well. This could be your native city, the city where you are now living, or any other city you know well. Write a paragraph or two of suggestions for a visitor to this city. You can include any kind of suggestions such as places to visit, how to travel in this city, what clothes to bring there, where to find a good hotel or restaurant, etc.

Be sure to include some different kinds of suggestions, some strong ones and some not so strong ones. Use the modals and semimodals from this lesson (*should/ought to/had better/could/might*) as much as possible in your writing.

After you write your paragraph, check your work for the following.

- ❏ You have included different modals and semimodals in your advice (*should/ought to/had better/could/might*).
- ❏ You checked the form of all your modals, semimodals, and the verbs that followed (no endings on any of them).
- ❏ You used *could* and *might* for your suggestions that were not as strong.
- ❏ You used *had better* for your strongest recommendations.

LESSON 17: WHAT'S NECESSARY?—DISCUSSING OBLIGATIONS AND REQUIREMENTS

Focus: must/have to/have got to

Preview

- Think about obligations you have in your life (things that are necessary for you or things you cannot say "no" to). What obligations do you have?
- Are there obligations in your country or your family that you may not have in other places or with other people?
- Think about your school or your job situation. Are there any things you are obligated to do at school or on your job?

Discuss your answers in groups of three people.

Presentation

The following information comes from an employee handbook of a manufacturing company. Read the information and then answer the questions that follow.

BADGES AND VISITOR CONTROL

something you wear for identification/name tag

employees/workers

All employees must wear an employee *badge* at all times while on company property. A badge with an orange triangle shows permission to be in the offices and factory. Only authorized *personnel* will have these badges. If you do not have your badge with you, you should request a temporary badge from Payroll Administration at the beginning of your work day.

building where goods are received, stored, and shipped

permission

limited

All visitors must wear a visitor's badge. They also have to sign the visitor log at the reception desk in the lobby. Non-employees are not allowed in the factory or beyond the shipping and receiving area in the *warehouse*. Visitors must have *authorization* from company officers to enter *restricted* areas. Employees should be aware of the security of these premises and should question any person in the plant without proper identification.

QUESTIONS

1. What are some recommendations for employees in this company? How do you know they are recommendations? (What words tell you this?)
2. What are some obligations of employees in this company? How do you know they are obligations? (What words tell you this?)

Explanation

1. One modal and two semimodals often express **obligation** or **necessity** in English:

   MODAL: must   SEMIMODALS: have to
                                                   have got to

2. As with the other modals, **must** always comes before the verb and never changes form. The verb that follows this modal also will not add any endings. Never add **to** between the modal and the verb.

   All visitors **must wear** a visitor's badge.
   All employees **must wear** an employee badge at all times while on company premises.

3. The semimodals **have to** and **have got to** also come before the verb. These expressions change to fit the sentence. The verb that follows the semimodals does not add any endings.

   These semimodals change to fit the subject.

   They **have to sign** the visitor log at the reception desk.
   He **has to sign** the visitor log at the reception desk.
   We **have got to** sign the visitor log at the reception desk.
   She **has got to** sign the visitor log at the reception desk.

4. When **must** means obligation, we do not use it in the past. We use the past of **have to** (**had to**) to express past obligation or necessity.

   We **have to** sign the visitor log when we go there.
   We **had to** sign the visitor log when we went there.

5. You will probably hear **have to** and **have got to** more often than **must**. In conversation, you may hear the following short forms. (You should never write these forms, but you will hear native speakers use them in conversation.)
   - have to   You will hear **hafta**.
   - has to   You will hear **hasta**.
   - had to   You will hear **hadda**.
   - have got to   You will hear **gotta**.

6. To make a negative sentence with expanded verbs with the modal **must**, follow the rules in Lesson 14. **Must + not** has a strong meaning. It expresses that something is prohibited (not allowed). [For more information and practice with negative sentences, see Lesson 20.]

   You **must not (mustn't)** go into the office without a badge.
   You **must not (mustn't)** bring visitors into the plant.

   To make a negative sentence with the expanded form **have to + verb**, follow the rules in Lesson 4 (using "do"). This negative form means something is not necessary. [For more information and practice with negative sentences, see Lesson 20.]

   We **do not (don't) have to** sign the visitor log.
   You **do not (don't) have to** wear a badge here.

7. To make a question with expanded verbs with the modal **must**, follow the rules in Lesson 14. (For example: Must I wear a badge? Must we sign the visitor log?) [For more information and practice with this type of question, see Lesson 21.]

   To make a question with the expanded form **have to,** follow the rules in Lesson 4 (using "do"). (For example: Do I have to wear a badge in the plant? Does she have to sign the visitor log?) [For more information and practice with this type of question, see Lesson 21.]

LESSON 17: WHAT'S NECESSARY?—DISCUSSING OBLIGATIONS AND REQUIREMENTS

CHAPTER 4
MODALS AND
SEMI-MODALS

Practice

ACTIVITY ONE

Abdulmohsen wants to apply to a state university for his Bachelor's Degree. He asked his friend about how to apply and below are some of the answers his friend gave him. Read the information his friend gave him. Then choose the word(s) or expression(s) in parentheses that fits best. Circle the correct answer(s). In some cases more than one answer may be correct.

1. Applicants to undergraduate programs (have to/has to/must) use the undergraduate application form.
2. Each applicant (have/has/must) to supply all the required information on the form or the form will not be processed.
3. Applicants for certain majors (have/has/must) to file by the specific deadline dates listed in the application booklet.
4. To get financial aid, you (have got/has got/must) to complete and submit the special Financial Aid form before December 31st.
5. Last year the application fee was $55.00, so I (have/had/has) to send that money with the application. I think they've changed the fee. You should call the school to find out about the new fee. You (has to/have got to/must to) send the correct fee with the application.
6. Students not classified as residents of this state (has got to/have to/must) pay the higher tuition fees.

ACTIVITY TWO

If possible, add the modal or semimodal in parentheses to the sentences below. Then make any changes to the verb if necessary. Do *not* add any other words to the sentence. In some cases, it may be impossible to add the word(s) in parentheses to the sentence. In these cases, leave the line blank and go to the next one.

EXAMPLES (must)   I work every Saturday.
I must work every Saturday.

(have to)   He works every night from 6–11 P.M.
He has to work every night from 6–11 P.M.

(have got to)   Those people work every weekday from 8 to 5.
Those people have got to work every weekday from 8 to 5.

1. (must)   My husband wakes up every morning at 5 A.M. for work.
   _____

   (have to)   My son wakes up every morning at 6 A.M. for school.
   _____

   (have got to)   My best friend wakes up every morning at 7 A.M. to prepare her son for school.
   _____

LESSON 17: WHAT'S NECESSARY?—DISCUSSING OBLIGATIONS AND REQUIREMENTS

2. (must)   Many of my friends wear a suit and tie to work.
   _____

   (have to)   You wear a suit and tie to work at that office.
   _____

   (have got to) We wear a suit and tie to work every day.
   _____

3. (must)   Two weeks ago I went to Tokyo on a business trip.
   _____

   (have to)   My boss went to New York on a business trip last week.
   _____

   (have got to) Last month three supervisors went to Tokyo on a business trip.
   _____

LEARNING STRATEGY

Testing Hypotheses: Checking with native speakers whenever possible helps you to verify your understanding of short forms.

ACTIVITY THREE

Your teacher will read some telephone conversations between some teenagers two times. In each conversation you will hear these people talking about various obligations, using short forms.

- After the first time your teacher reads each conversation, check the "not past" or "past" space for the time of the information you heard.
- After your teacher reads the conversation a second time, write any short forms you hear as well as the verb that follows each one.

1. _____ not past   _____ past
2. _____ not past   _____ past
3. _____ not past   _____ past

Now compare and discuss your answers with a partner. Make any changes that you think are necessary.

ACTIVITY FOUR

Work with a partner for this exercise. Below you will find a list of things to do when driving and/or taking care of a car using a manual (stick) shift.

A. Read the list and then do two things:

- Decide if each one is a recommendation or a necessity. (Think about the laws/regulations that exist where you are now living.)
- Write each one in the appropriate column below.

change the oil every 2,000 miles
use the clutch to change gears
follow the speed limit
fill up with gas
wear your seatbelt
have car insurance
do a tune-up regularly
use premium gas
have air in the tires

RECOMMENDATION	NECESSITY

B. With your partner think of some other things that are necessary or recommended and add them to the lists.

C. Write some sentences discussing these recommendations and necessities, using the different forms you learned:

- **should/ought to/had better** for recommendations
- **must/have to/have got to** for necessities

EXAMPLES You should slow down for a yellow light.
  You have to (had better) stop at a red light.

After you write your sentences, look at the checklist on page 108.

LEARNING STRATEGY

Managing Your Learning: Working in steps to organize your thoughts is helpful before you produce the final product.

ACTIVITY FIVE

LESSON 17: WHAT'S NECESSARY?—DISCUSSING OBLIGATIONS AND REQUIREMENTS

Do this activity in groups of three or four people. Sometimes people look for jobs in the newspaper. Most newspapers have a classified ad section that contains advertisements from companies and businesses looking for workers. In these advertisements they describe the job and discuss what skills/abilities are needed. When a skill is necessary, they often say it is "a must" or "necessary." When a skill is recommended but not necessary, they often say it is "a plus."

A. Below you will find two advertisements from a newspaper in the United States. Read each one and discuss any new vocabulary or abbreviations that you don't understand. Then decide what skills are necessary and what skills are recommended. List these skills for each advertisement.

---

1. TECHNICAL WRITER:
Prefer degree–BS/BA. Candidate with formal writing courses in composition and good grammar are a must. Previous experience in developing and writing manuals and procedures is recommended. Desktop publishing experience or training is a plus. Must have strong computer skills. Job requires an interview and writing sample. Mail resume with cover letter to:
Job Search PO Box 52,
Los Angeles, CA

---

2. ADVERTISING:
Dynamic agency is looking for a creative person to develop ad campaigns. Must be highly motivated and a self starter. Ability to work under tight deadlines required. Must have a minimum of two years experience in advertising, with more than two years a plus. Experience with Mac-based graphics recommended. Send resume and letter of interest to:
Human Resources, 556 Lake Carmel Avenue, Chicago, Illinois

A MUST (necessary)	A PLUS (recommended)
#1	
#2	

B. Imagine that you must write an advertisement for the school or class you are now attending. What kind of person would be a successful student there? What things are necessary and what things are recommended to be successful there? List these below.

A MUST	A PLUS

With the others in your group, write your own advertisement for a successful student at this school.

C. Each group will read each advertisement to the class. The other people in the class will take notes about what is recommended and what is necessary to be a good student in each advertisement. Then each group should write a short paragraph that describes a good student, using some of these ideas.

Use the following checklist after you complete Activity 4 and Activity 5. Check your work for the following.

❏ You discussed both necessities and recommendations.

❏ You included all three modals and semimodals *(must/have to/have got to)* for necessities.

❏ You included different ways of making recommendations (using *should/ ought to/had better*).

❏ You checked the form of all your modals, and the verbs that followed (no endings on any of them).

❏ You made changes on the semimodals when necessary (to fit the sentence in time or for the subject).

LESSON 18: DRAWING CONCLUSIONS—MAKING INFERENCES AND ASSUMPTIONS

Focus: must

Preview

Read the following situations and answer the questions after each.

A. You see a man and woman entering a stretch limousine. The man is wearing a tuxedo and the woman is wearing a long evening gown and diamond jewelry. You don't know these people but you make some conclusions in your head about them. What conclusions can you make about:

- how much money they have?
- where they are going?

B. It is 3 o'clock in the afternoon and you are at an airport to pick up a friend. Your friend's plane hasn't arrived yet, so you are waiting at the gate. You see a man at the next gate. The sign at that gate says "Flight 53–Arrival 2:45 P.M." The man looks at his watch several times. He is walking back and forth from the gate to the window. What conclusions can you make about:

- how the man feels?
- the airplane from the next gate?
- what the man is doing?
- why the man is there?

Share your answers with the rest of the class. Your teacher will write some of these conclusions on the board.

Presentation

The following are some possible answers to the questions in the preview above.

A. They must be rich.
They must have a good amount of money.
They must be leaving now.
They must be going out to someplace expensive.
They must be spending a lot of money on this.

B. He must be waiting for that airplane.
The airplane must be late.
He must be upset about waiting.

QUESTIONS

1. Look at the sentences in both (A) and (B). What modal do you see in each conclusion? Do you think this modal means obligation or necessity in any of these sentences?
2. Look at the form of the expanded verbs in the first two sentences in A. Are there any endings on the modal or the verb that follows?
3. Look at the form of the expanded verbs in the second two sentences in A. Are there any endings on any of the words in these expanded verbs?

Explanation

1. Sometimes we have a limited amount of information about people or situations. Using this information, we can make a conclusion about the person or situation. We call this **inference** or **assumption.**
2. You have already learned about using the modal **must** for necessity or obligation. Sometimes we use **must** for inference when we want to make a conclusion about someone or something. (This conclusion is stronger than just a slight possibility.)

    EXAMPLE We see two people entering a limousine and they are wearing expensive clothing and jewelry. We conclude they are rich. (We don't know this for sure, but we think it could easily be true. There is a strong possibility this is true.)

    They **must be** rich.
    They **must have** a good amount of money.

3. In Lesson 14 you learned about words that show possibility (*could/might/may*). In some cases you might use these words for conclusions, but they are not as strong as **must** for this meaning.

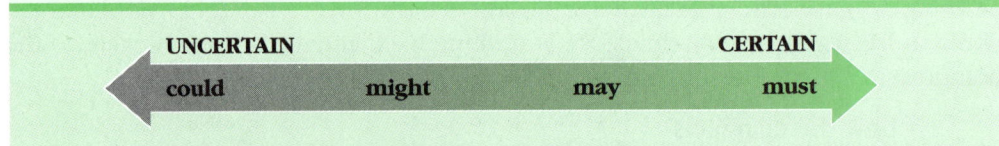

The plane **could/might/may be** late. (possibly or maybe)
The plane **must be** late. (probably)

   In the first example, the words **could/may/might** are not very strong. Only the **must** in the second sentence is a strong conclusion. In that sentence the speaker is fairly sure that this is true.

4. We can also use **must** for inference when we want to discuss something that is happening now. In this case we use the following pattern:

    must + be + verb (base) + -ing
    They **must be leaving** now.
    They **must be going** out to some place expensive.

5. To make a negative inference with expanded verbs with the modal **must**, follow the rules in Lesson 14. [For more information and practice with negative sentences, see Lesson 20.]

    He's not eating the pizza. He **must not be** hungry.
    They're wearing shorts and T-shirts. They **must not be going** to an expensive restaurant.

Practice

LESSON 18: DRAWING CONCLUSIONS—MAKING INFERENCES AND ASSUMPTIONS

ACTIVITY ONE

Below you will find a question and a sentence. Change each sentence from a fact to an inference by adding the modal **must** to the sentence. Then make any changes to the rest of the expanded verb if necessary. Do *not* add any other words to the sentences.

EXAMPLE Who are the people in the green uniforms? They work in that factory.

They must work in that factory.

1. Who is the man at the table? He is Bob's uncle from Chicago.

2. Why are so few people on line here? We are late for the 7 P.M. movie.

3. Why are those children standing on the corner? They are waiting for the school bus to pick them up.

4. Why do Sue's friends want to take a drive in the mountains? They have a new sports car.

5. Who is that lady at the computer? She is the new math teacher at the high school.

6. Where can we eat at this hotel? They are serving dinner in the dining room.

7. How does she keep in such good health? She eats healthy nonfattening food most of the time.

8. What flight is your brother taking home tomorrow? He's arriving on the 6 A.M. flight from Amsterdam.

CHAPTER 4
MODALS AND
SEMI-MODALS

ACTIVITY TWO

A. Each sentence below contains the modal **must**. In some cases the **must** means obligation or necessity and in other sentences it is an assumption or inference. Read each sentence. Then put a check (✔) next to each sentence that shows inference.

_____ 1. In the United States everyone must pay taxes and file tax returns by April 15.

_____ 2. Bill's father says he must finish his homework before he goes to the movies.

_____ 3. Jose is not answering his telephone. He must be studying at the library.

_____ 4. That young boy with the red hair must be Jill's son.

_____ 5. You must take your dirty shoes off before you enter the house.

_____ 6. You must be tired after hiking up that mountain.

_____ 7. Yuko must go to the airport at six o'clock in order to be on time for her flight.

_____ 8. Rogerio must like to exercise because I see him at the fitness center almost every day.

_____ 9. You must be very happy about finishing your college studies.

_____ 10. My neighbor must be cooking her food on the barbecue because I smell it.

*IT WORKS!
Learning Strategy:
Guessing Meaning
from Context*

B. Listen to parts of some conversations. In each one you will hear a sentence with the word **must**. In some cases the **must** means obligation or necessity and in other sentences it is an assumption or inference. Listen to each conversation carefully and decide if the meaning of must is necessity or assumption. Then write the word "inference" or "necessity" on the line next to the number.

1. _____

2. _____

3. _____

4. _____

5. _____

ACTIVITY THREE

Read each statement below. Then write a sentence that expresses an assumption or conclusion based on the information in the sentence. Use the modal **must** and the words in parentheses in each answer. Use the **must + be + base + -ing** pattern if possible in some of your answers.

EXAMPLE Joe buys a new Mercedes every year. (a lot of money)

> He (Joe) must have a lot of money.
> OR
> He must earn a lot of money.

1. That airplane leaves in five minutes. (on the runway)
2. Claudia and Nadia live next door to each other in the dormitory. (know each other)
3. Those passengers are showing the sky cap their plane tickets and giving him their baggage. (check in)
4. Those people are looking at a map and talking about it. (lost)
5. That man leaves that office building every day at 5 P.M. (work there)
6. The woman in the elevator is wearing a cast on her leg. (a broken leg)
7. Those two people are communicating in sign language. (hearing impaired)
8. My neighbor is looking under the hood of his car and he has some tools in his hand. (fix the car)
9. That food in the refrigerator smells terrible. (rotten)
10. The customer is taking her credit card out of her wallet. (pay the bill)

ACTIVITY FOUR

Work with a partner for this exercise.

Below are several photographs. Look at each photo and then answer the questions that follow with a conclusion about what you see. Be sure to use **must** in each conclusion. Then look at the checklist on page 114.

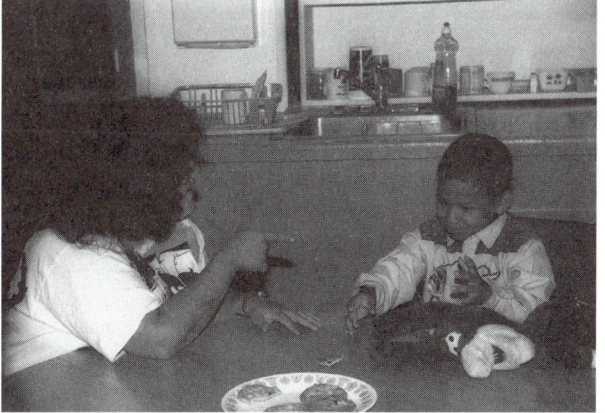

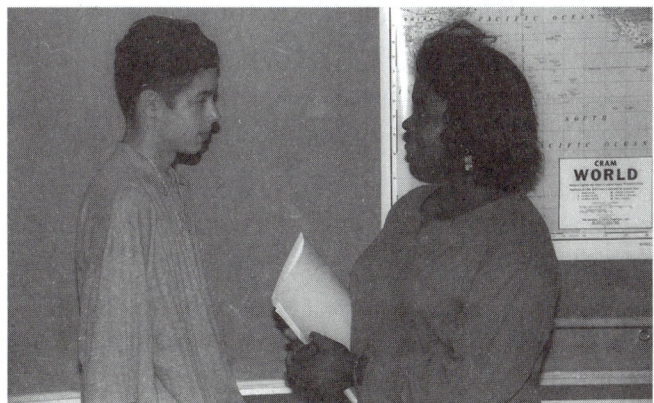

QUESTIONS

Answer the same questions for each photograph.
1. Who are these people?
2. Where are they?
3. Why are they there?
4. What are they doing?

LEARNING STRATEGY

Understanding and Using Emotions: Becoming aware of other people's thoughts helps you learn about other cultures.

ACTIVITY FIVE

A. Work in groups of three for this exercise. Look at the following photographs. In each one there is a woman using some body language. What message do you think she is sending with this body language? Write a sentence about the probable meaning or message using **must.** Compare your answers with the others in your class.

EXAMPLE   She **must be** happy.
               It **must mean something** positive.
               She **must be saying** something is good.

B. Think about the kind of body language that people use in your country. What kinds of gestures do people make with their hands? What kinds of facial expressions are typical? Share these with the rest of your class by showing these examples of body language. Your classmates will make conclusions about the meaning of this body language.

After you write your conclusions for Activity Four and Activity Five, check your work for the following:

❑ Each of your sentences is a strong conclusion (inference/assumption).

❑ Each of your sentences contains the modal *must.*

❑ You have followed all the grammatical rules about using modals.
- no ending on the modal, no ending on the verb that follows, no *to* after the modal
- when necessary, you have followed this pattern:
must + be + verb (base) + -ing

LESSON 19: GETTING HELP AND PERMISSION—MAKING REQUESTS

Focus: would/could/will/can/may

Preview

LEARNING STRATEGY

Testing Hypotheses: Relating something new to something familiar is one of the best ways to understand the new information.

Imagine that you need to find directions to get somewhere. You don't have a map, but some other people do. Look at the list of people below; each has a map that you want to look at. **In your native language,** how will you ask each person to see the map? Write your requests on the lines below.

1. your best friend
   _____

2. your grandfather
   _____

3. your teacher
   _____

4. your younger sister
   _____

5. your boss
   _____

6. a stranger on the street
   _____

CHAPTER 4
MODALS AND
SEMI-MODALS

Presentation

A. Now work with a partner. Imagine the same situation as in the Preview. How will you ask each person below to see the map **in English**?

Look at the following ways you can make your requests in English. Which will you use for the different people below?

Would you please show me your map?   Can you show me your map?
Will you show me your map?   Could you show me your map?
Show me your map.   Please show me your map.

Write your requests on the lines below. If you are not sure, just take a guess. (You may want to use some of the requests above more than one time.)

1. your best friend

   _____

2. your grandfather

   _____

3. your teacher

   _____

4. your younger sister

   _____

5. your boss

   _____

6. a stranger on the street

   _____

B. Share your answers with the class. Write some of your classmates' answers below if they are different from yours. Your teacher will also write some of these sentences on the board.

QUESTIONS

1. Look back at your answers in your language.
   - Did you write the exact same request for each person?
   - Can you explain why these requests were or were not the same?

   Look back at your answers in English.
   - Did you write the exact same request for each person?
   - Can you explain why these requests were or were not the same?

2. Compare the requests you wrote in your language with the requests you wrote in English.
   - Were some more formal or more polite than others? If so, which ones were the most formal in each language?
   - Were the formal and informal requests for the same people in your language as in English? If there were differences, can you explain why?

3. Look at the first word in each of your requests in English.
   - Did you use different modals?
   - Which modals did you use in the more formal requests and which modals did you use in the more informal requests?
4. Look at the answers that your teacher wrote on the board. What kind of word order do you see in each request?

Explanation

1. When you want to make a request (ask for something), you will often use modals. Some of these modals are: **would/could/will/can.**
   - In requests, some modals are more formal or more polite than others.
   - If you want to be very direct (and most informal), you can also make a request using an imperative form. [See Lesson 3 for more information about imperatives.]
   - You may also want to add *please* to your requests when you want to be more polite.

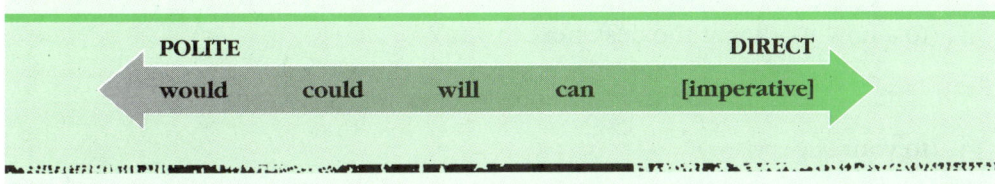

Would you please show me your map?   more formal
Could you show me your map?
Will you show me your map, please?
Can you show me your map?
Please show me your map.
Show me your map.   less formal

2. When you want to make a request for permission, you can use different modals as well.

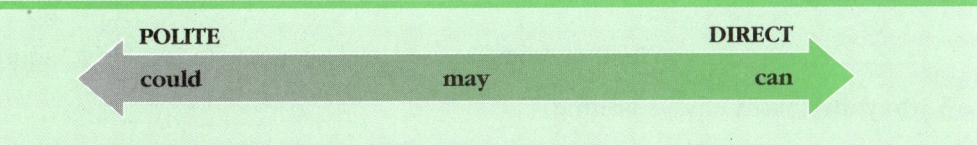

Could I borrow your map, please?   more formal
May I borrow your map?
Can I borrow your map?   less formal

NOTE Some people feel that it is not acceptable to use **can** for permission, but native speakers often use it this way.

3. Most requests are in the form of a question. This means that you must follow question word order. [See Lesson 21 for more information about this.] Use the following pattern at the beginning of your request:

modal + subject + verb (base form)

Practice

ACTIVITY ONE

A. It is time for lunch and you are at work. You are hungry, but you have no money to buy lunch. You want to borrow money to buy some food. Look at the list of modals below and choose one for each sentence. Think about how formal or polite you want to be for each one. Be prepared to explain your answers. (Some answers may have more than one possibility.)

    can   would   could   may   will

1. (to your best friend at the office)

   _____ I borrow $5 for lunch?

2. (to another worker—you don't know her very well)

   _____ you lend me some money for lunch today?

3. (to a new worker at the desk next to you)

   _____ you lend me some money for lunch today?

4. (to your supervisor)

   _____ I please borrow some money for lunch?

B. You are at home on a day off from school or work and you want to go to a movie. You have $5, but the movie costs $7. You will ask some people for the $2 you need to see the movie.

1. (to your mother or father)

   _____ I borrow $2 to see a movie?

2. (to a neighbor you have known most of your life)

   _____ you lend me some money to see a movie today? I'm $2 short.

3. (to your cousin who is visiting)

   _____ you please lend me $2 to see a movie?

ACTIVITY TWO

You are going to hear several telephone messages. After you hear each one, answer the following:
- What is the request in each message? In some cases, there may be more than one request.
- What is the relationship between the caller and the person she or he is calling?

Share your answers with the class. Ask your teacher to repeat the messages if necessary.

LEARNING STRATEGY

Overcoming Limitations: Role-playing specific situations helps you prepare for conversations outside class.

ACTIVITY THREE

Do this activity in small groups. Imagine you are in the following situations. What will you say for each one? Be sure to use the requests from this lesson (using *would/could/may/will/can/an imperative*). In some cases, there may be more than one possible answer. Discuss the different possibilities. Share your answers with the rest of the class.

1. You are cooking dinner and you realize that you need two eggs, but you don't have any. You go to your neighbor's house to ask for some eggs.
2. You are leaving a store and carrying a few packages. You get to the door and you can't open it. There is another person at the door. You want to ask him or her for help.
3. You are a salesperson in a store. You want to ask the customer if she or he needs any help.
4. Your sister is coming to visit you and you want to meet her at the airport today. This means you have to leave work early. How will you ask your boss for permission to go to the airport?
5. You are at a restaurant and you want to ask the waiter for more napkins. What will you say?

ACTIVITY FOUR

Do this activity with a partner.

A. Imagine that you are eighteen years old and living with your family in your country. Look at the following situations. Will you ask for permission from your parents to do these things? Discuss this with your partner.

- You want to drive your parents' car to see a movie tonight.
- You want to take a two-week vacation to another country.
- You want to go to another country to study for six months.
- You want to marry your boyfriend or girlfriend.

Do you think the answers are the same for people in the United States? If not, how might they be different?

B. With your partner, write a request for permission for each situation above. Try to use a different modal for each request. Then look at the checklist on page 120.

ACTIVITY FIVE

Do this activity in groups of three or four. Read the following situations. For each situation you must make a request or ask for permission about something. Think about the situation and the people involved. Then write the answers to the questions for each situation. Use one of the modals from this lesson in each of your answers. Try to use as many of these words/forms (*can/may/could/would/will/an imperative*) as possible.

A. You are in a movie theater, watching a very interesting and enjoyable movie. The people in front of you are constantly talking and it is difficult for you to hear the movie. The theater is crowded and you cannot change seats. You want to ask these people to be quiet. What will you say?

These people did not pay attention to your first request and they are continuing to talk. How will you ask them to be quiet again?

These people are still talking. Now you are going to the manager of the theater. How will you make a request to him or her?

B. You are in the waiting room at a doctor's office. A large window is open and the room is getting cold. How will you ask the receptionist or nurse to close the window?

You are at a friend's house and the window is open. You are getting cold. How will you ask your friend to close the window?

You are at home in your brother or sister's room and the window is open. You are getting cold. How will you ask your brother or sister to close the window?

C. You are at a supermarket and you want a certain kind of toothpaste. This toothpaste is on the top shelf in the back and you cannot reach it. Another shopper is next to you. How will you ask this person to get the box for you? How will you ask your son or daughter (who is taller than you are) to get this box for you?

D. You are shopping at a clothing store and you want to try on some clothes. How will you ask the salesperson for permission to try on the clothes?

You have decided to buy the clothing, but you have some other questions. How will you ask about the following:

- returning it if you change your mind
- asking them to hold it until six o'clock

Look back at your answers for Activity 4 and Activity 5.
Check your work for the following:

ACTIVITY 4
❏ Your requests for permission use the modals *may, could,* or *can*.

ACTIVITY 5
❏ Your requests use the modals *would, could, may, will,* or *can*.

ACTIVITY 4 and ACTIVITY 5
❏ Each request follows the pattern: *modal + subject + verb (base form)*.

Negatives/Question Formation

CHAPTER 5

LESSON 20: EATING HABITS/HEALTHY EATING— MAKING NEGATIVE STATEMENTS

Focus: be/have/do/modal + not

Preview

Below you will find several questions about food and eating habits of people in the United States. Answer each question by checking "true" or "false." (If you're not sure of the answer, make a guess.) Then share your answers with the class. You can find the correct answers to these questions at the end of the lesson.

1. Americans have been eating less and less cereal every year for the past fifty years.
   ❏ true   ❏ false

2. Men have eaten slightly more cereal than women, but children have eaten the most of all.
   ❏ true   ❏ false

3. Americans can choose from more than fifty kinds of cereals on the shelves at a supermarket.
   ❏ true   ❏ false

4. On average, Americans are eating as many vegetables as they should today.
   ❏ true   ❏ false

5. Potatoes, lettuce, onions, and tomatoes are the favorite vegetables of Americans.
   ❏ true   ❏ false

6. In a typical supermarket you could probably find hundreds of different frozen vegetables.
   ❏ true   ❏ false

7. On average, in the last five years each person in the United States has eaten fifty pounds of candy a year.
   ❏ true   ❏ false

8. People should have some concern about calories, fat, and cavities from eating candy.
   ❏ true   ❏ false

Presentation I

LESSON 20: EATING HABITS/HEALTHY EATING—MAKING NEGATIVE STATEMENTS

Imagine that each statement in the Preview is false and each one should be negative as follows:

1. Americans have not been eating less and less cereal every year for the past fifty years.
2. Men have not eaten slightly more cereal than women, but children have eaten the most of all.
3. Americans can not choose from more than fifty kinds of cereals on the shelves at a supermarket.
4. On average, Americans are not eating as many vegetables as they should today.
5. Potatoes, lettuce, onions, and tomatoes are not the favorite vegetables of Americans.
6. In a typical supermarket you could not find hundreds of different kinds of frozen vegetables.
7. On average, in the last five years each person in the United States has not eaten fifty pounds of candy a year.
8. People should not have some concern about calories, fat, and cavities from eating candy.

QUESTIONS

1. Look at each statement in the Preview. In the chart below write the auxiliary and the verb in the *Preview* column. Then look at each statement in the Presentation. Write the auxiliary, verb and word in between them in the *Presentation* column of the chart. Sentence #1 has been done as an example.

PREVIEW	PRESENTATION
1. *have been eating*	*have not been eating*
2. _____	_____
3. _____	_____
4. _____	_____
5. _____	_____
6. _____	_____
7. _____	_____
8. _____	_____

2. Look at the verbs in the preview column. Are most of them simple or expanded verbs?
3. Can you think of a rule about how to make a sentence negative in English with expanded verbs? Write your rule below.

_____

CHAPTER 5
NEGATIVES/QUESTION FORMATION

Explanation

1. In the first three chapters you learned about simple verbs and expanded verbs. The following are examples of expanded verbs you have already learned about:
   - Americans **are eating** as many vegetables as they should.
   - Americans **can choose** from more than fifty kinds of cereals.
   - Children **have eaten** the most cereal of all.

2. When you want to form a negative sentence using an expanded verb, put the **not** to the right of the auxiliary. Follow this pattern:

   auxiliary + not + verb
   - Americans **are not eating** as many vegetables as they should.
   - Americans **can not choose** from more than fifty kinds of cereals.
   - Children **have not eaten** the most cereal of all.

   If the expanded verb contains more than one auxiliary, put the **not** after the first auxiliary. Follow this pattern:

   auxiliary + not + auxiliary + verb
   - Americans **have been eating** less and less cereal for the past fifty years.
   - Americans **have not been eating** less and less cereal for the past fifty years.

3. You also learned (in Lesson 1) about using **BE** with complements. The following sentences contain the complements you learned about in Lesson 1 (in bold letters) and *be* as the verb of the sentence.
   - Potatoes and onions were **my grandfather's favorite vegetables.**
   - Sweet potatoes are **at many supermarkets.**
   - Sweet corn is **delicious.**

   When you want to make these kinds of sentences negative, put the **not** after the form of be. Follow this pattern:

   auxiliary (be) + not + complement

   Potatoes, lettuce, onions, and tomatoes **are** the favorite vegetables of Americans.

   Potatoes, lettuce, onions, and tomatoes **are not** the favorite vegetables of Americans.

4. Native speakers often use contractions with negative statements when they are speaking.
   - Americans **aren't eating** as many vegetables as they should.
   - Americans **can't choose** from more than fifty kinds of cereals.
   - Americans **haven't been eating** less and less cereal for the past fifty years.
   - Lettuce **isn't** the favorite vegetable of Americans.

Practice

LEARNING STRATEGY

Personalizing: Linking new material with something from your daily life can help you learn.

LESSON 20: EATING HABITS/HEALTHY EATING—MAKING NEGATIVE STATEMENTS

ACTIVITY ONE

A. Answer each of the following questions about your own eating habits by checking "yes" or "no." If your answer is yes, go to the next question. If your answer is no, write out your answer in a complete negative statement.

1. I have been eating more cereal during the past few months (or years).
   ❏ yes   ❏ no

2. I can find more than fifty kinds of cereals at any supermarket (or food store) in my city.
   ❏ yes   ❏ no

3. I am eating as many vegetables as I should these days.
   ❏ yes   ❏ no

4. Potatoes, lettuce, onions, and tomatoes are my favorite vegetables.
   ❏ yes   ❏ no

5. I could probably eat frozen vegetables every day.
   ❏ yes   ❏ no

6. I have eaten a lot of candy in the last few days.
   ❏ yes   ❏ no

B. Share answers with a partner. Did you have the same answers? With your partner, find all the statements for which you both answered "yes." Change these to negative sentences.

Presentation II

Here are some other statements about eating habits of people in the United States. Choose the one you think is correct by circling A or B. You can find the correct answers to these questions at the end of the lesson.

1. A Americans ate fewer vegetables in the past than they do today.

   B Americans didn't eat fewer vegetables in the past than they do today.

2. A Americans consume an average of 11.2 pounds of cereal a year.

   B Americans don't consume an average of 11.2 pounds of cereal a year.

3. A The average American eats one serving of vegetables a day.

   B The average American doesn't eat one serving of vegetables a day.

4. A Customers take their food home to eat from most fast food chains.

   B Customers don't take their food home to eat from most fast food chains.

5. A Most Americans (90 percent) eat candy.

   B Most Americans (90 percent) don't eat candy.

6. A The average American eats more candy on Friday than on any other day.

   B The average American doesn't eat more candy on Friday than on any other day.

CHAPTER 5
NEGATIVES/QUESTION
FORMATION

QUESTIONS

1. Look back at each A statement and then look at each B statement on page 125. In the chart below write everything at the beginning of each sentence up to the verb. (Do not write what comes after the verb.) You will find sentence #1 below as an example.

A	B
1. *Americans ate*	*Americans didn't eat*
2.	
3.	
4.	
5.	
6.	

2. Look at the verbs in the A column. Are they simple or expanded verbs? Look at the words in column B. Why do you think *do* has been added to the negative sentences?
3. Can you think of a rule about how to make a sentence negative in English with simple verbs? Write your rule below.

_____

Explanation

1. Another way to form a negative statement is to add a form of the auxiliary **do** (*does/do/did*). We add this auxiliary if the sentence contains a simple verb and has no auxiliary word.

   Americans **consume** an average of 11.2 pounds of cereal a year.
              simple verb

   Americans **do not consume** an average of 11.2 pounds of cereal a year.

2. When you add a form of the auxiliary **do**, you must change it to fit the subject and the time of the sentence if necessary. Then you will **not** add an ending to the verb. (This is because we need the ending only one time.)

   Follow this pattern when you use **do** in negative sentences:
       do/does/did + not + verb (no ending)
       auxiliary

   Customers do not take their food home to eat from most fast food chains.
   The average American does not eat one serving of vegetables a day.
   Americans did not eat fewer vegetables in the past than they do today

   For imperative sentences, follow this pattern: Do + not + verb

   Do not eat any of those vegetables.

3. We do **not** add the auxiliary **do** when we have the be + complement pattern. This is because a form of **be** (*am/is/are/was/were*) can act like the other auxiliaries and work with the **not** to form a negative statement.

   They are not in the kitchen right now.
   She was not in the restaurant yesterday.

4. Native speakers often use contractions with negative statements when they are speaking.

   Customers don't take their food home to eat from most fast food chains.
   The average American doesn't eat one serving of vegetables a day.
   Americans didn't eat fewer vegetables in the past than they do today.
   Don't eat any of those vegetables.

LESSON 20: EATING HABITS/HEALTHY EATING—MAKING NEGATIVE STATEMENTS

Practice

ACTIVITY TWO

People often take vitamins and other supplementary pills in order to try to stay healthy. Below you will find two labels from bottles of vitamins and supplements.

- Read each label.
- Fill in the blanks in the sentences that follow with the words listed below the label. Try to use a different answer for each sentence.
- Try to think of any other negative statements you can make using the information on these labels.

1.
   Advanced Formula Vitamins

   Recommended Intake: Adults one tablet daily
   Warning: Close tightly and keep out of reach of children. Contains iron, which can be harmful or *fatal* to children in large *doses*. Store at room temperature.
   Expiration Date: April 1998

   deadly/causing death
   amounts/portions

   might not   do not   should not   is not

   a. You _____ keep the lid open on a bottle of vitamins.

   b. _____ keep this bottle of vitamins in the refrigerator.

   c. A large dose of iron _____ be good for children.

   d. You _____ want to use these vitamins after April 1998.

man-made/not natural
chemicals that keep food from going bad
addition/something extra

stamped

2.

Vitamin C   500 mg.   250 tablets

No *Artificial* Colors • No Artificial Flavors • No *Preservatives*
Suggested Use: As a dietary *supplement,* take one tablet daily with a meal. Keep bottle tightly closed. Store in a cool, dry place, out of reach of children.
Check *imprinted* seal under cap before opening and using.

You will use one of the choices below two times.

don't   doesn't   aren't   shouldn't

a. This bottle _____ contain 1000 mg tablets.

b. Artificial colors or flavors _____ in these vitamins.

c. You _____ keep these vitamins in a warm or wet place.

d. You _____ need to take more than one vitamin a day as a dietary supplement.

e. _____ use these vitamins if the seal under the cap is broken or missing.

ACTIVITY THREE

A. Sometimes people take surveys to find out about eating habits of Americans. Below you will find some sentences about results of a survey from 1994. Change each sentence to a negative statement.

1. Americans often pay extra money for fat-free or all-natural foods.
2. Americans eat more carefully at restaurants than they do at home.
3. Americans are particularly worried about eating too much fat.
4. More women than men have made a great deal of effort to include less fat in their diets.
5. In 1994 younger people cut down on fat more than older people.
6. The most popular way to lower fat intake is buying low-fat versions of products.
7. About 60 percent (of the people in the survey) have discontinued buying certain products because of their fat content.
8. In 1994 Americans lost more weight than they gained.

B. Work with two or three other students in the class. Compare your answers with the others in your group. Decide which statement is the real survey result (the positive or the negative sentence). The correct answers are at the end of this lesson.

ACTIVITY FOUR

Below you will find a chart from an article "Eating Wisely at the White House." This chart shows how President Clinton changed his diet to a healthier one. Read the chart and write some negative sentences about his new and old eating habits and the food he was eating and is eating. Then share your answers with the class.

EXAMPLES   In his new diet he doesn't eat double cheeseburgers.
In his old diet he didn't have fat-free dressing with his salad.

THE OLD DIET	Fat	Cholesterol	Calories	THE NEW DIET	Fat	Cholesterol	Calories
Double cheeseburger	51.3g	163mg	804	Soyburger with bun	1.5g	1.7mg	216
Regular French fries, fried	18.3g	16mg	355	Baked potato, cut into "fries," broiled	.2g	0mg	220
Salad with regular dressing	25.6g	36mg	269	Salad with fat-free dressing	0g	0mg	33
TOTAL	95.2g	215mg	1428	TOTAL	1.7g	1.7mg	469
*Soyburger without bun has no fat or cholesterol, but it does have 84 calories.							

ACTIVITY FIVE

Think about your personal eating habits, either in the country where you are now or your native country. (Or think about the eating habits of people in your native country.) Think about the things you do and do not eat. Think about how you cook your food or how you eat it. Write a paragraph about your personal eating habits (or typical eating habits of people in your country). Be sure to have some negative statements in your paragraph.

Look back at your paragraph for Activity 5. Check your work for the following:

❑ You have written about your personal eating habits or typical eating habits in your native country.

❑ Some of your sentences are negative statements and some of them are positive.

❑ In your negative sentences with expanded verbs, you have added the word *not* after the first auxiliary.

❑ In your negative sentences with the *be + complement* pattern, you have added the word *not* after the *be*.

❑ In your negative sentences with simple verbs, you have added the correct form of *do* and the *not* before the verb.

*IT WORKS!
Learning Strategy:
Writing About
People You Are
Familiar With*

Answers to Preview Section
1. false (They have been eating more and more cereal in the last fifty years.)
2. true   3. true   4. false   5. true   6. false
7. false (The average has been 21 pounds.)   8. true

Answers to Presentation II Section
1. B   2. A   3. A   4. B   5. A   6. A

Answers to Activity Three
Sentences #2, #5, and #8 should be negative. All other sentences are true according to the results of the survey.

LESSON 20: EATING HABITS/HEALTHY EATING—MAKING NEGATIVE STATEMENTS

LESSON 21: QUESTIONNAIRES/APPLICATIONS—ASKING AND ANSWERING QUESTIONS—PART ONE

Focus: yes/no questions

Preview

Discuss the following with a partner. Think about some of the questionnaires/applications that you have completed in the past. Look at the following situations. Have you ever filled out questionnaires or applications in these situations? If so, what kind(s) of information did you need in order to complete them?

- registering for a school
- getting a passport or visa
- opening a bank account
- getting a credit card
- completing a warranty or information card about something you bought

In what other situations have you needed to fill out questionnaires, surveys, or applications?

Presentation I

Below is part of an application to an English language school. Read through these questions and then answer the questions that follow.

a. Have you ever attended this school before?   Yes _____   No _____

b. Are you planning to study at this school for one term only?   Yes _____   No _____

c. Will you need help with finding housing?   Yes _____   No _____

    Should we send you housing information about: _____ residence halls?

                                                                    _____ host families?

                                                                    _____ apartments?

d. Are you presently a student in your country?   Yes _____   No _____

QUESTIONS

1. What kind of answer will the student give for each of these questions?

   _____

2. Look at the first word of questions a–c. Then find the verb that works with this word in each one. Write these words (for each question) in the space below.

   _____

   _____

   _____

   In each case, did you find a simple verb or an expanded verb?

3. Look at question d. What is the first word in this sentence? What is the verb in this sentence? Is this a simple verb or an expanded verb?

Explanation

1. There are different ways to form a question in English. The way you make a question depends on the kind of answer you want to receive.

   Sometimes the answer will be a piece of information and sometimes the answer will be "yes" or "no." When the answer is "yes" or "no," the question is called a "yes/no question." In this lesson you will learn about forming this type of question.

2. In Lesson 20 (negative formation) you reviewed expanded verbs and simple verbs. This review is useful for learning about forming questions as well.

   When you want to form a question using an expanded verb, put the auxiliary to the left of the subject.

   Follow this pattern: auxiliary + subject + verb

   - **Is she applying** for a new job today?
   - **Should she apply** for a new job soon?
   - **Has she** already **applied** for a new job?

   If the expanded verb contains more than one auxiliary, put the first one to the left of the verb.

   Follow this pattern: auxiliary + subject + auxiliary + verb

   - She **has been applying** to many companies for a new job.
   - **Has she been applying** to many companies for a new job?

3. In Lesson 20 you also reviewed using **be** with complements. When you want to form a question with these kinds of sentences, put the form of **be** to the left of the verb.

   Follow this pattern: auxiliary (be) + subject + complement

   - **Is he** a law student at that school?
   - **Was he** at school almost every day last year?
   - **Is he** often tired and overworked?

LESSON 21:
QUESTIONNAIRES/
APPLICATIONS—ASKING
AND ANSWERING
QUESTIONS—PART ONE

CHAPTER 5
NEGATIVES/QUESTION
FORMATION

Practice

ACTIVITY ONE

Complete this activity with a partner or in a small group. Below you will find some questions from an application for a teaching job with some blanks. You will also find a list of auxiliaries and a list of verbs.

Choose the auxiliary and verb that best fit each question and write these words in the blanks. In some cases, you may need to add an auxiliary only. You will need to use some words on these lists more than once. In some cases, more than one answer may be possible. (Remember to use a capital letter if the auxiliary is the first word in the question.)

AUXILIARIES	VERBS
have	provide
are	working
may	show
can	teaching
	contact

1. _____ you currently _____?
2. If so, _____ you been _____ for at least one year?
3. _____ we _____ your present employer?
4. _____ any of your relatives _____ for this school district?
5. _____ you _____ us with three references as evidence of your teaching success?
6. _____ you a U.S. citizen?
7. If not, _____ you _____ proof of your legal right as a noncitizen to remain and work in the United States?

ACTIVITY TWO

- Change the following statements to questions that you might find on a questionnaire.
- After you write your questions, discuss them with the rest of the class. Are there any questions in this group that you would not find on a questionnaire in your country? Discuss this with your classmates.

1. You are presently married.

   _____

2. You have changed your marital status in the past six months.

   _____

3. Your household income is more than $25,000.

   _____

4. Our Marketing Department should keep your name on our mailing list.

   _____

5. We may give your name to other companies for their mailing lists.

   _____

Presentation II

LESSON 21: QUESTIONNAIRES/ APPLICATIONS—ASKING AND ANSWERING QUESTIONS—PART ONE

Below is another part of the application in Presentation I. Read through these questions and then answer the questions that follow.

> **VISA INFORMATION**
> a. Do you need an I-20 form to obtain a student visa or to transfer from another U.S. school?   Yes _____   No _____
> b. Are you presently attending a U.S. school?   Yes _____   No _____
> c. Can you obtain a student visa with an I-20 issued from our school?   Yes _____   No _____
> d. Do you want our office to mail your visa to the address on this application?   Yes _____   No _____

QUESTIONS

1. What kind of answer will the student give for each of these questions?
2. Look at the first word of questions b and c. Then find the verb that works with this word in each one. Write these words (for each question) in the space below.

   _____

   _____

   In each case, did you find a simple verb or an expanded verb?
3. Look at questions a and d. What is the first word in these sentences?
   Now think about these two sentences as statements and not questions. When they are statements, is the verb a simple verb or an expanded verb?
   Why do you think *do* has been added to questions a and d?

Explanation

1. Another way to form a "yes/no" question is to add a form of the auxiliary **do** (*does/do/did*). We add this auxiliary if the sentence contains a simple verb and has no auxiliary word to put at the beginning of the question.

   You **need** an I-20 form to obtain a student visa or to transfer from
       simple verb
   another school.
   Do you **need** an I-20 form to obtain a student visa or to transfer from another U.S. school?

2. When you add a form of the auxiliary **do,** you must change it to fit the subject and the time of the sentence if necessary. Then you will **not** put an ending on the verb. (This is because we need the ending only one time.)
   Follow this pattern when you use **do** in questions:

   do/does/did + subject + verb (no ending)
   auxiliary

   He **needs** an I-20 for his visa.
   Does he **need** an I-20 for his visa?
   He **needed** an I-20 for his visa.
   Did he **need** an I-20 for his visa?

3. We do **not** need to add the auxiliary **do** when we have the be + complement pattern. This is because **be** (*am/is/are/was/were*) acts like the other auxiliaries and can begin a question.
   Were you a student in your country?

Practice

ACTIVITY THREE

Below you will find seven questions from a company survey about appliances and warranties. Each question should begin with a form of the auxiliary *have* or a form of the auxiliary *do*. Fill in the blank at the beginning of each question with the correct form of one of these auxiliaries.

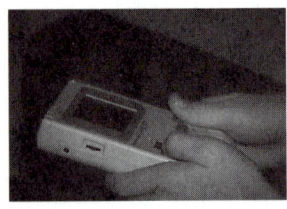

keeping a machine in good working order

fail/work improperly

a guarantee of quality

1. _____ you taken an appliance for *servicing* in the last year?
2. _____ anyone in your household plan to purchase any kind of camera in the next year?
3. _____ you bring any of your *malfunctioning* appliances to a repair service?
4. _____ you return any of your malfunctioning appliances directly to the manufacturer?
5. _____ you ever delayed making a purchase to wait for a sale?
6. _____ you think manufacturers' *warranties* run out too soon?
7. _____ you ever had to return a product because it malfunctioned during the warranty period?

ACTIVITY FOUR

Below you will find some questions from a computer company's questionnaire. The words in parentheses (in the first part of each question) are not in correct order. Change the order of these words to form questions. Be sure to capitalize the first word of each question.

1. (purchase / you / did) the 100 model or the 200 model?
   _____

2. (a factory representative / did / sell) this product to you?
   _____

3. (you / will / use) this product at home or at work?
   _____

4. (in your household / does / buy / anyone) products from our mail order catalog?
   _____

5. (planning / are / you) to purchase another computer over the next twelve months?
   _____

6. (computer system / your / is) part of a network?
   _____

7. (owned / you / have / your computer system) for more than one year?
   _____

8. (learn about / you / did) this product from a company advertisement?
   _____

ACTIVITY FIVE

Some of the questions from the following home safety survey are correct and some are not. Find the ones that are **not** correct and change them.

1. Do you live in a house or an apartment?
2. Has you *installed* a smoke *detector* in each bedroom of your home or apartment?
3. Does your *residence* contains a fire extinguisher?
4. Is your *electrical outlets* and wires in good condition?
5. Is the temperature of the hot water from your water heater less than 120 degrees F?
6. Does your community have a Poison Control Center?
    If so, did you have this telephone number available at all times (such as near your telephone)?
7. You does have a properly installed carbon monoxide detector near the sleeping area of your home?
8. Should this council sends you a free Home Safety Information Booklet?

LESSON 21:
QUESTIONNAIRES/
APPLICATIONS—ASKING
AND ANSWERING
QUESTIONS—PART ONE

set up/put in place and make it work

an instrument that finds/discovers something

place where someone lives/dwelling

places to put plugs in to get electricity

IT WORKS!
Learning Strategy:
Identifying
Problems in
Grammar

ACTIVITY SIX

Change the following statements to questions for a survey. Compare answers with a classmate.

1. You have a high school education.
2. Someone in your household has earned a college degree.
3. Both you and your spouse (or partner) work outside the home.
4. Someone in your family is an educator.
5. You usually use credit cards to buy large appliances.
6. We are thinking about buying some of your new products.

LEARNING STRATEGY

Forming Concepts: Talking with other people about a specific topic gives you new information.

ACTIVITY SEVEN

A. Do this part of the activity in small groups of three or four people. You are going to learn about your classmates' families by asking them questions.

First, with your group, write a short questionnaire of "yes/no" questions about families. Your questions should be about a classmate and any of his or her relatives. You should have at least five or six questions.

Now look back at your questions and check your work for the following:

❏ The answer to each question will be "yes" or "no."

❏ Each question begins with one of the following auxiliaries:
be (*am/is/are/was/were*)
have (*has/have*)
a modal (*can/could/should/will/might/must*)
do (*does/do/did*)

❏ The beginning of each question follows one of these patterns:
• auxiliary + subject + verb
• auxiliary + subject + auxiliary + verb
• a form of *be* + subject + complement

❏ The verbs in your questions have correct endings or no endings.

For questions with the auxiliaries **have, be,** or **do:**

❏ The auxiliary agrees with the subject and the time of the sentence.

B. You will do this part of the activity with a partner. You must choose someone from another group to be your partner. Then ask this person the questions your group wrote. If necessary, write the answers down because you will be sharing them with the rest of the class.

If you have enough time, find another partner and ask him or her the same questions.

C. Tell the class what you learned about one of your partners, without saying his or her name. Have the class guess which classmate you spoke to.

LESSON 22: NATIVE AMERICANS—ASKING AND ANSWERING QUESTIONS—PART TWO

Focus: wh question

Preview

What do you know about the Native Americans (Indians) from the United States and Canada? Have you ever seen movies or read books about these people? Discuss this with a partner.

Presentation I

People often ask . . .
1. **Who is considered an Indian? Who makes this determination?**
   Different tribes use different ways to determine that. The decision may be based on *ancestry* or blood. Some tribes require only a *trace* of Indian blood while others require as much as half.

   family background/ heritage

   a very small amount

2. **How many Indians are presently living in the United States?**
   In 1990, the U.S. Census Bureau counted 1.9 million American Indians and Alaska natives living in the United States.
3. **What is a reservation?**
   Indian reservations are lands some tribes received when they were forced to give up other land areas to non-Indians.

QUESTIONS

1. Look at the first word of each of the questions in bold above. (Look at the first two words in question #2.) Write these words in the left column below. Then write what kind of information you find in each answer in the column on the right. (The first one has been done for you as an example.)

WORD(S)	KIND OF INFORMATION
who	which person or people (identifies)

2. Each of these questions is asking about a piece of unknown information about Indians. In which part of each question is the "unknown" information?
3. What word(s) do you find right after the question word?

CHAPTER 5
NEGATIVES/QUESTION
FORMATION

Explanation

1. In Lesson 21 you learned about "yes/no" questions. We use these questions when the answer is "yes" or "no."
    Sometimes the answer to a question is a piece of information. In this case, we use a "wh" or information question.
2. Sometimes the piece of information we are asking about is a subject. In this case we use the following pattern:

    question word + auxiliary + predicate

    What is a reservation?
    (ANSWER: Indian reservations are lands some tribes received.)
3. Sometimes there is no auxiliary in the question. This is because the sentence contains a simple verb (not *be*).

    Who makes this determination?
    (Different tribes make this determination.)
4. There are several question words that can begin this kind of question. Choose the question word that will fit the answer you are looking for as follows:
    - who = identifies a person (or people)
    - what = identifies another piece of information (not a person)
    - how many/how much = tells you a number or quantity

    [See Lesson 23 for more information about using *much* and *many*.]
5. Often in informal speech native speakers will make contractions of the question word and the auxiliary that follows.

    Who's living on the reservations?
    What's a reservation?

QUESTION WORD = SUBJECT	AUXILIARY	PREDICATE
What		happened to you?
Who		watches television?
Who	's	got a purse? ['s is contracted has.]
Who	's	talking? ['s is contracted is.]

Presentation II

More questions people often ask . . .

1. **Where do Indians live?**

    Indians can and do live anywhere in the United States. In 1993 about 950,000 people lived on or near Federal Indian reservations.

2. **What language does an Indian speak?**

    There are many different tribal languages. Today, more than 200 of these languages are still spoken.

3. **When did Indians become U.S. citizens?**

In 1924, the U.S. Congress extended citizenship to all Indians born in the United States and its territories. Before then, they were not citizens of the United States.

4. Why are some people referring to Indians as Native Americans today?

The term came into use in the 1960s. It refers to American Indians and Alaska natives (Indians, Eskimos and Aleuts of Alaska). "Indian" was the name the Europeans gave to these people.

QUESTIONS

1. Look at the first word of each of the questions in bold above. Write these words in the left column below. Then write what kind of information you find in each answer in the column on the right (the same way you did for Presentation I).

2. Look at the words after the question word. What pattern do these words

WORD	KIND OF INFORMATION
_____	_____
_____	_____
_____	_____
_____	_____

follow?

3. What do you think is the same or different about these questions and the yes/no questions you learned in Lesson 21?

Explanation

1. Often information we are asking about is not a subject. In this case we use the following pattern:

   question word + auxiliary + subject + predicate (including verb)
   Where do Indians live?
   Why are some people referring to Indians as Native Americans today?

2. There are several question words that can begin this kind of question. Choose the question word that will fit the answer you are looking for as follows:
   - who = people
   - what = things/ideas
   - when = time
   - where = place
   - why = reason
   - how = method
   - which = what specific one (of several things)
   - how much/how many (uncountable/countable nouns) = quantity
   [For information on countable and uncountable nouns, see Lesson 23.]

3. When you follow this pattern for information questions, you must have an auxiliary.
   If the verb in the sentence is an expanded verb, put the first auxiliary to

QUESTION WORD	AUXILIARY	SUBJECT	PREDICATE	UNKNOWN INFORMATION
Who	do	you	have for history?	[people]
What	are	you	going to study there?	[things/ideas]
When	did	you	graduate?	[time]
Where	were	you	born?	[place]
Why	do	you	like kids?	[reason]
How	did	you	like it?	[method/quality/quantity]

WH-PHRASE	AUXILIARY	SUBJECT	PREDICATE
Phrases beginning with *wh*-words ask for more specific information.			
What high school	did	you	go to?
What kind of classes	are	you	taking?
How many words a minute	can	you	type?
Which other sports	do	you	like to watch?
How many years	have	I	been studying English?

the left of the subject. If the verb is *be,* put the *be* to the left of the subject.

Why **are** some people referring to Indians as Native Americans today?
Why **have** some people been referring to Indians as Native American since the 1960s?
Why **is** the name Native Americans popular today?

If the verb in the sentence is a simple verb (not *be*), you must use the auxiliary **do.**

The auxiliary **do** changes to agree with the time and the subject. The verb does not have any endings when you use **do.**

Where **do** Indians **live**?
What languages **does** an Indian **speak**?
When **did** Indians **become** U.S. citizens?

4. In informal speech, native speakers sometimes make contractions of the question word and the auxiliary that follows:

Why're some people referring to Indians as Native Americans today?
Where'd Indians live 300 years ago?

5. Sometimes in informal speech native speakers use the reduced form *whaddya* for questions that begin with *what.* This reduced form can mean two things:

- what do you
  Whaddya know about Native Americans?
  (What do you know about Native Americans?)
- what are you
  Whaddya learning about Native Americans?
  (What are you learning about Native Americans?)

Sometimes in informal speech you may hear native speakers ask information questions without any auxiliaries at all. This is only for informal speech.

LESSON 22: NATIVE
AMERICANS—ASKING
AND ANSWERING
QUESTIONS—PART TWO

WHEN YOU'RE TALKING

In informal speech, you will hear native speakers ask information questions without auxiliaries. In formal speech, however, it is considered an error to omit the auxiliary.

QUESTION WORD	ABSENT AUXILIARY	SUBJECT	PREDICATE
Where	[are]	you	going?
When	[are]	you	going?
What	[are]	you	going to study there?
How	[are]	you	doing in psychology?
Which other sports	[do]	you	like to watch?

Practice

ACTIVITY ONE

In 1993 a magazine printed an interview of U.S. Senator Ben Nighthorse Campbell of Colorado. He is a Northern Cheyenne and he talked about how life is changing for Native American Indians. Below you will find parts of his interview.

Each part of the interview begins with a question. In each question you will find a blank. A short answer follows each question. Do the following:

- Read each answer first. If you are not sure about the meaning of an answer, discuss it with a partner or ask your teacher.
- Then read each question. Fill in the blank with the correct question word from the list below. Some questions may have more than one possible answer. You will use one question word two times. (Be sure you use each question word at least one time.)

Question Words: how   why   what   where

_____ are some of the *misceptions* about American Indians today?   *misunderstanding/mistake*

One of the most common is that Indians are a civilization that is gone. The other misconception is that all Indians live on reservations.

_____ do you think these misconceptions come from?

Most schoolbooks that were used for years and years defined Indians as an ancient culture that was no longer here. Also, a lot of old-time movies *generate*   *create/produce*
misconceptions. They always show Indians as *villains*. Indians have rarely had   *bad person*
the chance to tell their side of the story.

_____ is that changing?

Many more books are coming out by Native American authors. Many of the new movies are showing Indians in a much *fairer light*. People are learning   *more positively*
more about what real Indians are like.

_____ is interest in Indian heritage growing among young people today?

This is because young Indians are no longer ashamed of their background as they were taught to be for a long time.

_____ has life for American Indians changed since you were a boy?

It's much better. There are many more opportunities for young Indians. More are now attending school and staying in school.

CHAPTER 5 NEGATIVES/QUESTION FORMATION

ACTIVITY TWO

Read the two paragraphs below about the Eskimos and Aleuts and the Hopi tribe of Arizona. Then form questions about the information in these paragraphs using the words given next to each number. Be sure to put the words in the correct order and to capitalize the first word of each question. (Some questions may have more than one possible answer.)

(1) Eskimos and related Aleuts lived in the Arctic regions of North America. (2) They were the only non-Indian *aborigines* in North America when European explorers arrived. (3) They were different from the Indians in appearance, language, and culture. (4) Surprisingly, the Eskimos followed a *uniform* lifestyle across the entire continent. (5) Through cleverness and *adaptability*, they managed to survive in one of earth's harshest environments.

people native to an area

the same

ability to change or adjust

EXAMPLE in the Arctic regions / lived / who

Who lived in the Arctic regions?

(The numbers refer to the sentence number in the paragraph that contains the answer to the question.)

1. live / the Eskimos and Aleuts / did / where

2. to explore / who / the Arctic area / came

3. different / were / the Eskimos and Aleuts / how / from North American Indians

4. the Eskimo's lifestyle / surprising / is / what / about

5. did / live in / kind of environment / these people / what

(1) The Hopi Reservation occupies a large area in the center of the vast Navajo Reservation of northeast Arizona. (2) The Hopi people are famous for weaving, pottery, and jewelry. (3) One of the most interesting places on this reservation is the village of Old Oraibi. (4) Old Oraibi is possibly the oldest of the present Hopi villages; it is probably the oldest continuously inhabited city in the United States. (5) People have been living there since 1100, but now the village is partially in ruins.

1. the Hopi Reservation / does / occupy / what / area

2. famous for / is / weaving, pottery and jewelry / who

3. village / an interesting place / which / on this reservation / is

4. Old Oraibi / why / an interesting / is / Hopi village

5. people / begin living there / did / when

ACTIVITY THREE

Listen to some questions from or about this lesson. Your teacher will read them at normal conversation speed with contractions. She or he may also say some questions with the reduced form *whaddya* (as in informal speech). After you hear each question, write it down in more formal style. Do not write contractions or reduced forms. Your teacher will read each question two times.

1. _____
2. _____
3. _____
4. _____
5. _____
6. _____
7. _____

Compare answers with a classmate. Ask the teacher to repeat the questions if necessary.

ACTIVITY FOUR

A. Read the paragraph below about the Native Americans of the Plains area of North America.

(1) The Spaniards brought horses to the New World. (2) These animals began to change life on the southern plains in the late seventeenth century. (3) By the early 1800s [most tribes of the northern plains], including the Cheyenne and the Blackfeet, were following a new life of highly efficient horseback hunting. (4) [Most tribes] [*enforced*] [*strict* hunting laws]. (5) They made [these laws] [in order to keep the great bison herd *intact*]. (6) They needed these animals for their food, clothing, and shelters. (7) This culture *flourished* for less than a century. (8) However, many people still think of the Plains horseman as the typical North American Indian.

make people obey
strong/severe
whole/undamaged
grow strong

- Read sentences (1) and (2) again. Then complete each question below by asking about the information in these two sentences. (One example has been done for you.) Compare answers with a partner.

1. What *did the Spaniards bring to the New World?*

   Who _____

   Where _____

2. When _____

   What _____

   Where _____

LESSON 22: NATIVE AMERICANS—ASKING AND ANSWERING QUESTIONS—PART TWO

IT WORKS!
Learning Strategy:
Verifying Short
Forms with Native
Speakers

B. Complete this part with your partner.

In sentences (4) and (5) you will find a word or group of words in brackets. Write "wh-" questions that ask about each of these pieces of information. You should have a different question for each word or group of words in brackets.

Begin your questions with any of the following words. (Some questions may begin with the same word.) Compare answers with other classmates.

    who   what   why

EXAMPLE (from sentence (3) "most tribes of the northern plains")
Who was following a new life of highly efficient horseback hunting by the early 1800s?

C. Complete this part in groups of three or four people.

Write some wh- questions about the information in the other sentences (6)–(8) in this paragraph. Share your answers with the class.

ACTIVITY FIVE

Work in pairs or small groups for this activity.

A. Below you will find several paragraphs about dwellings of different groups of Native Americans. Each pair or group will read *one* of these paragraphs and do the following:

- Go over the paragraph with your group (or partner) and discuss any new or unknown vocabulary.
- Write at least five wh- questions about the information in your paragraph. Try to use as many different question words as possible.
- Now look back at your questions and check your work for the following:

❏ The answer to each question is a piece of information in your paragraph.

❏ Each question begins with one of the following question words:
who / what / when / where / why / how / which

❏ The beginning of each question follows one of these patterns:
- question word + auxiliary + predicate
- question word + auxiliary + subject + predicate

❏ The verbs in your questions have correct endings or no endings.

For questions with the auxiliaries *have, be,* or *do:*

❏ The auxiliary agrees with the subject and the time of the sentence.

1. The Plains Indians made tipis to fit their housing requirements. Since they hunted buffalo, they traveled often to follow the herds. The buffalo-skin tipi was a portable, waterproof tent. It was easy to take a tipi down, carry it to the next encampment and put it back up. You could even keep a fire burning inside one of these shelters.

2. The Pawnees used earth lodges as their homes. These were permanent multifamily dwellings. They had a *framework* of posts and *beams.* Then they covered these over with layers of willow branches, *sod,* and mud. These lodges were more than forty feet in diameter. They even provided shelter for prized horses!

3. The Iroquois called themselves *hodinonhsonih* or "housebuilders." They built great houses of *poles* covered with *slabs of bark.* These "longhouses" sometimes stood 20 feet wide and 150 feet long. Each longhouse sheltered several related families or clans. Each family lived in a *compartment* of the longhouse. These compartments faced each other across shared fireplaces along the aisle.

---

*IT WORKS!
Learning Strategy:
Working with
Other Language
Learners*

a structure used to support other things

large piece of metal or wood used to make buildings, bridges, etc.

dirt with grass

long piece of wood/post/stick

thick piece or section of outer covering of a tree

section/chamber

4. Pueblo Indians of the Southwest lived in apartment complexes made of *adobe brick.* These apartment buildings were *terraced.* One man's roof was another man's balcony. The individual rooms in these buildings were small. When they needed more living space, these Indians added rooms *haphazardly.*

building material (from clay and straw) dried in the sun

in rows on different levels

without a plan or system

5. Eskimos throughout the central Arctic region lived in snowhouses during the winter months of October to May. A man could build one of these *domed* shelters for his family in about one hour. He did this by placing blocks of wind-packed snow in an inward-leaning *spiral.* The builder cut most of the blocks of snow with a long-bladed snow knife of *antler* or bone. Then he made a small hole in the roof so the *stale* air could escape. A stone lamp and body heat kept this dwelling fairly comfortable.

with a rounded roof

a kind of curve that gets larger or smaller as it goes around

horn of some animals (deer/elk)

not fresh or new

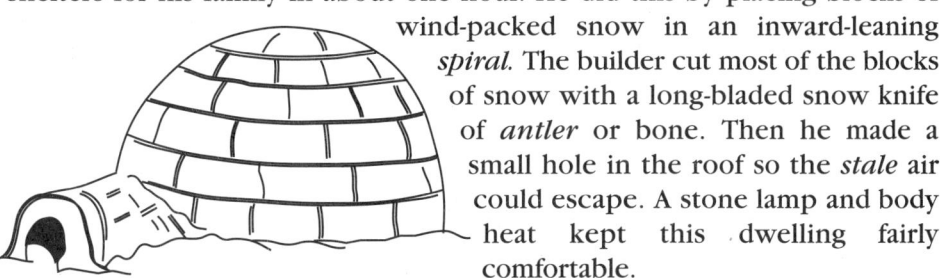

B. Each group or pair will share its questions with the rest of the class. Your classmates will try to answer the questions according to the information in the paragraphs.

C. Each pair or group should think of another kind of dwelling. It can be from your native country or any other place or time. Your classmates will ask you questions about this dwelling in order to try to guess what it is. The questions can be yes/no or wh- questions.

Noun Phrases

CHAPTER 6

LESSON 23: TAKING INVENTORY—DISCUSSING QUANTITY

Focus: nouns—singular/plural/countable/uncountable

Preview

With a partner take inventory in your classroom. How many of each of the following do you have in your room today?

- blackboards
- board erasers
- wastebaskets
- television sets
- light switches
- windows
- teachers
- students

Now look at the following picture. Take inventory in this room. Write down how many of each of the different items in this room you see.

Presentation I

Bill wants to make a salad. He has the following vegetables and fruit in his refrigerator. Discuss any unfamiliar items with others in your class. Which ones do you think Bill should include in his salad?

1 head of lettuce	5 small tomatoes
4 green onions	2 apples
8 radishes	1 orange
15 cherries	1 carrot
1 cucumber	3 peaches
3 potatoes	1 pickle

QUESTIONS

1. Put a check next to each item that Bill has only one of.
2. Look at the endings on the other items on this list (the items you did not check). Are they all the same or how are they different?

Explanation

1. A noun can be a person, place, thing, or idea. A noun can be singular (one item) or plural (more than one item). We use an **-s** ending to make a noun plural.

   1 carrot 3 carrot**s**
   1 apple 2 apple**s**

2. Some nouns make a change when you add the **-s** ending. Look at the following chart for information about making nouns plural.

Add -s alone:	This is the regular way, used for most nouns e.g., day/day<u>s</u>, district/district<u>s</u>, language/language<u>s</u>, teacher/teacher<u>s</u>
Add -es:	This is used for nouns that already end in -s as well as for ones that end in -ch, -sh, -x, or -z e.g., class/class<u>es</u>, tax/tax<u>es</u> It is also used for many nouns that end in -o e.g., hero/hero<u>es</u>, tomato/tomato<u>es</u>
Drop -y and add -ies:	This is used for nouns that end in a consonant (b, c, d, f, g, etc.) followed by -y. The -y is removed and -ies added. e.g., city/cit<u>ies</u>, company/compan<u>ies</u>
Drop f and add -ves:	This is used for some, but not all, nouns that end in -f. e.g., half/hal<u>ves</u>, knife/kni<u>ves</u>, wife/wi<u>ves</u>.

3. Some very common nouns in English are irregular. This means they do not use the **-s** ending at all in the plural form.

SINGULAR	PLURAL	SINGULAR	PLURAL
man	men	mouse	mice
woman	women	louse	lice
child	children	foot	feet
ox	oxen	goose	geese
person	people	tooth	teeth

Other nouns do not change form. In other words, they have the same form for both singular and plural.

NAMES OF NATIONALITIES	NAMES OF ANIMALS
Chinese	antelope
Japanese	deer
Portuguese	fish
Swiss	sheep
Vietnamese	shrimp

4. Some nouns are always in pairs in English as follows:
   - glasses   • pajamas   • scissors   • trousers/pants/jeans/slacks/shorts
5. Remember to make the verb in the sentence agree in number with the noun.

   A cucumber **is** in the refrigerator.
   Five cucumbers **are** in the refrigerator.
   The little girl **is** in the room.
   The little girls **are** in the room.
   The scissors **are** in the drawer.

Practice

LEARNING STRATEGY

Testing Hypotheses: Saying or writing something even if you are not sure about its correctness is good for learning. After all, you may be right.

ACTIVITY ONE

Do both parts of this activity with a partner.

A. Write the plural form for each of the following nouns.

> beach   ski slope
> museum   subway
> skyscraper   potato
> deer   computer software company

Look at the list of places below. Do you know where all of these places are? Discuss this with your partner. Then write each plural noun from the first part of this activity next to the name of the place you associate it with. (You can put more than one noun for some places.)

> New York City
> Hawaii
> Idaho
> San Francisco
> Rocky Mountains
> Silicon Valley, California

B. Write the plural form for each of the following nouns.

> bird   sheep
> glasses   child
> foot   trousers
> tax   mouse
> tooth   blueprint
> fish   bridge

Look at the following list of jobs. How many of these do you know? Discuss them with your partner. Write the name of the noun from the first part of this activity next to the name of the job you associate with this noun. Choose a different noun for each job below. (Write each noun only one time.)

> podiatrist
> pediatrician
> engineer
> veterinarian
> optician
> architect
> dentist
> tailor
> certified public accountant (CPA)
> laboratory researcher
> ornithologist
> marine biologist

ACTIVITY TWO

A. Pronunciation Practice

The plural *-s* on the end of regular nouns can have different sounds. Sometimes you will hear this ending sound like a buzz and other times it will sound like a hiss. Practice pronouncing the plural nouns in the lists in the Preview and Presentation sections of this lesson.

B. Listening Practice

You are going to hear a few short conversations. In each one you will hear some numbers and some plural nouns. Each time you hear a number and a plural noun, write these words down.

EXAMPLE You will hear:
Did you rent that apartment you looked at today?
No, it only had three bedrooms and four people will share the apartment. We're going to see two houses tomorrow, though.

You will write:
3 bedrooms   4 people   2 houses

Presentation II

Bill has made his salad and now he wants to make a dressing for it. Look at the following things he has in his kitchen. Which ones do you think he should use in his salad dressing?

oil	lemon juice
poppy seeds	yogurt
vinegar	raisins
salt	strawberries
pepper	mayonnaise
olives	sunflower seeds
sugar	mustard

QUESTIONS

1. How many of the nouns above have the plural *-s* ending? Put a check next to these words.
2. Look at all of the other nouns. Why do you think these words do not have the *-s* ending?

Explanation

1. Some nouns are **countable** (sometimes called count). This means you can count them or think of them as individual or separate items. These nouns follow the rules for plurals you discussed and practiced in the first part of this lesson.

1 olive	12 olives
1 strawberry	10 strawberries

2. Some nouns are **uncountable** (sometimes called noncount). This means we don't think of these things as separate or individual. This is because these items are often too small to count or they are substances, activities, or conditions.

   The following list shows some uncountable nouns in English.
   - liquids:
     coffee/tea/water/milk/oil/paint/perfume
   - small, granular things:
     sugar/sand/dust/rice/salt/pepper/other spices (like cinnamon)
   - materials:
     gold/cotton/wood/glass/steel/plastic/rubber/coal/wool/soap
   - gases:
     air/hydrogen/pollution/smog
   - some foods:
     bread/fish/cheese/meat/chicken/beef/lamb
   - abstract nouns:
     knowledge/intelligence/health/truth/honesty/courage/wealth/poverty/happiness/trouble/luck/fun/life/beauty
   - subjects:
     mathematics/physics/economics/biology/psychology/history/chemistry/engineering/French/Spanish/English/Chinese
   - other:
     advice/communication/information/news/work/homework/grammar/vocabulary/traffic/transportation/weather/rain/snow/crime/agriculture/garbage

3. Some uncountable nouns are categories or groups of things. The category or group is uncountable, but the individual parts in the group are countable.

GROUP	INDIVIDUAL PARTS
furniture	chairs/tables/lamps/desks
jewelry	necklaces/rings/bracelets/pins

   Some other groups are: equipment/fruit/food/money/clothing/makeup

4. Uncountable nouns will **not** have a plural form. Do not add an *-s* ending to these nouns. The verb in the sentence with these nouns will be singular.

   The **homework** tonight **is** not very difficult.
   The **bread** from that bakery **is** always delicious.

5. There are several words or expressions of indefinite quantity we use with nouns. We use these with uncountable nouns because they will not have a specific number. We can also use these expressions of quantity with countable nouns when we do not want to use a specific number. Some of them are the same for countable and uncountable nouns, but some of them are different. Look at the chart below for some of these words and expressions.

COUNTABLE ONLY	UNCOUNTABLE ONLY	BOTH COUNTABLE AND UNCOUNTABLE
a couple of	a little	no
a few	a great deal of	any (for questions & negatives)
several	much	some
many		a lot of/lots of (informal)

   I'm going to buy **a few pencils.**
   I'll probably buy **a little sugar.**
   They don't have **much furniture** in their new apartment.
   There are **many chairs and desks** in that classroom.

Practice

LESSON 23: TAKING INVENTORY— DISCUSSING QUANTITY

LEARNING STRATEGY

Personalizing: Applying this grammar to yourself and your life will make it more meaningful.

ACTIVITY THREE

Do all parts of this activity with a partner.

A. Look back at the list of ingredients in Presentation I and Presentation II. You are going to tell Bill which items on the list he should use in the salad and the dressing. You should also tell Bill how much or how many of each item he should use.

Make two lists, one of the items for the salad and one of the ingredients for the dressing. For the countable items use numbers. For the uncountable items use the words and expressions of quantity for your amounts. (Bill doesn't have any cups or spoons to measure these ingredients.) Try to use as many different words or expressions as possible.

B. Read the following sentences about some university students. Choose the word or expression in parentheses to fit each one. Circle the correct answers.

1. Marie is taking a class in Japanese. Japanese (is/are) a difficult subject for her, so she studies hard. For her, the (grammars/grammar) (is/are) the most difficult part of learning the language, but she thinks the (vocabulary/vocabularies) (is/are) not so difficult. She hopes she doesn't have (much/many) (troubles/trouble) with this class.

2. Antoine is not sure about which classes to take. He needs (many/a little) (information/informations) about requirements for his major. He plans to see a counselor so he can get (many/some) (advice/advices). He doesn't have an appointment with his counselor, but he will try to see her anyway. He hopes he'll have (a little/a few) (luck/lucks) so he can see her today.

3. Roberto has a class about meteorology this semester. The (work/works) (is/are) easy for him because he likes to study about weather and weather patterns. The teacher assigns (a great deal of/several) (homeworks/homework) every night for this class. He is glad to do the work because his (knowledge/knowledges) (is/are) improving (so much/so many) from this class.

C. Now think about the classes you are taking this semester or have taken recently. List these classes and think about the following for each one:

- new information
- homework
- new vocabulary
- difficult grammar
- test/quizzes
- trouble
- luck
- papers/essays

Tell your partner how much or how many you have (or had) of the above for these classes. Use words or expressions of indefinite quantity but not specific numbers when you discuss this with your partner.

ACTIVITY FOUR

Next to each number below you will find an uncountable noun. Make a list of any nouns that you think might fit in this category. Compare your list with others in the class. Then answer each question with a complete sentence. Use some of the words and expressions of indefinite quantity in your answers.

EXAMPLE jewelry   rings/bracelets/necklaces/earrings/pins/watches

- How much jewelry do you wear every day?
  I wear a little jewelry every day.
- How many necklaces are you wearing right now?
  I'm not wearing any necklaces right now.
  OR *I'm wearing no necklaces right now.*
- What specific pieces of jewelry do you wear every day?
  I wear two rings and three earrings every day.

1. fruit _____
   - How much fruit do you eat each day?
   - How many apples do you eat a day?
   - How many bananas do you eat a day?
   - Name another fruit you usually eat and write a sentence about how many of this fruit you eat in a week.

2. clothing _____
   - How much clothing do you have in your closet?
   - How many sweaters do you own?
   - How many pairs of jeans do you have?
   - Write a sentence about another piece of clothing you own and how many you have of this item.

3. money (list the kind of money you have in the country you are now living in)
   _____
   - How much money do you usually carry with you to school?
   - How many _____ (insert name of currency, such as "dollars" in the blank) do you have with you right now?
   - How many _____ (insert name of coin, such as "dimes" in the blank) do you have with you right now?
   - Do you have any other money with you right now? If yes, what kind of money and how much of it do you have?

4. furniture _____
   - How much furniture is there in the room you are now in?
   - How much furniture is in your room or the apartment or house you are now living in?
   - How many chairs are in the room you are now in?
   - Name another piece of furniture in this room. Write another sentence about how many pieces of this kind of furniture you see in this room.

5. sports equipment _____
- How much sports equipment do you keep in your house or apartment (or room)?
- How many basketballs do you have at home?
- How many golf clubs do you own?
- Name another piece of sporting equipment you own. Write a sentence about how many of these you have.

ACTIVITY FIVE

You will do both parts of this activity with a partner.

A. One of you will be Partner A and the other will be Partner B. Each partner will look at different pieces of information for this part of the activity. Each partner should read his/her information below.

PARTNER A

Below you will find three lists of things your partner needs. Next to some of the items you will find specific amounts and next to other items you will find indefinite amounts. Try to guess what your partner plans to do with the items on each list. (Your partner has the answers.)

EXAMPLE Look at the following list. What do you think your partner will do with these things?

1 green onion   4 bouillon cubes
a couple of carrots   1 can of tomatoes
a few green beans   a little salad oil
several cups of water

(ANSWER: She or he will make some vegetable soup.)

LIST 1   LIST 2
3 lemons   a few flat pieces of wood
3 cups cold water   one electric drill
several ice cubes   10 screws
a little sugar   some space on a wall

LIST 3
one large backpack
one sleeping bag
some travel pots and pans
several shirts
2 pairs of jeans
many matches

Answers to Partner B's lists:
List 1: She or he will hang a picture on the wall.
List 2: She or he will go to the beach (or take a vacation to a tropical area).
List 3: She or he will make a chocolate dessert (chocolate brownies).

LESSON 23: TAKING INVENTORY— DISCUSSING QUANTITY

PARTNER B

Below you will find three lists of things your partner needs. Next to some of the items you will find specific amounts and next to other items you will find indefinite amounts. Try to guess what your partner plans to do with the items on each list. (Your partner has the answers.)

EXAMPLE Look at the following list. What do you think your partner will do with these things?

1 green onion	4 bouillon cubes
a couple of carrots	1 can of tomatoes
a few green beans	a little salad oil
several cups of water	

(ANSWER: She or he will make some vegetable soup.)

LIST 1	LIST 2
some space on a wall	2 bathing suits
one frame with 2 small nails	a couple of books
one bracket with holes for 2 nails	a great deal of sunblock
one hammer	several pairs of shorts
one larger nail	a pair of sunglasses

LIST 3
some sugar
several eggs
2 cups of flour
a little vanilla extract
some oil
3 squares of chocolate
a few walnuts

Answers to Partner A's lists:
List 1: She or he will make some homemade lemonade.
List 2: She or he will put a shelf on the wall.
List 3: She or he will go camping outdoors (or go to the mountains).

B. Together with your partner make up your own list of things. Give this list to other people in your class and ask them to guess what you might do with these items.

Look back at your list for Activity 5. Check your work for the following:

❑ You have included some countable and some uncountable items on the list.

❑ You used the *-s* ending with any plural countable nouns.

❑ You did not use the *-s* ending with any uncountable nouns.

❑ You have numbers with some of your countable items.

❑ You have indefinite quantifiers with the uncountable items (and possibly some countable items).

LESSON 24: SHOPPING AT THE MALL—INDICATING SPECIFIC AND NON-SPECIFIC NOUNS

Focus: articles—the/a/an/zero article

Preview

LEARNING STRATEGY

Understanding and Using Emotions: Focusing on what you do know rather than on what you don't know will give you the confidence to continue learning.

Below you will find a map of a shopping mall with many different kinds of stores. You will also find a list of things that you and a friend want to buy today. You can find some of these things at the mall, but other things on the list you can't find there.

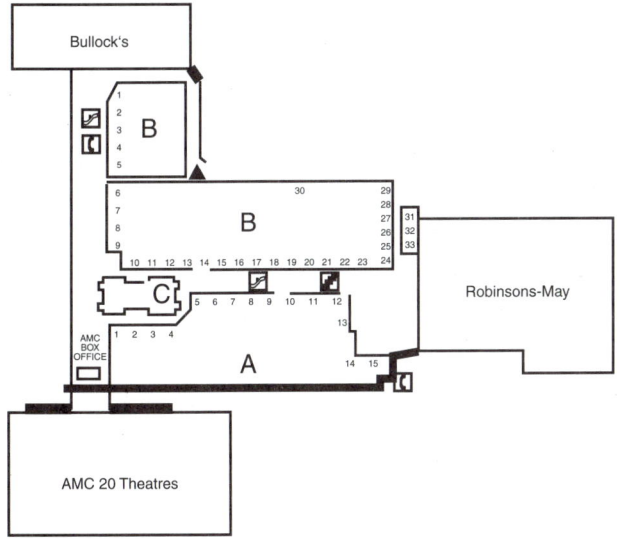

Department & Anchor Stores
Bullock's
Robinsons-May

Entertainment
AMC 20 Theatres

Women's Apparel
B-10 Casual Corner
C Charlotte Russe
B-14 Compagnie Internationale Express
A-11 Judy's
B-15 Lane Bryant
A-6 Lerner New York
B-22 The Limited

Men's Apparel
B-6 Gingiss Formalwear
B-18 J. Riggings

Children's Specialty Shops
A-2 Kay Bee Toy and Hobby
B-21 Limited Too

Fashion Specialty Shops
B-17 Gap
B-3 Miller's Outpost
B-13 Wilsons The Leather Experts

Shoe Stores
A-1 Athletic X-Press
B-22 Cathy Jean
B-19 Foot Locker
B-11 Wild Pair

Jewelry
A Ben Bridge Jeweler
B-7 Claire's
B-16 Kaleidoscope
B-20 Merksamer Jewelers
B-30 Zales

Music & Electronics
A-9 Sam Goody's Musicland
B-4 Sun Coast Motion Picture
A-5 Wherehouse Records

Specialty Foods
B-24 Coffee Collection
B-8 General Nutrition Center
B-25 Mrs. Fields Cookies
B-26 Pretzel Time
B-33 Sweet Factory

Restaurants
A-15 Canyon Cafe
B-27 Dairy Queen/Karmel Korn/Orange Julius
  Dimitri's - Inside Bullock's
A-14 Guacamole Mexican Cafe
A-13 Legends Cafe & Grill

Housewares & Home Furnishings
B-32 Lechters Housewares
B-2 Posters And Frames

Cards & Gifts
A-3 Coach House Gifts
A-12 Elam's Hallmark
B-1 The Confetti & Card Company
B-12 Things Remembered

Miscellaneous Specialty Shops
A-7 B. Dalton Bookseller
B-28 Bath & Body Works
B-29 Max Photo, Camera & Video
B-9 Natural Wonders
A-10 Oshman's Sporting Goods
A-8 Software Etc.

Read this list and do two things:

1. Put a check next to the item if you think you can buy it at this mall. (If you think you cannot buy it there, do nothing.)
2. Write the name of one or two stores where you can find each item.

ITEM   STORE(S)

earrings

rice

camera equipment

dishes

bread

CDs (compact discs)

running shoes

bananas

T-shirts

157

CHAPTER 6
NOUN PHRASES

Presentation

Below you will find a conversation between two friends at a mall. Read this conversation and then answer the questions below it.

Jean: I hope I can find everything I need today. I've got to get shoes for the party at the office next weekend. I also need a necklace for the new dress I bought yesterday.

Diane: I'm not buying clothes today. I just got a new stereo system, so I'm looking for CDs. I'd like to get the CDs on sale if possible. I also have to buy a book for my night class. Is there a book store in this mall?

Jean: Is that for the computer class on Thursday nights at the community college? I've taken computer classes there. Maybe I have the book.

Diane: No, it's not for the computer class. I already have that book. I'm also taking an English class. It's a speed-reading course.

Jean: I'm sure there's a bookstore here. Let's find a mall directory.

Diane: There's one right behind you.
(one minute later)
I found a bookstore. It's number 23 on the map. It's the store just next to the coffeehouse. I'll go there with you. I'm always looking for an interesting book to read.

Jean: Okay. And maybe we'll have time for coffee after that.

QUESTIONS

1. List the things that Jean needs to buy. Then list the things that Diane needs to buy.
2. Look back at the conversation and find each of the nouns you listed in #1. Do you see the words **a** or **an** or **the** before any of these nouns? Write each one you see in the conversation (*a/an/the*) next to each noun on your list.

    Which items on your list in #1 do not have *a* or *an* or *the* before them in the conversation? Are these words singular or plural? Are they countable or uncountable?

3. Look back at the conversation again. Jean uses several nouns in the first part of the conversation. Look at the following list and answer the questions that follow.
    • shoes   • party   • office   • necklace   • dress

    Is she talking about something specific (something she knows about) or something more general (it could be any one of this thing) for each of these nouns? Put each noun in the correct column below.

GENERAL	SPECIFIC
_____	_____
_____	_____
_____	_____
_____	_____

Explanation

LESSON 24: SHOPPING AT THE MALL—INDICATING SPECIFIC AND NON-SPECIFIC NOUNS

1. In Lesson 23 you learned about different kinds of nouns. You also learned about some words that can come before these nouns (indefinite quantifiers). Indefinite quantifiers are not the only words that can come before nouns.

    Often you will find articles before nouns. In this lesson you will learn about and practice when to use articles and when not to use them with different kinds of nouns.

2. When you are thinking about using articles, you have four choices as follows:

a or **an**	**the**	**no article**
indefinite article	definite article	zero article (0)

3. We can use indefinite articles (*a/an*) for singular countable nouns. These nouns are not specific, but are more general. We can use the indefinite article when the listener or speaker is not familiar with or doesn't know the noun we are talking about.

    I also need **a necklace** for the new dress I bought yesterday.

    We do **not** use indefinite articles with the following: plural nouns/uncountable nouns/most proper names.

    We use the **an** form of the indefinite article when the following word has a vowel sound.

    I'm also taking **an English** class.

    Remember: The **an** goes before a vowel **sound,** not before every vowel. Sometimes you will also find **an** before a consonant because it has a vowel sound.

    (If you are not sure of the pronunciation of the words in bold, ask your teacher or a native speaker of English to pronounce these words for you.)

    He works in **an office.**   She is **an honest** person.
    She wears **a uniform** to work.   She works in **a hotel.**

4. We can also use an indefinite article when we are talking about something for the first time. When we mention this item again, we use the definite article. (See #5 below for more information about definite articles.)

    I also have to buy **a book** for my night class.
    Maybe I have **the book.**

5. We can use the definite article before the following kinds of nouns:
    - singular countable
    - plural countable
    - uncountable

    The computer classes are at **the community college.**
    We can get **the coffee** at **the new coffeehouse.**

    We use the definite article (*the*) for specific nouns. The listener or reader knows the noun that the speaker or writer is talking about. There are several ways that the listener or reader may know this as follows:
    - There is only one of these things in the world (**the** sun).
    - There is only one of these things in the specific environment you are talking about (**the community college**).
    - You have already mentioned this item and the reader or listener now knows about it. (See # 4 above.)
    - You give more information about this noun (**the** party at **the** office next weekend). This information makes the noun more specific.

6. We use no article (zero [0] article) when we have general plural countable or uncountable nouns.

    I've got to get **shoes** for the party.

CHAPTER 6
NOUN PHRASES

IT WORKS!
Learning Strategy:
Analyzing Context
of Grammatical
Forms

Practice

ACTIVITY ONE

Do all three parts of this activity with a partner.

A. Look back at the conversation in the Presentation part of this lesson. Find nouns that fit the categories below. Write the nouns and articles that you find in the conversation in the correct columns.

NOT SPECIFIC (singular countable)	SPECIFIC (singular or plural countable/uncountable)
a necklace	*the new dress*
an English class	*the community college*

B. Which general plural countable or uncountable nouns in this conversation have zero article (no article at all)?

_____

C. Can you find examples of nouns in the conversation that are mentioned twice, first as something indefinite and then as something more definite? Write any examples of this below.

_____

ACTIVITY TWO

Sometimes when native speakers talk quickly, it can be difficult to hear all of the words. This is often true with the indefinite article *a*. You will listen to several people talk about things they bought today. Listen carefully for information about the items they bought and the stores where they got these things. Next to each number below write both the articles (*a/an/the*) and the nouns you hear in each one.

1. _____

2. _____

3. _____

4. _____

5. _____

Now compare answers with a classmate. Do you have all the same answers? If necessary ask your teacher to repeat the sentences.

ACTIVITY THREE

Next to each number below you will find some information about things that several people bought or will buy. Fill in each blank with one of the articles from this lesson (*a/an/the*). If you think no article is necessary, write a 0. (In some cases, there may be more than one possible answer.)

1. Juliana wants to buy _____ new VCR. She will look for the name of _____ electronics store near her house in the telephone book. She wants to find _____ discount store because she doesn't have much money. She wants to buy _____ VCR for _____ good price.

2. Roberto bought _____ baby present for _____ old friend. He bought _____ colorful baby toy. He also bought _____ electronic game for _____ older child in the family. Now he needs to buy _____ batteries for _____ game.

3. Steve went shopping this morning at _____ large supermarket near his house. He bought _____ cereal, _____ bread, and _____ ice cream. He forgot to buy _____ dessert for dinner, so he'll go back to _____ store later.

4. Sue is ordering _____ pizza for dinner. She wants _____ onions and _____ olives on _____ pizza, but her children want _____ pepperoni. She has decided to get two pizzas and _____ order of garlic bread to make everyone happy.

LEARNING STRATEGY

Forming Concepts: Focusing on how specific words are used in a sentence helps you use them correctly.

ACTIVITY FOUR

Work with a partner for both parts of this activity. You will need to look at the map of the shopping mall at the beginning of this lesson to complete them.

A. Below you will find the names of several people. Each person wants to buy something at this mall. First decide what type of store this person should look for and write a sentence about it. Use the article *a/an* in your sentence. Then write something about a specific store in this mall using *the*.

EXAMPLE Yuko   birthday card
Yuko should look for a card store. She can go to the Elam's Hallmark in this mall. The Hallmark store is near the Legends Restaurant.

1. Jorge   sweet snack
2. Jonathan   dress shirt
3. Sylvia   camera film
4. Hiroshi   video games
5. Ellie and Richard   lunch

B. Think of something (or more than one thing) that you want to buy. Tell your partner what you want. Your partner will tell you what kind of store you need and then give you some specific information about where to go at this mall.

ACTIVITY FIVE

A. Do this activity in groups of three people. Look at the pictures of items on sale below. Discuss with your group the names of these items. As a group, decide which one of these you might buy. Why did you choose this item? What will you use it for? (How will you use it?)

B. As a group, write a few sentences about your answers to A. If possible, use some specific nouns and some general nouns in your sentences. Be sure to use the correct articles (*a/an/the*) or zero articles with your nouns.

After you finish writing, check you sentences with the checklist at the end of this lesson.

ACTIVITY SIX

A. Look at the following cartoon and think about why it might be funny. Can you answer these questions about it?

"Well... so much for your two semesters of French."

- Who are the people in this cartoon?
- Where are they?
- What things are on the table? Why are they there?

B. Share your answers to Part A with a partner. Do you have the same story?

C. Think about your own experiences in a restaurant or another kind of shopping situation. Have you ever had a funny experience similar to the one in the cartoon? (This could be an experience from any kind of misunderstanding, including one about language.) Tell this experience to others in the class. Then write it down in a short essay.

Look back at your sentences for Activity 5 and your essay for Activity 6. Check your work for the following:

❏ You talked about some general nouns and some specific nouns.

❏ You used *a/an* for the general singular countable nouns.

❏ You used *an* if the following word had a vowel sound.

❏ You used *the* for specific nouns (singular countable/plural countable/uncountable)

❏ You used no article (zero article) with general plural countable or uncountable nouns.

LESSON 25: MUSIC AND DANCE— MAKING REFERENCES

> Focus: pronouns—subject/object/reflexive

Preview

1. Look at the list of different kinds of music. Are you familiar with all of these? Can you think of an artist or group associated with each kind?

rock and roll	bluegrass	heavy metal
jazz	country western	rap
classical	folk	techno
opera	reggae	rhythm and blues (R & B)

   What kind of music is traditional in your native country? What kind is most popular in your native country? Do you play a musical instrument? If so, what do you play?

2. Do you like to dance or watch dance performances? What kind of dancing is your favorite to do or watch? What kind of dancing is most popular in your native country?

Presentation

Following are some people's ideas about their favorite music. Read the information and then answer the questions that follow.

1. We've always liked bluegrass music best. It can be very lively, but it can also make **us** relax at times.
2. My son likes to listen to the oldies, mostly from the 60s. He especially likes The Beatles, The Doors, and Jimi Hendrix. When he goes out, he often takes his tapes and walkman with <u>him</u>. That way he can listen to them anywhere he goes.
3. I enjoy listening to various female singers, especially Natalie Merchant and Annie Lennox. They write some interesting songs and I try to understand them. What happened to <u>them</u> in their lives and why did they write these songs?

QUESTIONS

1. Look at the word "we" in the first sentence in #1. What position in the sentence is this word?

   Look at the word "I" in the first sentence in #3. What position in the sentence is this word?
2. Look at the bold word (*us*) in the second sentence in #1. What position does this word have in that sentence?
3. Find the underlined words (*him* and *them*) in #2 and #3. What word comes just before the word *him*? What word comes just before the word *them*?
4. Can you think of any rules about when to use each of the following words in an English sentence: *I* and *we*   *us* and *him*? Discuss your ideas with the others in your class.

Explanation

1. We use pronouns to take the place of nouns. When we use a pronoun, we often want readers or listeners to think of something or someone they know about already.

    Have you seen **Mary** today?
    Yes, I saw **her** in school this morning.

    There are several different kinds of pronouns in English. In this lesson we will discuss and practice **subject, object,** and **reflexive pronouns.**

2. You will find **subject** pronouns in the subject position of a sentence. These pronouns include the following:

    I   you   she/he/it   we   they

    (*NOTE* We always use a capital letter for the pronoun **I.**)

    I enjoy listening to various female singers.
    We've always liked bluegrass music best.

    Sometimes you will use the first person singular (I) with another word, such as a noun or another pronoun. In this case you should (for politeness) put the pronoun **I** second.

    Joe and I have always liked bluegrass music best.
    He and I have always liked bluegrass music best.

3. You will find **object** pronouns in the object position of a sentence. These pronouns include the following:

    me   you   her/him/it   us   them

    It can also make **us** relax at times.

    You will also find an object pronoun after a preposition. [For more information about prepositions, see Chapter 7.]

    He often takes his tapes and Walkman **with him.**
    What happened **to them** in their lives?

4. **Reflexive** pronouns refer back to something or someone mentioned before, most often the subject of the sentence. These pronouns include the following:

    myself   yourself   himself/herself/itself   ourselves   yourselves   themselves

    Nobody wanted to sing the song with me, so **I** sang it **myself.**

5. English, like other languages, has three basic sets of pronouns as follows:

SET	SUBJECT	OBJECT	REFLEXIVE
First person			
singular	I	me	myself
plural	we	us	ourselves
Second person			
singular	you	you	yourself
plural	you	you	yourselves
Third person			
sing. masc.	he	him	himself
sing. fem.	she	her	herself
sing. neuter	it	it	itself
plural	they	them	themselves

a. You use the first person set to talk about yourself (alone or with other people).

I/We enjoy listening to various female singers.
You needed **me/us.** You gave it to **me/us.**
I did it **myself.** We did it **ourselves.**

b. You use the second person set for people you are talking or writing to.

You danced with Joe.
I danced with **you.** I can give it to **you.**
You did it **yourself/yourselves.**

c. You use the third set to talk or write about other people or things.

She/he listens to the oldies from the 60s.
When's your birthday? **It's** next week.
They listen to the oldies.
We'll dance for **her/him/them.**
He sang it **himself.** She sang it **herself.**
The cat was cleaning **itself** after the meal.

NOTE In the past it was common to use the pronoun *he* to refer to people and animals if the writer or speaker was not sure about the sex. More recently, many people feel you should not use *he* so often. This is because it seems to exclude (leave out) females.

You can do several things to avoid this problem:
- Repeat the noun phrase.
- Change your subject to a plural one. This way you will use the pronoun "they." (For example, change "person" to "people.")
- Use he and she together as follows:
he and she/he or she
s/he
(s)he

You need to be careful with all of the above suggestions. It can become clumsy to use one way too many times.

6. In conversation, native speakers often use the wrong pronoun. You should not write these mistakes as they are incorrect. You should be aware that native speakers sometimes use them this way. For example, you may hear sentences like the following:

Me and my brother went to the movies.
He gave the package to my sister and I.

What is the correct form for each of the incorrect pronouns in the sentences above?

Practice

ACTIVITY ONE

A. Look back at the Presentation on page 164 and do the following:

- Find all the subject pronouns. Put a circle around each one.
- Find all the object pronouns after a verb. Put a line under each one.
- Find all the object pronouns after a preposition. Put an X on each of these pronouns.

B. Find each pronoun in bold. Draw an arrow from each one of these pronouns to the noun each one refers to. (Be careful! One of them may have two possible answers.)

1. We've always liked bluegrass music best. **It** can be very lively, but it can also make us relax at times.
2. My son likes to listen to the oldies, mostly from the 60s. **He** especially likes The Beatles, The Doors, and Jimi Hendrix. When he goes out, he often takes his tapes and Walkman with him. That way he can listen to **them** anywhere he goes.
3. I enjoy listening to various female singers, especially Natalie Merchant and Annie Lennox. **They** write some interesting songs and I try to understand **them.** What happened to **them** in their lives and why did they write these songs?

ACTIVITY TWO

Read each of the following short conversations and fill in each blank with a pronoun. Use any of the pronouns from this lesson (subject/object/reflexive). You will have to use some pronouns more than one time.

1. A: I've got tickets to see a ballet tonight. Would you like to go with _____?

   B: No _____ can't. _____ have to study for a big test tomorrow. Maybe next time.

   A: Okay. Sorry _____ can't make it. I'll probably just go by _____.

2. A: Let's look in the Arts section of the paper. Maybe _____ can find a good concert for next weekend.

   B: Good idea. Here's one. Do _____ like folk music? There's a big concert at the park next Saturday. Would you like to see _____?

   A: Not really. Can _____ look at that paper?

   B: Sure. Here _____ is. _____ can look for _____.

3. A: Hi Mara. _____ tried to call _____ last night, but _____ weren't home.

   B: _____ know. My husband and _____ were at a Broadway show. My parents took _____ out for our anniversary.

   A: What about your daughter? Where did you leave _____?

   B: _____ slept at a friend's house. Of course _____ couldn't leave her home by _____.

LESSON 25: MUSIC AND DANCE—MAKING REFERENCES

ACTIVITY THREE

Do both parts of this activity with a partner.

A. Look at the following Dennis the Menace cartoon. Can you explain it? What errors in grammar can you find? How can you correct these errors?

DENNIS THE MENACE ® used by permission of Hank Ketcham and © by North America Syndicate.

B. Read the following short paragraphs. Some of the sentences have mistakes in pronouns and others are correct. Find the mistakes and correct them.

1. I saw an opera last night and it was great. My brother and me went together. We went by ourselfs because our friends couldn't come with us. Next time we'll be sure to take they.

2. A group of dancers and musicians from Bali will be at the Performing Arts Center next weekend. Joe and his wife are planning to go. She went to Bali last year but Joe couldn't go with him. While she was there, she saw these dancers and musicians perform. Now she wants he to see their performance. He will enjoy watching themselves very much.

LEARNING STRATEGY

Remembering New Material: Practicing different forms in realistic contexts helps you remember them better.

ACTIVITY FOUR

A. You are looking in the newspaper for a place to go for entertainment one night this weekend. You see the following advertisement. Decide which night you want to go to this place. Write one or two sentences about what you want to do and why you chose this particular night or activity. Use some of the pronouns from this lesson (subject/object/reflexive) in your sentences.

B. Do this part of the activity in groups of three or four people.

- Share your answers to Part A of this activity with the others in the group.
- Write some sentences about the plans of various people in the group. Be sure to use different pronouns in your sentences. For example, use *she* or *he* to talk about one other person in the group and use *we* for plans you may have in common with another person (or other people) in the group, etc.
- Share your sentences with other groups in the class. Which activity is the most popular in the class?

```
THE REVOLVING DOOR
1200 Main Street
Open 'til 2 A.M.

FRIDAY NIGHT
Karaoke
$2.00 admission charge

SATURDAY NIGHT
Live Music—Local Bands
$3.00 cover charge

SUNDAY NIGHT
D.J.
No admission/No cover charge!
```

LEARNING STRATEGY

Understanding and Using Emotions: Associating your own feelings and experiences with particular grammatical structures helps you learn those structures more quickly.

ACTIVITY FIVE

Have you ever gone to a live performance of music or dance? Have you ever performed yourself (dancing/singing/playing an instrument)?

Describe a time when you performed or watched or listened to a performance. Talk about how you felt, what you saw or did, and what you enjoyed or did not enjoy about this experience. Write a paragraph or two about your experience. Try to use pronouns from all three groups discussed in this lesson in your writing.

Look back at your writing for Activity 5. Check your work for the following:

❏ You wrote about a musical or dance performance (your own or someone else's).

You used pronouns from all three groups in this lesson.

❏ You used some subject pronouns: *I/you/she/he/it/we/they.*

❏ You used some object pronouns: *me/you/her/him/it/us/them.*

❏ You used at least one reflexive pronoun: *myself/yourself/himself/herself/itself/ourselves/yourselves/themselves.*

LESSON 26: ADVERTISING AND CONSUMERS—SHOWING OWNERSHIP/POSSESSION—PART ONE

Focus: possessive nouns

Preview

1. What kind of a consumer are you? Do you buy expensive things when you go shopping? Do you look for sales sometimes? Does advertising influence your decision to buy things? (Do you make a decision to buy something because of the advertising?)
2. What are some of your most important or favorite possessions? Why are they so important or your favorites?

Presentation

Read the following advertisements and then answer the questions that follow.

Bring in any store's price and Clark will beat them all . . . or the product is yours **FREE**

Carter Bed's red tag sale—*One Day Only*

George's Furniture Store
–no down payment–no interest–no monthly payments for 6 months

---

Chicago's largest arts and crafts store
—Mitchell's—
Anniversary Sale today!

Jones' warehouse
proudly serving the area since 1978

Celebrate With Us
the Zoological Society's 100th birthday party continues this month

---

The city's best selection of furniture is on sale today at Porter's

QUESTIONS

1. Look at the **'s** and **s'** (apostrophe -s and -s apostrophe) on some of the words in these advertisements. Write some of these words below.

   _____

   _____

   What information does the **'s** give you? (Why are they at the end of these words?)
2. Look at the end of the advertisement for George's Furniture Store. Why doesn't the word "months" have an apostrophe before the -s?
3. Look at the **apostrophe** (') in the advertisement about Jones' Warehouse. Why is this apostrophe after the -s in this word?

Explanation

1. A possessive noun shows ownership. It tells you who or what something belongs to.
2. The most common form in English for a possessive noun is **'s** (apostrophe -s).

   George**'s** Furniture Store
   the Zoological Society**'s** 100th birthday party

   If a singular noun ends in an **-s**, you may find the apostrophe -s (**'s**) ending or just the apostrophe after the -s (**s'**). This often depends on how awkward the pronunciation of the word is with the **'s**.

   my boss**'s** office
   Jone**s'** warehouse
3. When a noun is plural and ends in -s, you should add an apostrophe only.

   the store**'s** sale (one store)
   the store**s'** sales (more than one store)

WHEN YOU ARE WRITING

When you make a noun phrase into a possessive, ask yourself these questions:

1. Is the noun singular or plural?
2. Have you added an -s?
3. Have you put the apostrophe in the right place?

Remember that the apostrophe should be **before** the -s on a singular noun and after the -s on a regular plural one.

NOTE Be careful when you are using the possessive form for irregular noun plurals such as *women*, *children*, and *men*. These forms do not have the plural -s ending because they are irregular. Therefore, they follow the regular rule about adding the **'s** (the **women's** department).

4. If two people own the same thing, only the second person adds the apostrophe -s.

   He is sailing on **John and Alice's boat.**

LESSON 26: ADVERTISING AND CONSUMERS—SHOWING OWNERSHIP/POSSESSION—PART ONE

5. A possessive will usually have at least two words

Bob's boat

George's Furniture Store

You will sometimes see the name "noun phrase" for these words. For example, "Bob's boat" is a noun phrase and "George's Furniture Store" is a noun phrase.

Sometimes you will find only one word in a possessive, especially after a noun phrase has already been mentioned. Then the speaker or writer may not repeat the noun.

Is this **Bob's boat**? No it's **Carol's**. (It is not necessary to repeat the word "boat" in the second sentence.)

6. You will often find possessives with names of people, places, or companies ("proper nouns").

Chicago's largest arts and crafts store—**Mitchell's**—Anniversary Sale today!

We also usually use possessive nouns for other living things (such as animals) and a few nonliving things such as time and nature.

See **nature's gifts** at the zoo.

Two years ago the zoo introduced live trout into the **bears' pools.**

You should wear sunscreen for protection against the **sun's rays.**

We do not usually use possessive nouns for other nonliving things (such as things or ideas). For these, we use the preposition "of." [For more information about this preposition see Chapter 7 (Lesson 31).]

I love the color of that house.

Practice

ACTIVITY ONE

A. Look at the following advertisements and do two things:
- Circle the possessives.
- Put a line under the plural nouns.

1. Bill's Garage Doors—$529 installed—windows extra—579-0236
2. Free nights and weekends—cellular phones
3. Miami's Own—Jack's Sound Stereo—Factory Warehouse Sale
4. Mattress Sale—This President's Day rest assured with us!
5. Luby's automotive specials available at two locations
6. Fabric City's final sale days—all fabrics 50-60% off
7. Half price days—dozens of items throughout the store

B. Read the following advertisements. Some of them have possessive nouns without the apostrophe before or after the -s ('s or s'). Find the possessive nouns and add the apostrophe in the correct place. (Some of the advertisements may have more than one possessive noun.) Some advertisements do not need an apostrophe. In these cases, write nothing. Share your answers with a partner.

1. Visit Acapulco—Mexicos First class resort—Winter rates—50% off until March 31
2. Orange Countys Used Car and Truck Superstore—over 250 quality used cars and trucks in stock
3. Savings for all your office needs!

IT WORKS!
Learning Strategy:
Focusing on How
Forms Are Used in
Sentences

4. For the Lowest fares call: The Cruise Center—the citys #1 cruise source
5. Come see our interactive display with 54 computers plugged-in and ready to play.
6. Today only—20-30% off luggage from your travel experts
7. Come to our Valentines Day Sale for the best selection of chocolates and flowers
8. Hurry to Michelles Spring Sale of leather and suede products
9. As seen on TV—Barbara Johnsons famous "No Makeup" Makeup system. Try Barbaras makeup FREE for 30 days

ACTIVITY TWO

You are going to hear several sentences. Each sentence has at least one possessive noun in it. Write down each possessive noun as you hear it. (Remember, you may hear more than one possessive in a sentence.)

Now check your work with another student. Did you both put the apostrophe in the same place for each possessive you heard? If necessary ask your teacher to repeat the sentences.

ACTIVITY THREE

Below you will find some information about a cruise ship. There are several possessive nouns in this information, but some of them are not correct. Find the mistakes and correct them. Look for the following kinds of mistakes:

- a noun with the apostrophe -s ('s or s') that should not be possessive
- a possessive noun that needs 's or s'

The Floating Palace Company has everything for your next cruise. The Floating Palace's newest boat is 75,000 tons, one of the largest ships afloat. The ships creative team tried to find things of interest for all kinds of travelers. Here are some of the things they offer:

- The ships workout room has high-tech equipment to use for exercise and windows to offer beautiful views'. These help take the exercisers mind off the work and pain.
- The childrens' program on the ship gives young artists' all their supplies and an ocean view.
- A "virtual" sports center lets you "play" some of the worlds best teams on large video screens.
- Quiet traveler's can sit in the Reading Room's beautiful furniture. You can bring your own books or borrow from the ships 2,000 books sitting in bookcase's.

LEARNING STRATEGY

Overcoming Limitations: Applying new forms in different contexts will help you understand and use these forms quickly.

CHAPTER 6
NOUN PHRASES

ACTIVITY FOUR

A. Think about something you bought recently or something you own that you like very much. State what this item is and write a short description below.

EXAMPLE I have a new television.
It has a 15-inch screen. It gets 153 cable channels.

State the item you bought or own.

_____

Describe this item in one or two sentences.

_____
_____

B. Work with a partner for this part of the activity. Tell each other the information from above (in part A). Write your partner's information down and then tell the class what you learned in one or two sentences. Use a possessive noun in each sentence you write.

Suzanne's new television gets 153 cable channels.
Suzanne's new television's screen is 15 inches.

ACTIVITY FIVE

Do this activity in groups of three or four people.

A. Think about a place you like (or want to) visit. It can be any kind of place, such as a city, a country, a company, an amusement park, a museum, a restaurant etc. Think about what things this place has to see or what you can do there that might be interesting. Write some of these ideas down.

B. With your group, write a short description or advertisement (three to five sentences) for the place you discussed above. Be sure to use some possessive nouns in your description or advertisement.

C. Share your work with the rest of the class.
Look back at your description or advertisement for Activity 5. Check your work for the following:

❑ You chose one place for your advertisement.
❑ You used some possessive nouns in your work.
❑ You used apostrophe -*s* (*'s*) for single nouns with no -*s* on the end.
❑ You put the apostrophe after the -*s* (*s'*) where appropriate.

LESSON 27: FAMILY TIES/GENEALOGY—SHOWING OWNERSHIP/POSSESSION—PART TWO

Focus: possessive pronouns

Preview

What is genealogy? How much do you know about your family's history? Look at the family tree below and fill in as many names as you can about your family. (If you need more boxes for brothers and sisters, you can add them in.)

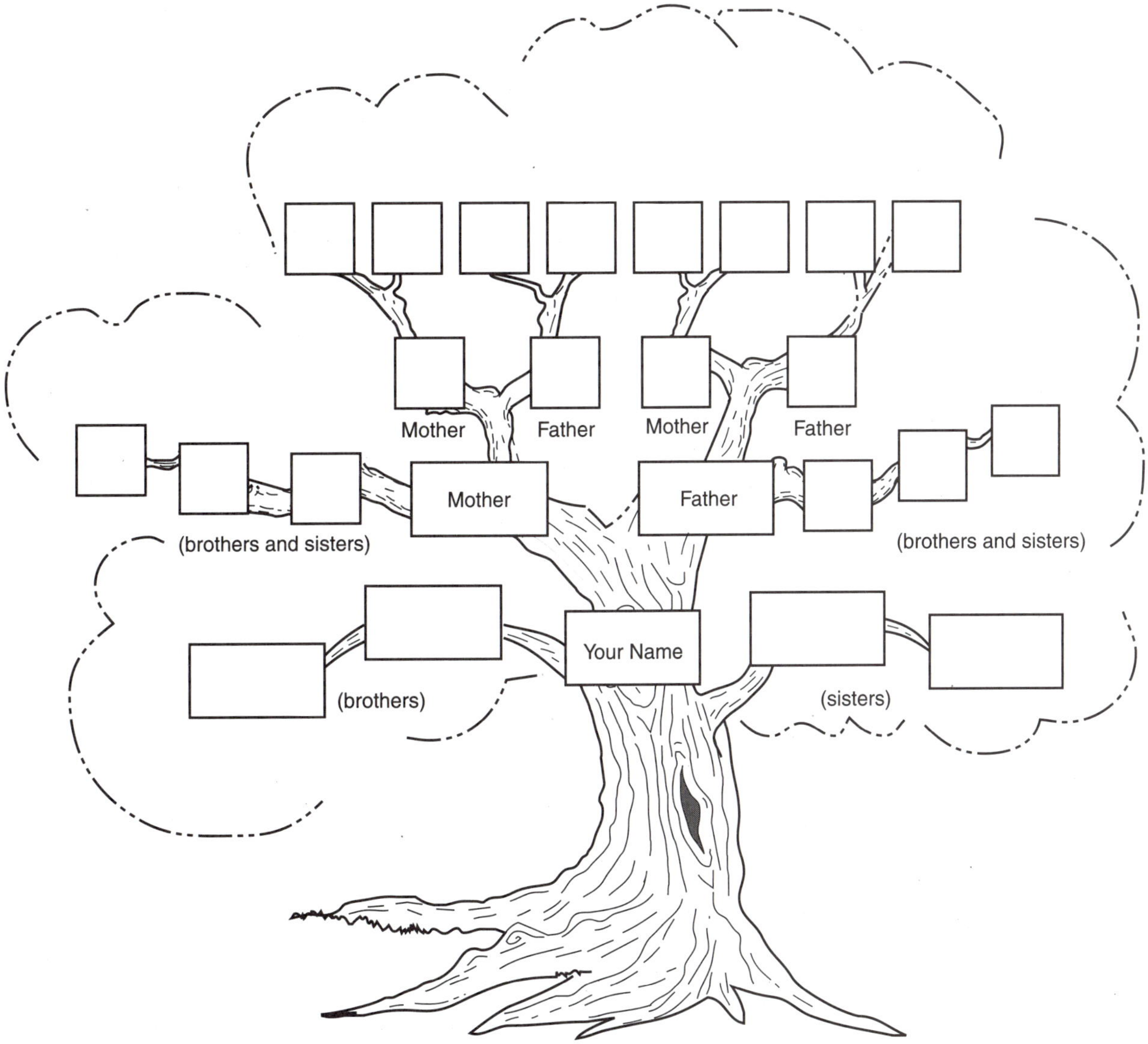

CHAPTER 6
NOUN PHRASES

Presentation

Below you will find Charles Ross' family tree and a list of words related to family. Look at both of these and then read the instructions that follow for A and B.

FAMILY WORDS
wife
brother
son
father-in-law
grandparents
father
grandson
great-grandson
husband
daughter
mother
parents

A. The following is a short description of part of Charles' family. Fill in each blank with the correct word from the list of family words above. Be sure to use a different word for each answer.

Paul is his _____ and Evelyn is his _____. Evelyn's _____ on her father's side are Jean Smith and Lawrence Storm. Her _____ are Gloria Mitchell and Ben Storm. Charles is their _____ .

B. Now imagine you are Betty Little on this family tree. Fill in the blanks about your family with more of the words from the list above. Use a different word for each answer and do not repeat any words from A above.

George Ross is my _____ and our _____ is Paul. My _____ is Samuel Ross and his _____ is Lynn Porter. Their _____ is Charles Ross.

QUESTIONS

1. Find the possessive nouns in the Presentation above. Write them below.

   _____
   _____

   Can you find any other words that show possession in this Presentation? Write them below.

   _____
   _____

2. Look carefully for apostrophes in the words you wrote in #1 above. Which words have the apostrophe and which words do not?

Explanation

1. Possessive pronouns take the place of possessive nouns. Unlike possessive nouns, possessive pronouns do not include an apostrophe.

   George is **Paul's** father.
   George is **his** father.

2. There are two groups of possessive pronouns in English as follows:

SET	POSSESSIVE	POSSESSIVE
First person		
singular	my	mine
plural	our	ours
Second person		
singular	your	yours
plural	your	yours
Third person		
sing. masc.	his	his
sing. fem.	her	hers
sing. neuter	its	—
plural	their	theirs

   REMEMBER: Do **not** put an apostrophe on any of the pronouns in this chart.

   NOTE Be especially careful about using the word **its** as a possessive (without an apostrophe) and **it's,** the contraction of *it is* or *it has*. You should only use the apostrophe if you can change the word to *it is* or *it has* in the sentence.

   I like genealogy. **It's** (**it is**) a fascinating subject.
   It's (**it has**) been years since I last saw you.
   I want to learn more about my family and **its history**

3. One group of possessives comes before the noun of possession.

   Lynn and Samuel are **his parents.**

4. When you use the other group of possessives, you do not include the noun. (This possessive is only one word.) Speakers often use this pronoun when they do not want to repeat the noun of possession. You will usually find these possessives in speaking and only rarely in writing,

   George's parents live in Ohio.
   Mine live in Florida.

   Sometimes you will find this group of possessive pronouns at the end of a sentence.

   The family tree in this lesson is **mine.**

Practice

ACTIVITY ONE

A. Mary, Charles Ross' sister, decided to become the family historian. Below you will find some information about how she began to do this. Choose the correct word in parentheses for each sentence.

Mary found two local genealogy clubs and went to a few of (theirs/theirs'/their) meetings. She joined one club because it gave a lot of help to (it's/its/its') new members. She became friends with one of the members and attended (his'/his/his's) workshop for beginners. He explained step-by-step how to begin a family search and Mary became anxious to start (her/her's/hers).

After the workshop, she called (hers/her's/her) parents and asked them to write down the names of all of (their/theirs/theirs') relatives. Then she asked (her/her's/hers) mother to contact some of (her/hers/her's) family and (her's/hers/her) father to contact some of (his/his'/his's) for more information.

B. Mary's parents contacted several relatives and some of them sent responses. Below you will find some of the responses. Each response has some problems with a possessive noun or pronoun. Find the mistakes and correct them.

1. Pauls grandparents sent a copy of theirs marriage certificate. They also sent a few pictures of their wedding's day.
2. Evelyn's sister sent the front page from her familys old Bible. She wrote, "This page has part of ours family tree on it. It's not complete, but maybe you can compare it with your's. I hope this helps."
3. Pauls' mother sent him a copy of his birth certificate with this note:

   "Here's a copy of yours birth certificate. I thought I had a copy of my too, but now I can't find it. I'll keep looking for it."

ACTIVITY TWO

Sometimes when people want to learn more about their family, they begin with an "oral history." They do this by taping interviews with relatives. Below you will find some information about how to do this. Fill in each blank with one of the following possessive pronouns: (You will use most of these possessives more than one time.)

my   your   his   her   our   their

ASK RELATIVES TO TELL STORIES

To put a family history on tape, you need to talk to family members. Talk to _____ parents and greatgrandparents about _____ experiences. Don't forget to talk to aunts, uncles, and parents as well. They have _____ own stories to tell.

Tips to get started:

- Ask a relative to take the time to talk to you about _____ or _____ life story.

- Ask your relatives to gather _____ old pictures, news clippings, journals, and other papers. Then they can tell stories about these.

- Help _____ relatives recall _____ stories. Ask them questions like, "Remember when we did that?" or "Remember _____ vacation to New York?" Share _____ own memories of these times to help them remember.

- Ask _____ other relatives for stories about the person you interview. That way you will get a more complete picture of _____ or _____ life.

- Begin each tape with an introduction. It might be, "This is Bob Jones. I'm interviewing _____ grandmother, Ruth Jones, on June 2, 1996. This is _____ 65th birthday. We are talking about _____ life and about _____ family in general."

- Organize all _____ tapes. Write on the tape box the dates and names for all of _____ interviews.

LEARNING STRATEGY

Forming Concepts: Paying attention to new language forms helps you understand how they work and when to use them.

LESSON 27: FAMILY TIES/GENEALOGY—SHOWING POSSESSION/OWNERSHIP—PART TWO

ACTIVITY THREE

You are going to hear some information about different families. In each case you will hear some possessives. Some of these will be possessive nouns and some will be possessive pronouns from this lesson. Listen carefully and write down all the possessives you hear in the correct column below. Write the possessives and the noun that follows (if any).

POSSESSIVE NOUN	POSSESSIVE PRONOUN
1. _____	_____
2. _____	_____
3. _____	_____
4. _____	_____
5. _____	_____
6. _____	_____

ACTIVITY FOUR

IT WORKS!
Learning Strategy:
Applying New
Grammar to
Personal Situations

Write a few sentences about some of the people in your family. Write each sentence using a different possessive. Use each of the following possessives:

my   his   her   our   their

EXAMPLES My mother's name is Evelyn.
Her family lives in Toronto.
Our family visits my grandparents often.

ACTIVITY FIVE

A. Look back at the family tree you completed in the Preview part of this lesson. Add any more information you can about brothers, sisters, aunts, uncles, and their families.

B. Discuss your family tree with a partner. Tell your partner some information about some of the people in your family using the possessives from this lesson (my/your/his/her/our/their).

C. Share some of the information you and your partner discussed with others in the class. Each partner should tell the others some of the information she or he learned about both families. Use as many of the possessives from this lesson as possible (from both groups).

ACTIVITY SIX

Think of an interesting or funny story about any of the people in your family. Write a paragraph about this. Use as many possessives from this lesson as you can in your story.

Look back at your paragraph for Activity 6. Check your work for the following:

❏ Your story is about some people in your family.
❏ You used some possessives from this group: *my/your/his/her/our/their.* These words come before a noun.
❏ You used some possessives from this group: *mine/yours/hers/his/ours/theirs.* A noun does not follow these words.
❏ You did not put an apostrophe on any of these possessives.

LESSON 28: SETTING RECORDS—DESCRIBING AND COMPARING

Focus: adjectives—comparatives/superlatives

Preview

Look at the following list of activities. Have you ever tried to do any of these?

Put a check next to the ones you have tried or done.

_____ drove a car over 90 mph

_____ ate a whole pie or cake by yourself (at one time)

_____ ran a race that was more than 10 miles

_____ talked on the telephone for more than two hours (to the same person)

_____ drank three glasses or more of anything (in one sitting)

Presentation I

Read the following short story and answer the questions that follow.

One day a **strange** visitor arrived at the office of Mark Young, editor of the "Guinness Book of Records." The man wanted Mark to watch him do an **unusual** *feat*. The man planned to lie on a bed of nails.

Usually these kinds of "beds" have many nails, so the body won't rest too heavily on any **single** point. But this man was *determined* to set the record for using fewer nails than anyone before. His bed had only four nails.

The man put out his bed and he did as promised. He lay on it and he did not get hurt. Editor Mark Young thought this was a **fine** accomplishment, but he could not put it in the record book. It was too dangerous. A reader might try the trick and hurt himself/herself. "Sorry," he told the man with the **thick** skin. No record there.

Not every person hoping to break into the **famous** "Book of Records" comes to Mark's office in New York City. Most people just write a letter. In fact, Mark gets about 100 letters from record *seekers* each week. This book now lists more than 2,000 records. That's a lot of records to *keep track of. Updating* this book every year keeps the staff of several people busy full time.

an action that's not ordinary/accomplishment

be sure you want to do something

someone who tries to find or get something

pay attention to something/watch

make current/modernize

QUESTIONS

1. Look at the bold words in the reading above. Which of these words describe something? Write each word that describes below.

   _____

   _____

2. What kind of word follows each of the words you wrote in #1 above?

3. Find the word "dangerous" in the third paragraph. What verb comes before this word? What comes after this word?

Explanation

1. Adjectives describe things and they can do this in several ways. They may describe by color, size, general appearance, or other qualities or characteristics.

    One day a **strange** visitor arrived at the office of Mark Young.
    "Sorry," he told the man with the **thick** skin.

    NOTE If you are using a dictionary, you will find the letters **adj.** for an adjective.

2. Adjectives usually come before a noun or in the complement position after a linking verb. [See Lesson 1 for more information about linking verbs and complements.]

    The man wanted Mark to watch him do an **unusual feat**.
    adjective noun

    It **was** too **dangerous**.
    linking verb   adjective (complement)

    Adjectives in English do not add any endings to agree with the nouns. DO NOT add the plural -s ending to an adjective.

    The man wanted Mark to watch him do **an unusual feat**.
    The man wanted Mark to watch him do **some unusual feats**.

3. Qualifiers can modify (make stronger or weaker) adjectives.

    One day a **fairly strange** visitor arrived at the office of Mark Young.
    qualifier
    The man wanted Mark to watch him do a **pretty unusual** feat.
    qualifier

    Some qualifiers are more common in speaking than in writing. Look at the chart below for some common examples of qualifiers for adjectives.

TYPICAL IN SPEECH	TYPICAL IN WRITING
a bit	about
awful(ly)	almost
kind of	especially
plain	fairly
pretty	hardly
real(ly)	nearly
sort of	only
terribly	quite
	rather
	somewhat

Be careful not to use the qualifier **very** too often or to confuse it with **too**. **Very** means **much** or **a large amount. Too** is more of an opinion. It means the speaker or writer feels there is an amount that is beyond a good amount.

What is the difference in meaning in the following examples?

The trick was *very* dangerous.
The trick was *too* dangerous for the book.

4. Sometimes you may want to use a qualifier and more than one adjective to describe a noun. The order you should follow is:

QUALIFIER	NUMBER	OPINION	SIZE	SHAPE	AGE	COLOR	ORIGIN
rather		unusual	large			blue	flower
	five	silly			old		songs
			small	round		red	rocks

Practice

LESSON 28: SETTING RECORDS—DESCRIBING AND COMPARING

ACTIVITY ONE

Below you will find some rules about record-breaking from the book "The Guinness Book of World Records 1996." Read these rules and then do two things:

- Find all of the adjectives in these rules. Circle each adjective you find.
- Look at the list of other adjectives below. Find adjectives in the rules with the same meaning as the adjectives on the list. Replace as many adjectives in the rules as you can with adjectives from the list. (You will not replace all of the adjectives in the rules.) Compare answers with a partner.

| common/prevalent | exact | weak/small | not the same | every |
| present | additional | tolerant/calm | real/genuine | lengthy |

THE SIX GOLDEN RULES OF RECORD-BREAKING

1. Try to make a new record for something that is in the current edition.
2. Remember if the record you want to beat is not in the book, your chances of getting in the book are slim. Make sure your record is measurable and it has plenty of *popular appeal*.   *interesting or pleasing to many people*
3. Check with the editors of the book before you proceed. The record you are thinking about may be different now.
4. Follow the specific rules and guidelines. These guidelines are long and you can get them by writing to an address in New York City.
5. Produce documents at each stage. You need all the authentic *proof* you can *gather*.   *evidence that something is true* / *collect/bring together*
6. Please be patient. It can take four to six weeks for the editors of the book to get back to you. Sometimes it can take longer if your claim requires extra research.

LEARNING STRATEGY

Personalizing: Adding your own information to new material makes the new material more meaningful.

ACTIVITY TWO

A. Complete each sentence below. Share your answers with a partner and if possible explain a little bit more about each answer. Then share your answers with the rest of the class.

1. I'm usually awfully _____.
2. I can be rather _____.
3. Sometimes I'm kind of _____.
4. I am especially _____ when _____.
5. I am never terribly _____.

B. Now think about one of your friends. Write a few sentences about this person. Use at least one adjective in each sentence. Also use one of the following modifiers in each sentence you write. (Use a different modifier in each sentence.)

a bit   pretty   sort of   fairly   quite   somewhat

Presentation II

Look at the following chart and fill in the blanks in the sentences that follow. Then answer the questions below.

AUTHENTIC LONGEVITY RECORDS				
Country	**Age**	**Name**	**Born**	**Died**
Japan	120 yr. 237 days	Shigechiyo Izumi	June 29, 1865	Feb. 21, 1986
France	120 yr.	Jeanne Louise Calment*	Feb. 21, 1875	
United States	116 yr. 88 days	Carrie White	Nov. 18, 1874	Feb. 14, 1991
United Kingdom	115 yr. 229 days	Charlotte Hughes	Aug. 1, 1877	Mar. 17, 1993
Canada	113 yr. 124 days	Pierre Joubert	July 15, 1701	Nov. 16, 1814
Australia	112 yr. 330 days	Caroline Maud Mickridge	Dec. 11, 1874	Nov. 6, 1987
Wales	112 yr. 292 days	John Evans	Aug. 19, 1877	June 10, 1990
Spain	112 yr. 228 days	Josefa Salas Mateo	July 14, 1869	Feb. 27, 1973
Norway	112 yr. 61 days	Maren Bolette Torp	Dec. 21, 1876	Feb. 20, 1989
Morocco	112 yr. +	El Hadj Mohammed el Mokri	1844	Sept. 16, 1957

*still living as of July, 1996

Fill in the blanks in the following sentences with information from the table above. (Some sentences may have more than one possible answer.)

1. Carrie White was younger than _____.

2. John Evans was older than _____.

3. _____ had an earlier date of birth than Josefa Salas Mateo.

4. _____ had a later date of birth than Maren Bolette Torp.

5. The oldest person on this list is _____.

6. The youngest person on this list is _____.

7. The earliest birthday on this list is for _____.

8. The person on this list with the longest name is _____.

Answer the following questions:

1. Which name is more difficult for you to pronounce: Carrie White or Shigechiyo Izumi?
2. Which name on this list is the most difficult for you to pronounce?

QUESTIONS

1. Find adjectives in the first four sentences. Write them below.

   _____

   What ending do you find on each one? What does this ending mean? What word do you find after each adjective in these sentences?

   _____

2. Find the adjectives in sentences 5–8. Write them below.

   _____

   What ending do you find on each one? What does this ending mean?

   _____

3. Look at the last two questions. What adjective do you find in both questions? Does this adjective have any endings? Can you explain this?

Explanation

1. Sometimes we want to compare people or things to one another. We can do this with adjectives. There are different ways to do this, depending on the adjective. There are also different ways to compare two things and to compare something to more than two things.

2. **Short Adjectives-Comparatives**

   Add the **-er** ending to a short adjective (one syllable or two syllables ending in -y) to compare two things.

   Carrie White was **younger** than Jeanne Louise Calment.

   Sometimes an adjective ends in a single consonant preceded by a single vowel. In this case, you will double the consonant when you add the **-er** ending.

   Your dog is big.
   Your dog is **bigger** than mine.

   If the adjective ends in **-y**, change the **y** to **i** when you add **er**.

   Shigechiyo Izumi was born **earlier** than Josefa Salas Mateo.

BASE	COMPARATIVE
big	bigger
early	earlier
great	greater
happy	happier
hard	harder
small	smaller

3. **Long Adjectives—Comparatives**

   For longer adjectives (two syllables or more) you do not add an ending to the word. Instead, you add the word **more** or the word **less** before the adjective.

   Which name is **more difficult** for you to pronounce?

   Be careful not to use **more** with an adjective that is already comparative.

   He is **older** than his brother.
   He is more older than his brother. (not correct)

LESSON 28: SETTING RECORDS—DESCRIBING AND COMPARING

BASE	COMPARATIVE
beautiful	more beautiful
difficult	more difficult
horrible	more horrible

4. When you mention both things that you are comparing, you will also use the word **than**. Be careful to spell this word correctly. Do not confuse it with the word "then" (for time).

John Evans was **older than** Maren Bolette Torp.

5. Short Adjectives—Superlatives

When you want to show that something is the top or bottom of a group of things (more than two things), you will use a different ending. In this case, add the **-est** ending for short adjectives. You will also usually use these forms with the definite article **the**.

The youngest person on this list is El Hadj Mohammed el Mokri.

BASE	SUPERLATIVE
big	biggest
early	earliest
great	greatest
happy	happiest
hard	hardest
small	smallest

6. Long Adjectives—Superlatives

For longer adjectives (three syllables or more) you do not add an ending to the word. Instead, you add the word **most** or the word **least** before the adjective.

The most difficult name for me to pronounce is Caroline Maud Mickridge.

BASE	SUPERLATIVE
beautiful	most beautiful
difficult	most difficult
horrible	most horrible

7. Two common adjectives have irregular comparative and superlative forms as follows:

BASE	COMPARATIVE
good	better
bad	worse

BASE	SUPERLATIVE
good	best
bad	worst

Practice

LESSON 28: SETTING RECORDS—DESCRIBING AND COMPARING

ACTIVITY THREE

A. Look at the following facts about movies and answer the questions in complete sentences.

- Average price of a movie ticket in 1933: 23 cents. In 1991: $4.89
- Cost of making "Snow White and the Seven Dwarfs" in 1937: $1.5 million. Cost of making "Aladdin" in 1992: $35 million.
- Average weekly movie attendance in 1933: 60 million. In 1991: 18.9 million.

1. Which movie was less expensive to make, "Snow White and the Seven Dwarfs" or "Aladdin"?
2. In what year was the average weekly attendance at movies higher, 1933 or 1992?
3. According to this information, when was the average price of a movie ticket lower, in 1933 or 1991?

B. The following facts from the Guinness Book of Records are missing a superlative. Can you guess the correct information for each one? Fill in a superlative from the list for each blank. (Use each one only one time.) The correct answers are at the end of this lesson.

| rarest | largest | most complex |
| most widespread | oldest | most common |

1. The _____ language in the world is Chinese.
2. The _____ language in the world is English.
3. Inuit is one of the _____ languages in the world. It has 63 forms of the present tense.
4. One of the _____ sounds in the world is the click from the southern Bushman language !xo.
5. The _____ letter is "O" because it hasn't changed its shape since the Phoenician alphabet.
6. The language with the _____ number of irregular verbs is English (283 verbs).

ACTIVITY FOUR

On page 188 you will find some charts about different natural features of the earth. Use these charts for this activity. Follow the directions for each part.

A. Look at the chart about rivers of the world and the sentences about the information on this chart. Fill in each blank in the sentences with the correct comparative or superlative form of the adjective in parentheses. Be sure to add any other words necessary to make a correct comparative or superlative.

RIVERS OF THE WORLD	
Name	Length in miles
Nile, Africa	4,132
Amazon, South America	3,915
Mississippi-Missouri, North America	3,741
Yangtze, China	3,424
Ob-Irtysh, Siberia	3,416
Yenisey-Angara, Siberia	3,100

1. The Yangtze River is (long) _____ the Ob-Irtysh River.
2. The Mississippi-Missouri is (short) _____ the Amazon.
3. The (lengthy) _____ river in the world is the Nile in Africa.
4. The Yenisey-Angara is (short) _____ river on this chart.

B. Look at the following adjectives and charts. Using these words, make some comparisons of the facts on the charts. Be sure to make your comparisons using the *-er* ending or *more* or *less*. Make at least two comparisons for each chart. Use a different adjective for each comparison you make.

ADJECTIVES: high/tall   big/large   deep   small   shallow   short

OCEANS AND SEAS OF THE WORLD		
Name	Area in Square Miles	Greatest Depth in Feet
Pacific Ocean	64,186,000	36,198
Atlantic Ocean	31,862,000	28,374
Indian Ocean	28,350,000	25,344
Arctic Ocean	3,662,000	17,880

PRINCIPAL MOUNTAINS OF THE WORLD	
Name	Height in Feet
Everest, Nepal-China	29,028
Godwin Austen (K2), India	28,250
Kanchenjunga, Nepal-India	28,208
Dhaulagiri, Nepal	26,810
Nanga Parbat, India	26,660

EXAMPLE   The Indian Ocean is deeper than the Arctic Ocean.

C. Use the same adjectives from A above to write sentences with superlatives. Be sure to use the definite article (*the*) and the *-est* ending or *most* or *least*. Write at least two sentences for each chart. Use a different adjective for each sentence you write.

LEARNING STRATEGY

Managing Your Learning: Working with others increases your chances for acquiring new information.

ACTIVITY FIVE

Do this activity in groups of three or four people.

A. Look back at the statements in the Preview part of this lesson. Share your answers with the others in your group. Has anybody in the group done these things?

Tell the others in your group what you have done related to these questions. For example, you might say: I drove 100 mph in my friend's car. OR I've never driven over 90 mph. I drove 85 mph one time.

Then do the following:

- Write two to three sentences comparing some of the things people in your group have done. Use comparative forms in your sentences.
- Write two to three sentences using superlatives about the things the people in your group have done. (Who has done the most or the least of something?)

Compare your answers with other groups in the class. Who has done the most (or the least) of any of these things?

B. You are going to try to find out more about the people in your class. To do this, you will write some ideas similar to the ones in the Preview. Try to think of some unusual things that people do. Write your ideas down and then give your paper to another group in the class.

C. Read the sentences from the other group. Try to find people in your group who have done these things. Discuss what people have (or have not) done in relation to these sentences. Make some comparisons. Write some sentences using comparisons. Write some sentences using superlatives about people's answers to this activity.

Look back at your sentences for Activity 5. Check your work for the following:

❏ You have adjectives in your comparisons.

❏ You have added the *-er* ending or the words *more* or *less* where appropriate.

❏ You have used some superlatives.

❏ You used the *-est* ending or the words *most* or *least* where appropriate.

Answers to B in Activity Three

1. most common
2. most widespread
3. most complex
4. rarest
5. oldest
6. largest

Prepositions

CHAPTER 7

LESSON 29: SCHEDULES—EXPRESSING TIME RELATIONSHIPS

Focus: prepositions of location—time

Preview

Do you work and go to school? Do you have a family to take care of? Do you usually have a very busy schedule?

Think about your daily activities and make a list of things you do in a typical day.

Presentation

Below you will find a schedule of a one-day business seminar. Look at the schedule and read the short paragraph that follows. Then answer the questions.

SEMINAR ON QUALITY ASSURANCE
TOTAL QUALITY MANAGEMENT
July 17, 1996

9:00– 9:30	Coffee and Participant Arrival
9:30– 9:45	Welcome and Introductions
9:45–10:15	Introductory talk—Guest Speaker "Quality Improvement Teams"
10:15–11:00	Focus Groups
11:00–11:15	Break
11:15–12:00	Discussion (all groups)
12:00– 1:30	Lunch
1:30– 2:30	Panel Presentation: "Cross Functional Work Groups"
2:30– 3:00	Question and Answer (all participants)
3:00– 3:15	Break
3:15– 4:00	Focus Groups
4:00– 4:30	Final Discussion and Review
4:30	Reception

Jack is participating in the seminar outlined above. He is describing the day's schedule to his boss. Read his description below.

The seminar is **on** Wednesday, July 17 and will take the whole day. We arrive **between** 9:00 and 9:30 A.M. and **at** 9:30 the seminar officially begins. The guest speaker will talk about "quality improvement teams" **from** 9:45 **to** 10:15. Then there will be a small-group discussion, followed by more discussion with the whole group. **In** the afternoon there will be a panel of four presenters discussing their companies' experiences with work teams. **Before** the final review, we will have small-group discussions again. **After** the final wrap-up, there will be a reception. I'm really looking forward to this seminar. I'm sure I can learn some new things and do some networking **during** the breaks and reception.

QUESTIONS

1. Read the following sentences (or parts of sentences) from Jack's description.
   - Find the subject and verb in each one.
   - Find the object (if any) in each one as well.
   - Look at the underlined phrases in each one. Are these phrases subjects or objects?
   a. The seminar is on Wednesday, July 17.
   b. We arrive between 9:00 and 9:30 A.M.
   c. Before the final review, we will have small-group discussions again.
2. Find all of the words in bold (dark) letters in the story above. Write them here.

   _____

   _____

   Do you know the meaning of any of these words? Discuss the meanings with others in your class.

Explanation

1. There are many **prepositions** in English, such as **in, at, on, to, from,** etc. These words connect nouns and pronouns to other parts of a sentence.

   Prepositions and the words that follow them are called **prepositional phrases.**

   The seminar is <u>on</u> Wednesday, July 17.
               preposition

   The seminar is <u>on Wednesday, July 17.</u>
              prepositional phrase

2. Prepositions also give information about the nouns and pronouns in a sentence. They can tell the relationship between a noun or pronoun and the rest of the sentence. Subjects and objects usually do not need prepositions.

   <u>The seminar</u> is <u>on Wednesday, July 17.</u>
     subject   prepositional phrase
                 (time relationship)

   <u>Before the final review</u> <u>we</u> will have <u>small-group discussions</u> again.
   prepositional phrase subject   object
     (time relationship)

   Prepositions can give many different kinds of information about nouns and pronouns in a sentence. In this lesson you will learn about prepositions of location in time.

3. Sometimes prepositional phrases can move around in a sentence because they don't always have a special place.

   <u>Before the final review</u> we will have small-group discussions again.
   We will have small-group discussions again <u>before the final review.</u>
   The guest speaker will talk about "quality improvement teams" <u>from 9:45 to 10:15.</u>
   <u>From 9:45 to 10:15</u> the guest speaker will talk about "quality improvement teams."

4. Two common prepositions of time are **from** and **to.**

   From tells you the **beginning** time.
   To tells you the **end** time.

   The guest speaker will talk about "quality improvement teams" **from** 9:45
                                                                             beginning
     to 10:15.
     end

5. **In, on,** and **at** are three other common prepositions of time. Often **at** is the most specific and **in** is the most general of these.

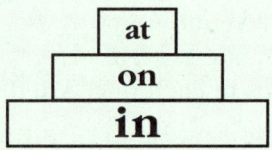

At 9:30 the seminar officially begins. (exact/specific time)
The seminar is **on** Wednesday. (day of the week)
The seminar is **on** July 17, 1996. (date)
In the afternoon there will be a panel discussion. (time of day)
He will go to the seminar **in** the summer. (time of year)
The seminar will take place **in** 1996. (year)

6. In Lessons 12 and 13 you learned about using **for** and **since** when talking about things that happened from the past to the present.

    (It's 10 o'clock on the day of the seminar.)
    Jack has been at the seminar <u>**for** one hour</u>.
                              prepositional phrase
                            time relationship—duration
    He has been listening to the speaker <u>**since** 9:45</u>.
                                   prepositional phrase
                                   time relationship—starting time

    Sometimes you will also find the preposition **for** meaning duration with other time frames.

    Jack was at the conference <u>**for eight hours today**</u>.
                             prepositional phrase
                          time relationship-duration

7. **Before, after, during,** and **between** are other prepositions of time.

    before = earlier than
    after = later than
    during = throughout that time/in the time of
    between = within two limits of time

    Before the final review, we will have small-group discussions again.
    After the final wrap-up, there will be a reception.
    I can do some networking **during** the breaks and reception.
    We arrive **between** 9:00 and 9:30 A.M.

Practice

ACTIVITY ONE

The following activity is about Jack's seminar. Fill in the blanks with the preposition that fits each one. Use each preposition at least one time. Some blanks may have more than one possible answer.

When you finish the activity, compare answers with a partner. If you had some different answers, discuss them.

    from   to   at   in   on   before   after   during   between

_____ July 17, 1996 Jack is attending a professional seminar. The seminar begins _____ the morning and he can arrive any time _____

9:00 and 9:30 A.M. He should be there _____ 9:30 because that's when the welcome and introductions begin. _____ 9:45 _____ 11:00 he will hear the guest speaker and participate in focus groups. _____ the afternoon there will be a panel presentation and more discussion time. _____ this seminar there will be some short breaks and a longer lunch break. _____ 4:00 _____ 4:30 there will be a final discussion and review for the day. _____ 4:30 _____ this last session there will be a reception. Jack hopes he can meet other people and talk to them _____ the breaks and reception time.

ACTIVITY TWO

You will hear two short conversations that take place at a dentist's office. In each conversation the receptionist and a patient are trying to make the patient's next appointment.

Below you will find a blank weekly schedule from an appointment book. Listen to each conversation and fill in the following information:

- Fill in all times that the patient is busy. Write the activity in the space for the correct time. For example, if the patient has a meeting at 10 A.M. on Monday, write the word "meeting" in that space.
- Write the word "free" for any time the patient says she or he is available.
- Fill in the correct space for the appointment the patient makes with the receptionist.

CONVERSATION I

	Monday	Tuesday	Wednesday	Thursday	Friday
8:00					
9:00					
10:00					
11:00					
12:00					
1:00					
2:00					
3:00					
4:00					
5:00					
6:00					

CONVERSATION II

	Monday	Tuesday	Wednesday	Thursday	Friday
8:00					
9:00					
10:00					
11:00					
12:00					
1:00					
2:00					
3:00					
4:00					
5:00					
6:00					

Compare answers with a partner. Ask your teacher to repeat the information if necessary.

LEARNING STRATEGY

Overcoming Limitations: Using simple sentences may help when you are having difficulty expressing yourself.

ACTIVITY THREE

Do this activity in groups of three. Your boss, Denise, has been out-of-town for the past three days. She has just called the office to find out about any telephone messages. Below you will find her messages. Read the sample message and the information to tell the boss. Discuss any questions you may have about the information with the others in your group.

Then do the following:

- Each person in the group chooses one of the other messages. Then each person writes the information from the message for Denise in sentences.
- Each person should be sure to use some of the following prepositions in the sentences: *on in at from to between before during after*
- Each person shares his/her written message with the others in the group.

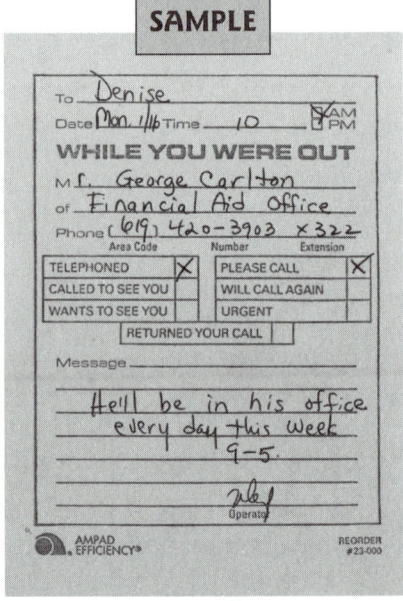

SAMPLE MESSAGE:

You will tell the boss:

Mr. George Carlton from the Financial Aide office called on Monday morning at 10 A.M. Please call him. His phone number is 619 420-3903, extension 322. He will be at his office every day this week from 9 to 5.

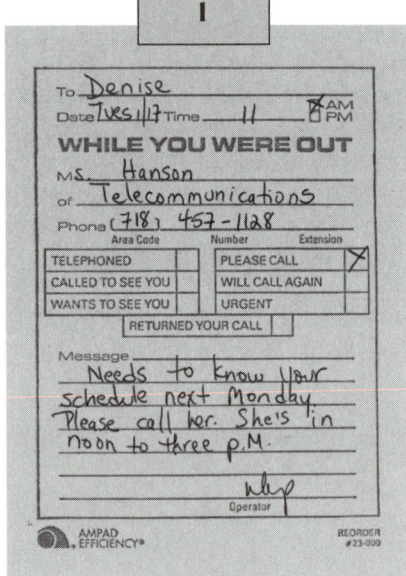

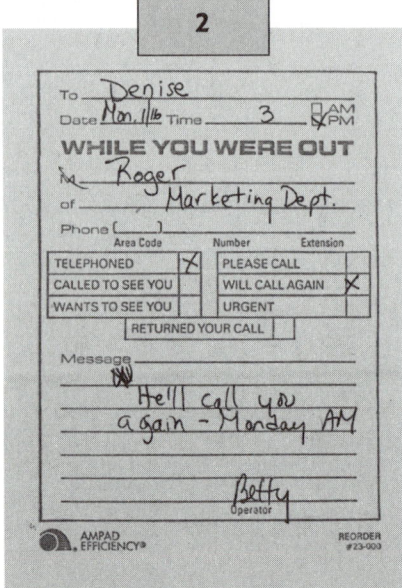

ACTIVITY FOUR

You will do this activity with a partner. You and your partner want to see a movie and you are trying to find a time that you are both available this weekend. You would like to find a time when there is a bargain price as well. Below you will find two things:

- a schedule for movies playing on Saturday and Sunday
- a personal weekend schedule for each partner

One of you will be Partner A and the other will be Partner B. Each partner should read only his or her own weekend schedule below. DO NOT LOOK AT OR READ YOUR PARTNER'S SCHEDULE. Look at the movie schedule and your own weekend schedule. Then together with your partner try to find a time that you can see a movie together. If possible, try to find a bargain price movie.

In your conversation, use as many of the prepositions from this lesson as possible (*from to at in on before after during between*).

PERSONAL WEEKEND SCHEDULE—PARTNER A

MOVIE SCHEDULE
Main Street Theatres   Bargain shows in ( )

Toy Story (G)   (11:20   1:20)   3:20   5:20   7:20   9:20
Mission Impossible (PG-13)   (11:00   1:15)   3:30   5:40   8:00   10:15
Cable Guy (PG-13)   (12:00   2:50)   5:45   8:30
Mr. Holland's Opus (PG)   (11:00   1:45)   4:25   7:10   9:50
Nixon (R) on 2 screens   (11:00   12:00   1:00   2:00)   3:00   4:00   5:00
                                        6:00   7:00   9:00
The American President (PG-13)   (11:30   2:15)   5:00   7:30   10:00
James & the Giant Peach (PG)   (12:00   2:30)   5:15   7:45   10:10

LESSON 29: SCHEDULES—
EXPRESSING TIME
RELATIONSHIPS

IT WORKS!
Learning Strategy:
Role-playing
Situations in Class

PERSONAL WEEKEND SCHEDULE—PARTNER B

ACTIVITY FIVE

Think again about the questions in the Preview section at the beginning of this lesson. Write a description of what you usually do on weekdays when you work and/or go to school. Then write a paragraph or two describing one day of a recent weekend or another day when you did not work or go to school. When you write these descriptions, be specific and use as many prepositions of time as you can.

Look back at your writing for Activity 5. Check your work for the following:

❑ You described a schedule for a typical day.
❑ You also described a weekend day or other "free" day.
❑ You used some of the following prepositions of time from this lesson in your descriptions: *from to at in on before after during between*.
❑ You checked that the meaning is correct for each preposition in your sentences.
❑ You did not use any prepositions with subjects and objects in your sentences.

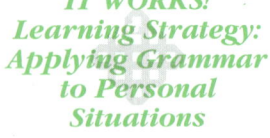

IT WORKS!
Learning Strategy:
Applying Grammar
to Personal
Situations

LESSON 30: GOING PLACES—EXPRESSING SPATIAL RELATIONSHIPS

Focus: prepositions of location—place

Preview

Answer the following questions. Then share your answers with the rest of the class.

1. What kind of transportation do most people use in your country for the following:
   • to go to work or school
   • for vacations

2. Are there any large bodies of water or rivers in your native country? How do people travel across them? Do they use boats or bridges most often? Are there any large or famous bridges in your native country?
3. Have you ever taken any kind of unusual type of transportation? If so, tell the class about it.

Presentation I

Read the following story and then answer the questions that follow.

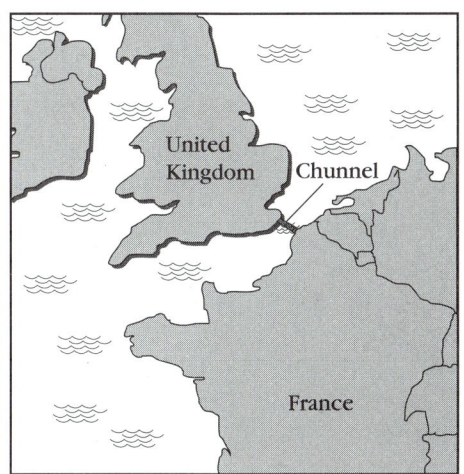

Eight thousand years ago (during the last ice age) you could walk **from** England **to** France **on** dry land. As *glaciers melted*, sea levels *rose* and created the English Channel. Travel **between** the two land areas was no longer easy.

When Frank Davidson was 12, he read about a wild idea. Someone wanted to build a *tunnel* **under** the English Channel and then people could travel back and forth without using a boat. People had suggested this idea before, and digging had even begun a couple of times. However, it was a big job, and nobody made much progress.

Frank Davidson grew up and became a lawyer, but he never forgot the wild idea. When it came up again in the 1950s, he helped write an agreement **between** France and England to plan a tunnel. The project started, but stopped when British officials changed their minds. Frank Davidson became a professor **at** the Massachusetts Institute of Technology **in** the United States and waited for the idea to become a reality. Years later, the two countries reached another agreement and work began again.

The Chunnel is now complete. It is 32.2 miles long, the longest underwater tunnel **in** the world. Tunnelers dug **through** solid rock, and *removed* 10 million *tons*. They developed special digging machines, called moles. Each mole weighed 1,500 tons and was 300 yards long.

river of ice
soften/change from ice to water
reached a higher level/went up

passage cut under or through something

take away/take off
a measure of weight (2,000 lbs—USA)

QUESTIONS

1. Read the following sentences (or parts of sentences) from the story. Find the subject and verb in each one. Find the object (if any) in each one as well.
   a. Eight thousand years ago (during the last ice age) you could walk from England to France on dry land.
   b. Tunnelers dug through solid rock, . . .
   c. They developed special digging machines.
2. Find all of the words in bold (dark) letters in the story above. Write them here.

_____

_____

Do you know the meaning of any of these words?

Explanation

1. As discussed in Lesson 29, prepositions give information about the nouns and pronouns in a sentence. In this lesson you will learn about prepositions of place.

2. Two common prepositions of place are **from** and **to.**

   From tells you the **beginning** place.
   To tells you the **end** place.
   Eight thousand years ago (during the last ice age) you could walk **from** England **to** France on dry land.

3. **In, on,** and **at** are three other common prepositions of place. Often **at** is the most specific and **in** is the most general.

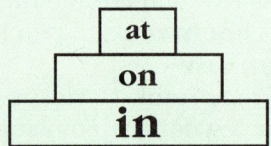

   She lives **at 356 Oak Street.** (specific address)
   She lives **on Mulberry Street.** (street name)
   She lives **in Washington D.C.** (city)
   She lives **in the United States.** (country)
   She lives **in North America.** (larger area)

4. **In** and **on** can also be used for the following meanings:
   a. **in** = inside
      on = on top of/the surface

   The tunnel is complete now, so you can travel **in** it.
   Eight thousand years ago you could walk from England to France **on** dry land.

   b. Sometimes you will use these prepositions with specific kinds of transportation as follows:
      in   car/taxi
      on   airplane/train/bus/motorcycle/bicycle

   He is riding **in** his father's new car to the baseball game.
   The passengers are all **on** the plane now.

5. **Under, between** and **through** are other prepositions of place.

   under = lower than (a position lower than)
   between = within two places
   through = from one end to another/in one side and out another

   Someone wanted to build a tunnel **under** the English Channel.
   He helped write an agreement **between** France and England to plan a tunnel.
   Tunnelers dug **through** solid rock, and removed 10 million tons.

Practice

ACTIVITY ONE

A. A woman is on a business trip and she has just arrived at the airport in Cairo, Egypt. She is at customs now and the customs officer is looking at her papers. Below is some of the information she has written. Read the information on her papers below.

Name: *Susan A. Peters*
Place of Birth: *Toronto, Canada*
Present Nationality: *Canadian*
Originating Airport: *Chicago, O'Hare airport*
Final Destination: *Cairo, Egypt—Cairo Airport*
Permanent Address: *7355 Mt. Vernon St.*
Detroit, Michigan USA
Local Address: *El-Gezira Sheraton Hotel*

IT WORKS!
Learning Strategy:
Focusing on a Few Forms

Now complete the activity by filling in the blanks after each preposition using the places listed below. More than one answer may be possible in some blanks. Try to use as many different pieces of information as possible.

Cairo	Toronto	Mt. Vernon St.	the United States
Egypt	O'Hare Airport	Detroit	Michigan
El-Gezira Sheraton	Cairo airport		

Ms. Susan Peters is a businesswoman from _____. She was born in _____ but now she lives in _____ on _____. She has just flown from _____ to _____. She will stay there for three days at _____. It is her favorite hotel in _____. After she finishes her business in _____, she will go home to _____.

B. Do this part with a partner.

- Tell your partner about where you live now by completing the following sentences.

    I live in _____. My apartment/house/dormitory is on _____. I live at _____.

- Now tell your partner where you lived in the past by completing the same sentences.

    I lived in _____. My apartment/house/dormitory was on _____. I lived at _____.

- Together with your partner describe the location of your school using the same sentences.

201

LESSON 30: GOING PLACES—EXPRESSING SPATIAL RELATIONSHIPS

ACTIVITY TWO

Look at the following photographs. Under each photograph you will see some numbers. Next to each number you will find two or more words: something from the picture and a preposition. Using these words, write a sentence about what you see in the picture or a conclusion you can make about what is happening.

EXAMPLE man at   *The man is at the counter.*

1. computer under
2. the man to from
3. papers on
4. counter between
5. two people at

1. these people on
2. carry-on luggage in
3. the plane to from
4. carry-on luggage under
5. airplane at
6. airplane in

Presentation II

LESSON 30: GOING PLACES—EXPRESSING SPATIAL RELATIONSHIPS

The Chunnel is actually three tunnels. Two have train tracks **in** them and carry high-speed trains to take people, cars, and *freight* **across** the English Channel. The third tunnel is a service *corridor* with a road **in** it. Trucks use it to carry supplies and workers **up** and **down** the tunnel area to keep the Chunnel in good shape.

goods/cargo
passageway/hallway

Most passengers will go **on** the train **in** their cars and stay **in** them for the 35-minute ride. Others will board train cars that have *bunks* and dining rooms. **At** the far end of the tunnel, people will drive **off** the train and go on their way **to** their final destinations.

small sleeping area/narrow bed

The Chunnel has no *escape routes* **to** the surface **between** one end and the other. What would happen in case of an emergency such as fire or flood **in** the Chunnel? The engineers say there is no need to worry and here's why:

way to get out

- The Chunnel goes **through** strong rock called "chalk marl." The tunnels are also lined with strong materials (such as steel-reinforced concrete or cast iron). A roof *collapse* is extremely unlikely.
- If a fire starts **on** a train, automatic doors will close to *contain* the *blaze*. Automatic extinguishers will put out the fire with foam.
- Having three separate tunnels is another safety feature. Every quarter mile, you will find a cross tunnel that connects all three. In an emergency, *conductors* could stop trains and lead the passengers **to** a different tunnel. **From** there, passengers could return **to** the surface **above** the Chunnel.

fall down/fall apart
hold back/keep in a small area
fire
people who work on the train/operators

QUESTIONS

1. Find all of the words from the beginning of this lesson in bold (dark) letters in the reading above. Write them here.
   _____
   _____

2. Find all the other words in bold in this reading. Do you know the meaning of any of these words?
   _____
   _____

Explanation

In Presentation I, you learned several prepositions of place and direction. In Presentation II, there are a few others as follows:

up = farther along/in a higher direction
down = farther along/in a lower direction
across = from one side to another/on the other side
off = in a direction away from/separated from
over = higher than (in a position higher than)
above = directly higher than something
below = directly lower than something
next to = closest to/beside
around = surrounding/encircling

EXAMPLES

Trucks use it to carry supplies and workers **up** and **down** the tunnel area to keep the Chunnel in good shape.
High-speed trains take people, cars, and freight **across** the English Channel.
The Chunnel goes **below** the Channel.
People will drive **off** the train and go on their way to their final destinations.
From there, passengers could return to the surface **above** the Chunnel.
An airplane can travel **over** the English Channel.
The service corridor tunnel is **next to** the other tunnel.
A boat can take you **around** the English Channel.

LEARNING STRATEGY

Remembering New Material: Playing with new words and associating them with visuals helps you remember them more easily.

ACTIVITY THREE

Look at the following map of the trolley system in a city in the United States. After the map you will see several sentences about this trolley system. Each sentence has a mistake of some kind. In some sentences you will find an incorrect preposition and in other sentences you will find some incorrect information after the preposition. Read each sentence, find the problem and correct it. (In some cases there may be more than one possible answer.)

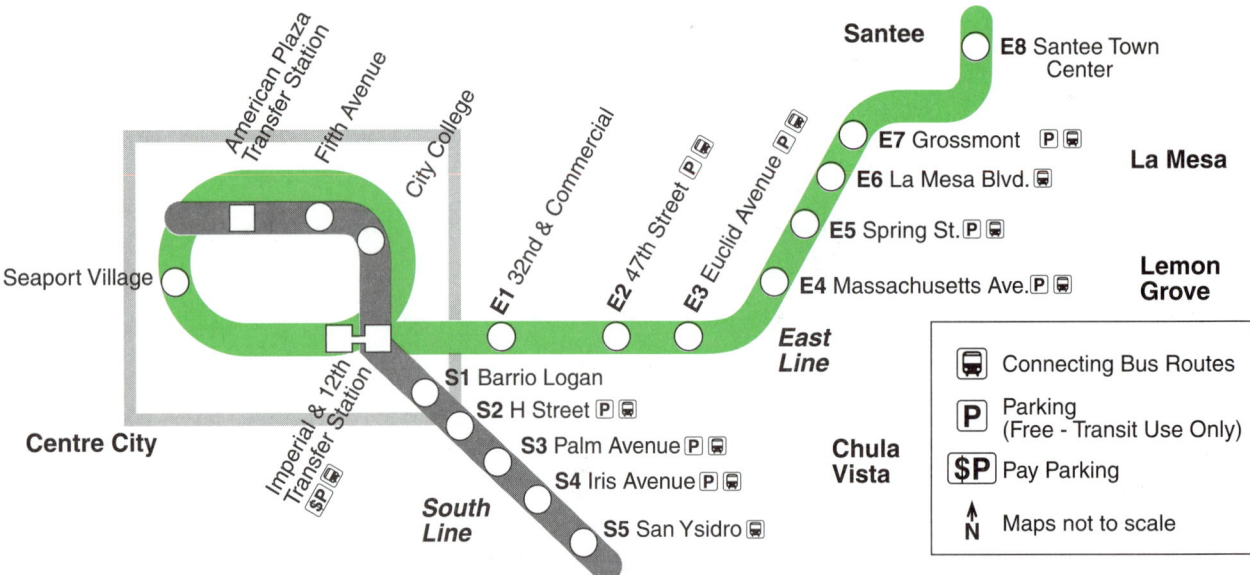

EXAMPLE I am a passenger at the Santee Town Center station (East Line) and I am going to Centre City. My trolley will stop at the Spring Street station <u>before</u> the La Mesa Blvd. station.   **not correct**

My trolley will stop at the Spring Street station <u>after</u> the La Mesa Blvd. station.

1. A passenger is shopping in Centre City and lives in Lemon Grove. He can take the trolley from Massachusetts Avenue to Seaport Village to get home.

2. The Euclid Avenue Station on the East line is between the 47th Street station and the 32nd & Commercial Street station.

3. On the map of the South Line, Palm Avenue is below Iris Avenue.
4. The City College station is in La Mesa.
5. You can find a transfer station at the Grossmont stop.
6. You are at H Street on the South Line map. You must look up on this map to find the San Ysidro stop.
7. The Fifth Avenue stop is next to the Barrio Logan stop on this map.
8. On this map the East Line goes around the South Line in the Chula Vista area.

ACTIVITY FOUR

A. Look at the following cartoon. It shows how a little boy and his grandmother walk through a park in different ways.

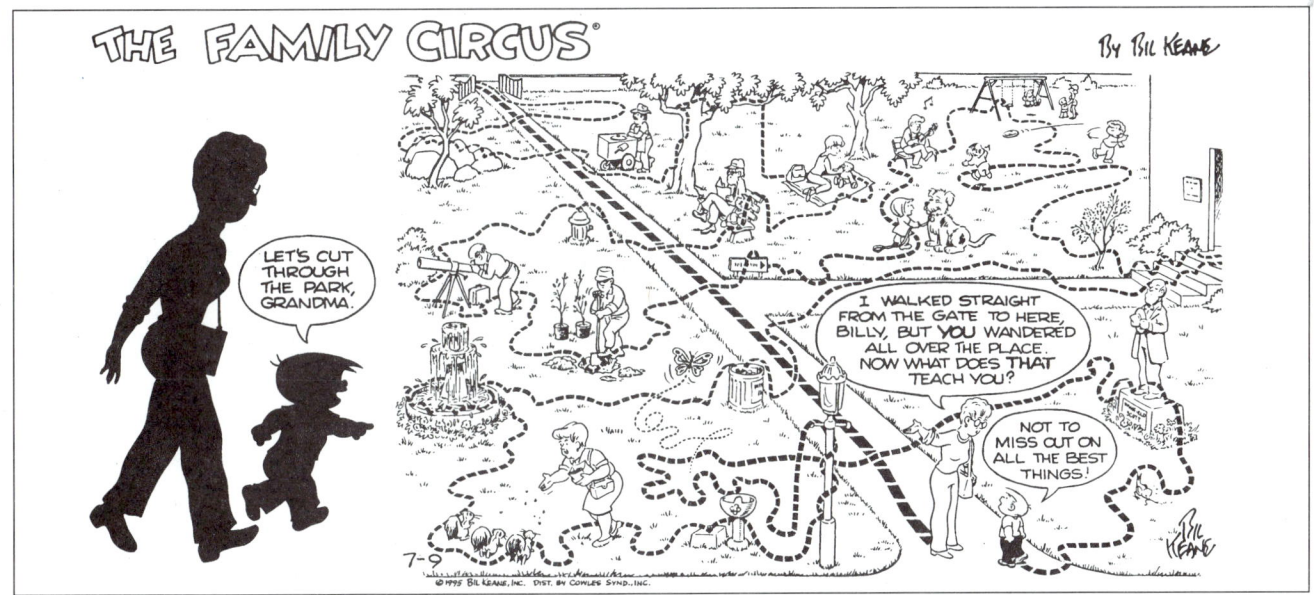

Reprinted with special permission of King Features Syndicate

Below you will find some sentences about the little boy's path from the beginning to the end. Fill in the blank in each sentence with a preposition that fits the cartoon. Choose your preposition for each sentence from the list below. Try to use as many prepositions as possible. You will not use all of these prepositions and some sentences may have more than one possible answer.

to   from   in   on   at   under   over   between   through
next to   below   above   up   down   across   around   on   off

1. The little boy goes _____ the gate _____ the entrance _____ the rocks.
2. He walks _____ the rocks and then _____ the path _____ a tree _____ the ice cream vendor.
3. He climbs _____ the tree and goes _____ the branches.
4. After he goes _____ the lady _____ the blanket, he crosses the path again.
5. He walks _____ the legs of the tripod of the telescope and later goes back _____ the path.

6. He steps _____ the sign and walks _____ the little girl and the dog.

7. Later he walks _____ the stairs, goes _____ the building, and then comes _____ the stairs.

8. He also walks _____ two of the squirrels and then goes _____ the woman.

9. He steps _____ the statue, walks _____ the statue's feet, and then goes _____ the statue and walks _____ the grass again.

10. He meets his grandmother _____ the path.

B. Share your answers to A with a partner. Then write numbers next to some of the things in this picture. Show these numbers to your partner and she or he will tell you a sentence about what the boy is doing for each number. Your partner must use a preposition in each sentence.

LEARNING STRATEGY

Understanding and Using Emotions: Realizing how much you have to learn can be frightening. Relax; you already know a lot about language.

ACTIVITY FIVE

A. Do this activity in groups of three or four people. Look at the map of the United States below. Choose one state on this map. Describe this state by giving information about its location. Write your description on a piece of paper.

Tell your description to the others in your group. Do not say the name of the state. They will guess which state you are talking about. Try to use as many of the prepositions from this lesson as possible.

B. Now choose a state together with your group and prepare a new description. Write this description down and then tell it to the class. The others in the class will guess the state you are describing.

EXAMPLE This state is in the southern part of the United States. On the map, this state is next to three other states. It is between Texas and Mississippi. If you go up on the map from this state, you will see Arkansas. If you go down, on the map, you will see water (the Gulf of Mexico). The Mississippi River goes across this state.

(ANSWER: LOUISIANA)

LESSON 30: GOING PLACES—EXPRESSING SPATIAL RELATIONSHIPS

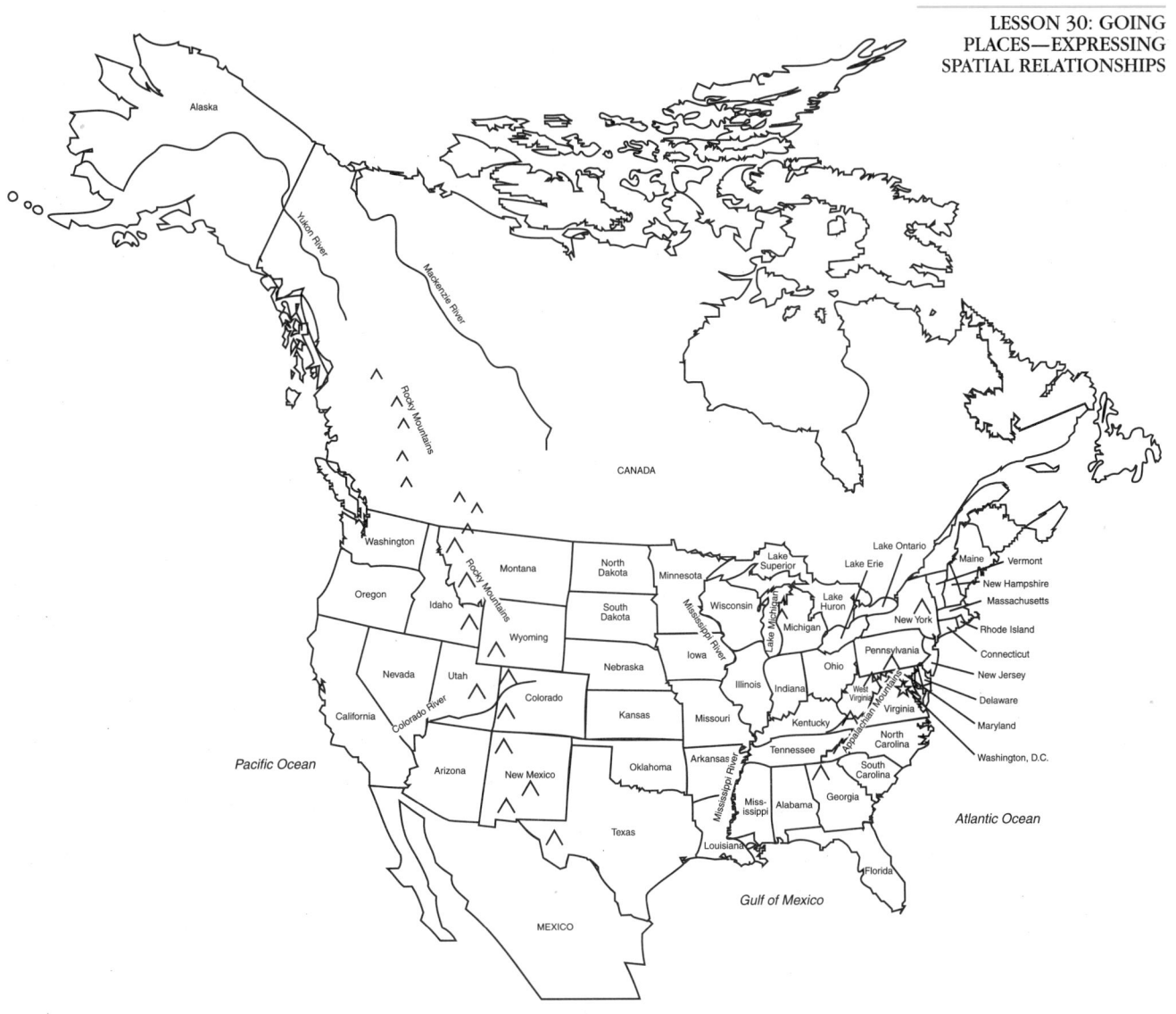

Look back at your descriptions for Activity 5. Check your work for the following:

❏ You have described two states on this map, using different prepositions.

❏ You used some of the following prepositions:

on at in under over above below beside around behind near across between to from through up down beneath

❏ You checked that the meanings are correct for each preposition in your sentences.

❏ You used these prepositions with nouns and pronouns, but not subjects and objects.

LESSON 31: WEDDINGS—OTHER NOUN/VERB RELATIONSHIPS

Focus: prepositions—for/with/by/of

Preview

LEARNING STRATEGY

Managing your Learning: Sharing information with others gives you more opportunity for learning.

Think about the following questions about weddings in your native country. Then share your answers with the class.

- What kind of ceremony do people usually have when they get married (for example, religious or civil)?
- Do most people have small or large weddings? Who plans and pays for the wedding?
- Do most people have a party after the ceremony? What kind of party is typical? Who pays for the party?
- Are there typical presents for the bride and groom? What are they?
- Is there a typical kind of honeymoon after the wedding?
- Does the bride or groom change her/his name after the wedding?

LESSON 31: WEDDINGS—
OTHER NOUN/VERB
RELATIONSHIPS

Presentation

Martha Parker and Kevin Webster were married on Sept. 15, 1996. Read the announcement that appeared in a local newspaper. Then answer the questions.

Parker-Webster

Martha Parker and Kevin Webster were married Sept. 15, 1996 at the home **of** the bride's parents in Lake Peekskill, New York. The bride is the daughter **of** Mr. and Mrs. Louis Parker and graduated from Cornell University, majoring in Graphic Communication. She is a *free-lance* illustrator and runs her own company, New Age Designs.

The bridegroom, son of Mr. and Mrs. Robert Webster, earned a B.A. in Mathematics from State University of New York at Albany and is now an Engineer **for** a large science applications company in New York City.

The bride wore a *gown* **of** ivory satin **with** a cathedral length *train*. She made her *veil* and head piece **by** hand **with** her own original designs. The bride also wore a pearl necklace and earrings that the bridegroom bought **for** her as an engagement gift. There were several attendants including the bride's sister, Jennifer Smith, as maid-of-honor, and the bridegroom's brother, Steven Webster, as best man. The bride's niece, Nicole Parker, participated in the ceremony as flower girl **with** her cousin, Stuart Sofia, as the *ring bearer.*

The couple went **by** limousine from the wedding to the airport **for** their honeymoon in Acapulco, Mexico. They will make their home in White Plains, New York.

*working independently/
self-employed*

*a long, formal evening
dress for women*

*an extension of a woman's
dress (often drags on the
ground)*

*piece of light material
worn over the face*

*person who holds the ring
at a wedding ceremony*

QUESTIONS

1. Find all of the prepositions in bold in this announcement. Write these words and the entire prepositional phrase for each one below:

   _____
   _____
   _____

2. Do you know the meanings of any of the prepositions in bold?

Explanation

1. Four other common prepositions in English are:

   for   with   of   by

2. Two common meanings for the preposition **for** are:

   for = help or benefit for someone else
   The bridegroom bought a pearl necklace and earrings **for** her.

   for = purpose
   They went from the wedding to the airport **for** their honeymoon.

3. Two common meanings for the preposition **with** are:

   with = people do something together
   The bride's niece, Nicole Parker, participated in the ceremony as flower
       girl **with** her cousin, Stuart Sofia, as the ring bearer.

   with = using an instrument or tool to help someone do something
   She made her veil and head piece **with** her own original designs.

4. The preposition **by** often tells you the method or how something is done. You will often see **by** with types of transportation.

She made her veil **by** hand.
The couple went **by** limousine to the airport.

5. The preposition **of** can have different meanings.
Sometimes **of** can show possession as follows:

. . . at the home **of** the bride's parents in Lake Peekskill, New York.
(This means the bride's parents' home.)

The bride is the daughter **of** Mr. and Mrs. Louis Parker.
(This means she is Mr. and Mrs. Louis Parker's daughter.)

Sometimes **of** can show a material or substance.
The bride wore a gown **of** ivory satin.

Practice

ACTIVITY ONE

Read the partial statements or questions in the column on the left. Then find the prepositional phrase on the right that finishes each one. Choose the letter of the correct answer and write it in the space next to each number on the left. In some cases, more than one answer may be possible. Use each letter only one time.

IT WORKS!
Learning Strategy:
Checking Meanings
with Native Speakers

_____ 1. Did you go to the engagement party
_____ 2. Yes, I went
_____ 3. I've been a friend
_____ 4. Nobody wanted to drive, so we went
_____ 5. What kind of present did you buy
_____ 6. I bought a beautiful crystal vase
_____ 7. It was a nice party, but we left early. It was mostly friends and relatives

a. with Susan's brother and his friend.
b. by taxi. It was expensive!
c. of their parents.
d. of the family for many years.
e. with Jean and Sharon.
f. for Susan and Ed last Friday night?
g. for them?

Compare answers with a partner. Discuss any different answers you may have.

ACTIVITY TWO

You will hear a story about a wedding two times. Listen and do the following:

- The first time you hear the story: write down the prepositional phrases that begin with: *for with of by.*

If necessary, ask your teacher to repeat the story so you can find as many of these prepositional phrases as possible.

- The second time you hear the story: choose the meaning you think fits for each prepositional phrase you wrote.

Choose from the following meanings:

for 1. purpose   2. help/benefit
with 1. together   2. tool/instrument
by   1. how   2. transportation
of   1. possessive 2. material

Compare answers with a partner. Make any changes you think might be necessary.

LESSON 31: WEDDINGS— OTHER NOUN/VERB RELATIONSHIPS

ACTIVITY THREE

Do this activity in groups of three. Judy and Greg are getting married in Washington D.C. next weekend. Below you will find several pieces of information about the wedding and specific tasks. Read the directions for Part A and complete that activity. Then read the directions for Part B and complete that activity.

IT WORKS! Learning Strategy: Applying New Material Immediately

A. Many relatives are coming to the wedding. Below is a list of a few people and where they live. Write a sentence about how each one will get there, using a different kind of transportation for each one. (If you are not sure about location of some of these places, look at the map of the United States in the previous lesson.)

EXAMPLE Jon, Greg's nephew, lives in San Diego, California.

Jon will go to the wedding by airplane.

1. Aunt Lydia lives in New York City, New York.
2. Cousin Paul lives in Virginia.
3. Judy's parents live in Washington D.C.
4. Greg's parents live in Miami, Florida.

B. Write sentences about the wedding using the words given next to each number. You should not change the words in parentheses, but you can change their order. You must also add one of the prepositions from this lesson (*with by for of*) to each sentence.

EXAMPLE *Judy's brother came with his wife and three children.*
(his wife and three children/Judy's brother/came)

1. _____
   (they/many/friends/invited/Greg's parents)

2. _____
   (danced/Judy/her new father-in-law)

3. _____
   (the wedding/rented/several men/tuxedos)

4. _____
   (cut/they/the cake/a special wedding knife)

5. _____
   (to the party/went/they/horse-drawn carriage)

6. _____
   (Greg and Judy/presents/bought/each other)

ACTIVITY FOUR

Do this activity in groups of three or four. Read the situation and then do the problem solving.

Often when people plan a large event such as a wedding, there are some last-minute problems and details they must take care of. Below you will find some problems and details Greg and Judy had before and during their wedding.

Your group wants to help them take care of these things. Read each problem or detail below and think of a solution or some help that you might be able to give. If you can think of more than one solution, write them both. Be sure to use prepositions from this lesson (*for with by of*) as many times as possible in your answers. Share your answers with the other groups in the class.

PROBLEMS
1. Judy and Greg plan to take a trip by car for their honeymoon. Several days before the wedding the car has a new mechanical problem and they don't have time to take it into the shop.
2. Judy's aunt and uncle are half an hour late for the wedding. All of the other guests have already arrived. They don't really want to begin the wedding without these people, but everyone else has arrived.
3. Greg's little niece is the flower girl, but she is only four years old and very shy. She is scared and too nervous to go through the ceremony by herself.
4. A guest arrives at the wedding with a friend. The guest did not tell anyone she was bringing a friend. Now there are not enough seats at the table for the relative and the friend.

ACTIVITY FIVE

Think about a wedding you have gone to in your country. If you haven't gone to one, think about a typical wedding or another kind of big celebration there. Describe the event in a paragraph or two. You may look back at the questions in the Preview section of this lesson to help you. Be sure to use the prepositions from this lesson (*for with by of*) as much as possible in your description.

Look back at your paragraph for Activity 5. Check your work for the following:

❑ You have written about a wedding or other big celebration in your country.

❑ You used all of the prepositions from this lesson: *for with by of*

❑ You checked that all of the meanings for these prepositions are correct for each sentence.

LESSON 32: SPECIAL DAYS AND GIFTS—REVIEW AND CHANGING WORD ORDER

Focus: preposition review and deleting—for/to (indirect objects)

Preview

Look at the following list of holidays and special days in the United States. Which ones do you know about? Which ones are new to you? Do you celebrate any of these same days in your country?

NOTE For the last two on this list, just answer the last question.

SOME HOLIDAYS AND SPECIAL DAYS IN THE UNITED STATES

New Year's Day
Martin Luther King Day
Valentine's Day
President's Day
St. Patrick's Day
April Fool's Day
Mother's Day
Memorial Day
Father's Day
Independence Day
Labor Day
Halloween
Thanksgiving Day
Christmas Day
your birthday
a wedding anniversary

Presentation

Read the following short paragraphs about some special days and celebrations in the United States. Then answer the questions.

VALENTINE'S DAY

(1) Valentine's Day is on February 14. (2) It is special because on this day people show they care about others. (3) Men and women often buy the special people in their lives presents. (4) Boxes of candy and bouquets of flowers are very popular gifts on this day. (5) Children often give their friends and classmates cards and small candies.

A SPECIAL BIRTHDAY

(1) Last week John Small celebrated his 65th birthday. (2) For this special birthday his children gave him a surprise party. (3) Many of his friends and family came to this party. (4) Some relatives came from out-of-town so they could be there with him. (5) Everyone brought John presents and they all watched as he opened them.

QUESTIONS

1. Find the following prepositions in the two paragraphs above and review their meanings:

   on   for   of   to   from   with

2. Look at sentence #3 in the first paragraph and sentence #2 in the second paragraph.
   - What is the subject of each of these sentences?
   - What is the verb of each of these sentences?
   - What is the object of each of these sentences? (What do men and women buy in sentence #3 and what did John's children give in sentence #2?)

   Can you think of another way to say these two sentences using the preposition **for**? If you can, share your sentences with the class.

3. Look at sentence #5 in the first paragraph and in the second paragraph.
   - What is the subject in each of these sentences?
   - What is the verb in each of these sentences?
   - What is the object in each of these sentences? (What do children give in the first paragraph and what did everyone bring in the second paragraph?)

   Can you think of another way to say these two sentences using the preposition **to**? If you can, share your sentences with the class.

Explanation

1. In Chapter 1, you learned about typical sentence patterns in English. You learned that often you will find the order of words in an English sentence as follows: subject   verb   object

   Men and women buy presents for their children.
       subject   verb   object

   She gave a present to her child.
   subject verb   object

2. In Lessons 29-31, you learned about prepositions and prepositional phrases. You learned how they can show different relationships between nouns or pronouns (not subjects or objects) and the rest of the sentence.

   Men and women buy presents <u>for their children</u>.
                                         prepositional phrase

   She gave a present <u>to her child</u>.
                     prepositional phrase

   You also learned that sometimes prepositional phrases can move in a sentence. (See Lesson 29 Explanation #3.)

   In this lesson you will review some of the prepositions from Lessons 29-31. You will also learn how two prepositional phrases can move in a special way.

3. Sometimes the prepositional phrases beginning with **for** and **to** can move next to the verb. When you move these phrases, you must delete (remove) the preposition. You can only make this change in the following ways:

   for = benefit or help a living thing   **to** = a living thing receives something

   Men and women often buy presents <u>**for** the special people in their lives</u>.
   Men and women often buy <u>the special people in their lives</u> presents.

   Children often give cards and small candies <u>**to** their friends and classmates</u>.
   Children often give <u>their friends and classmates</u> cards and small candies.

   NOTE Traditionally you will hear these words or phrases called "indirect objects."

4. You cannot make this change when these two prepositions have other meanings.

You *cannot* change the following:
Many of his friends came from out-of-town to the party. (correct)
Many of his friends came the party from out-of town. (not correct)
Many people came from out-of-town for his party. (correct)
Many people came his party from out-of-town. (not correct)

5. You will find this change with a small group of common verbs in English.

bring (to/for)	make (for)	show (to)
buy (for)	order (for)	take (to/for)
give (to)	sell (to)	tell (to)

6. Sometimes a sentence will have a pronoun as an object and one of the prepositional phrases from explanation #3 above. In this case, you <u>cannot</u> move the prepositional phrase next to the verb.

She bought **the present** for her brother.
       object
She bought her brother the present.
She bought **it** for her brother. (no change possible)
       object

Practice

LEARNING STRATEGY

Overcoming Limitations: Creating cards to identify difficult prepositions and their meanings and then placing them where you can see them will help you improve your English.

ACTIVITY ONE

A. Look back at the list of holidays and special days from the Preview section of this lesson. Write the following information for each one:
- When do people celebrate this holiday in the United States? First give the month and then the exact date if you know it. If you do not know about this holiday, just go to the next one.

    EXAMPLE   In the United States, Valentine's day is in February. It is on February 14.

- When do you celebrate this holiday in your country if it is a holiday there?

Share your answers with a partner. Try to find the exact dates for each one.

B. Look at the following invitations. The printer made some mistakes with some of the prepositions. Find these mistakes and correct them. (There may be several incorrect prepositions in each invitation.) There may be more than one way to correct these.

Then answer the following questions for each invitation:

- What is the occasion? (What is the invitation for?)
- Does this occasion require a present? If the answer is yes, what might be a good present to bring?

Discuss your answers with the class.

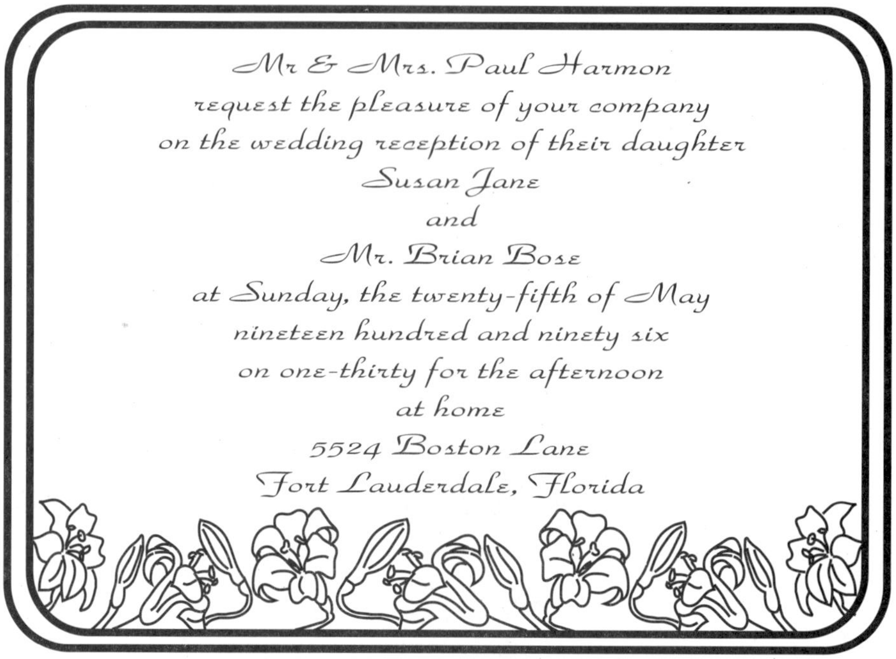

Mr & Mrs. Paul Harmon
request the pleasure of your company
on the wedding reception of their daughter
Susan Jane
and
Mr. Brian Bose
at Sunday, the twenty-fifth of May
nineteen hundred and ninety six
on one-thirty for the afternoon
at home
5524 Boston Lane
Fort Lauderdale, Florida

We invite you to share
a special day from our family
as we celebrate
the Golden Wedding Anniversary on
our parents
Mr. and Mrs. Gordon Simpson

Please join us for
a celebration
beginning in 7:00 o'clock at the evening
for dinner and dancing
on the
Lighthouse Restaurant
Harbor Drive
Seattle, Washington

LESSON 32: SPECIAL DAYS AND GIFTS—REVIEW AND CHANGING WORD ORDER

ACTIVITY TWO

A. Below you will find some sentences about a few of the holidays and special days from the Preview of this lesson. Read each one and do the following:

- Label all the subjects, verbs, and objects (if any) in each sentence with the letters S (for subject), V (for verb), and O (for object).
- Underline all of the prepositional phrases that begin with **for** or **to**.

EXAMPLE: Valentine's Day is in February on February 14. People often buy
                  subject   verb   subject   verb

their sweethearts presents on this day. Children give small candies to their friends
     object   subject verb   object

and classmates.

1. On April Fool's Day, people play tricks and fool other people. Sometimes they also tell people jokes and give silly presents to their friends.
2. Mother's Day is a special Sunday in the United States. Children often buy their mothers cards and give gifts to them. Sometimes school children make small crafts for their mothers in school. Then they bring them home to their mothers as gifts.
3. On Halloween many people wear costumes and go trick-or-treating in their neighborhoods. Sometimes parents buy the costumes and sometimes they make them for their children. Usually children go to their neighbors' houses and the neighbors give the children candy or pennies. Many children show their costumes to all of their friends.

B. If possible, change the prepositional phrases (with **for** or **to**) by moving them next to the verb and deleting the preposition.

EXAMPLE Children give small candies *to their friends and classmates*.
                 Children give their friends and classmates small candies.

- Find any phrases next to the verb that came from prepositional phrases with **for** and **to**. Circle these.

EXAMPLE People often buy (their sweethearts) presents on this day.
Share these answers with your partner. Make any changes you think are necessary.

*IT WORKS!
Learning Strategy:
Becoming Aware of
Other People's
Thoughts and
Cultures*

ACTIVITY THREE

Look at the following list of situations. Think about what you do for these situations or how you celebrate them in your country. Do you do something special for someone on these days? Do you buy a present for someone?

A. Write your answers to these questions in one or two sentences. Try to write some sentences using the prepositions **for** and **to.** Use some of these verbs:

bring   buy   give   make   show   tell

B. Can you change any of your sentences by moving prepositional phrases (with *for* or *to*) next to the verb?

> **EXAMPLE** Today is Mother's Day.
> *I buy a card for my mother. I buy my mother a card.*
> *I give a present to my mother. I give my mother a present.*
> *I take my mother to a nice restaurant for dinner.* (no change possible)

- Your sister just had a baby.
- Your best friend just moved into a new house.
- You are going to a dinner party at a friend's house tonight.
- Today is your brother's birthday.
- Today is your parents' wedding anniversary.
- Today is your last day of school and you want to do something special for your teacher.

Share your answers with the others in your class. Are your classmates' answers different from yours? What do you think the answers to these questions might be in the United States?

ACTIVITY FOUR

A. Do this activity with a partner. Choose a holiday or special day. You may want to look back at the list of days at the beginning of this lesson or you may want to choose a holiday from your country.

After you choose one special day, with your partner write a short description of that day. DO NOT write the name of the holiday in this description.

Think about the following when you write your description:

- When is this special day or holiday? What is the exact date?
- Why is this day important?
- What special activities take place on this day? (How do people celebrate this day?)
- Do people give gifts on this day?

Try to use the prepositions from Lessons 29–31 as much as possible. Try to move the prepositional phrases with *to* and *for* if possible.

Look carefully at your description. Check your work for the following:

❏ You described one special day or holiday from the list.

❏ You used some of the prepositions from Lessons 29–31.

❏ You checked that the meanings of these prepositions are correct for each sentence.

❏ You tried to move some prepositional phrases with *for* and *to* next to the verb (and deleted the preposition).

B. Read (or tell) your description to the class. DO NOT say the name of the holiday. The other students will guess the name of the holiday from your description.

ACTIVITY FIVE

Think about holidays in your country. How do people celebrate holidays there? Are they mostly religious days? Are any of them days or celebrations for giving gifts? What kinds of gifts are typical? Write a paragraph or two about holidays in your country. Discuss your favorite holiday or special day as well.

Check your work for the following:

❏ You used some of the prepositions from Lessons 29–31.

❏ You checked that the meanings of these prepositions are correct for each sentence.

❏ You tried to move some prepositional phrases with *for* and *to* next to the verb (and deleted the preposition).

Appendices

APPENDIX A: SCRIPTS FOR LISTENING

LESSON 1—ACTIVITY 3
1. She's my new friend.
2. My new friends love tennis and golf.
3. They're from northern Switzerland.
4. John's a new teacher at my school.
5. I'm tired and hungry.
6. Pablo plays three instruments very well.
7. You're a very interesting person.
8. My sister's in Las Vegas this week.

LESSON 3—ACTIVITY 1B
1. Wait for the dial tone.
   Put the coin into the slot.
   Dial the number.
2. Push the "on" button or switch on the machine.
   Turn on the monitor.
   Slip the disk in the drive.
3. Turn on the machine.
   Open the tray.
   Drop the disk in the tray.
   Close the tray.
4. Deposit nickels, dimes, or quarters.
   Press button for selection.
   Make another choice if red light appears.

LESSON 4—ACTIVITY 2A
1. *Grandma Moses—Artist*
   For many years Anna Mary Robertson Moses lived on a farm. At the age of 76 she began to paint in oil. She never had an art lesson in her life, but she became a famous artist. She painted many scenes of rural American life until she died at age 101.
2. *Harriet Beecher Stowe—Writer*
   Harriet Beecher Stowe wrote the book *Uncle Tom's Cabin*. This book showed her opposition to slavery. The book also helped people think about this issue before the American Civil War. When she met President Abraham Lincoln for the first time, he said, "So this is the little woman who made the big war."
3. *Sacagawea—Native American Woman/Explorer*
   In 1804 two men, Meriweather Lewis and William Clark, started to explore a large area of land in the Northwestern part of the United States. They brought with them only one woman, Sacagawea. Sacagawea was a Native American from the Shoshone tribe. She guided the explorers on their trip and helped them successfully travel through the area.
4. *Barbara Jordan—Politician/Educator*
   Barbara Jordan was both a politican and an educator. In 1966 she won an election and became the first black woman to serve in the Senate of the state of Texas. Later she also won election to the United States Congress. She earned attention and praise for several famous speeches, including one in 1992 against racism and intolerance.

LESSON 7—ACTIVITY 2
1. Scot said: I'll become an actor and act in many plays.
2. Susan said: In five years my husband will become the head coach of a football team.
3. Mike said: I'll play linebacker next year for the Balboa Raiders team.
4. Jon said: I'm gonna be a great and famous cook.
5. Jean said: My business will grow and many stores will carry my products.
6. Seth said: I'm gonna get my driver's license next year.
7. Jack said: My company is gonna offer me an important position in a plant in another country.

LESSON 8—ACTIVITY 2A
1. Scot said: I'm playing video games all weekend.
2. Jon said: Next week I'm going to a museum with my class.
3. Susan said: This summer we're going camping in Banff for a week.
4. Mike said: I'm gonna move to a new house in a few months.
5. Jean said: I'm going to go to Cape Cod for two weeks in July.
6. Seth said: I'm spending two weeks at a summer camp.
7. Jack said: I'm gonna go on a business trip for a few days in July.

LESSON 9—ACTIVITY 2
1. I was watching television all night from 8 P.M. until midnight. I heard nothing unusual.
2. My husband and I were taking a walk on 37th Avenue at about 8:30 P.M. At that time I noticed the light was on in apartment B5.
3. I was looking out my window at the moon for about 10 minutes last night. I saw a stranger leave the building at about 9 P.M.
4. I worked late last night. As I was arriving home at 9:30 P.M., I met Mrs. O'Brien at the entrance to the building.
5. My friends and I were having a party at that time last night. It was very noisy in my apartment, so we couldn't hear anything.

LESSON 10—ACTIVITY 2
1. My brother's taken several business trips to Bali, Indonesia.
2. I've written a new textbook for language learners.
3. Sixteen years ago we bought our first house in San Diego.
4. You've completed your first year at a new school.
5. Some of my friends took a trip to Yosemite National Park last month.
6. We've made several repairs to our house, both on the inside and outside.
7. In July 1969, people from Earth first walked on the moon.
8. He's entered some writing contests with the local newspaper.

LESSON 12—ACTIVITY 3
For the last few weeks Jordan's tried to follow his normal routine but it's been difficult. At school he has had to change his schedule because he can't go to some of his classes. He has also dropped his afternoon sports practices since the accident. Yesterday he went to the doctor to check his leg. The doctor said the leg's healed a little but not completely.

LESSON 13—ACTIVITY 2
On April 22, 1970 millions of environmental activists responded to a call for participation in a special event called Earth Day. On that day twenty million Americans listened to speeches by politicians and philosophers. These speakers talked about the horrible polluted condition of the world. Some speakers that day feared the enthusiasm of the day might fade away, but they shouldn't have worried.

There've been Earth Days each April 22 since then. In addition, several new laws have appeared in the law books, such as a stronger Clean Air Act and a Safe Drinking Water Act. Many individuals and small groups have been taking action on their own as well. These people've been educating others and taking strong action to help the environment for over twenty five years now.

LESSON 14—ACTIVITY 3

1. I'm going straight to the music store. I got some money for my birthday and I can't wait to buy some new CDs.
2. I might go to a music store too, but I don't really have much money with me today. I may just do some window shopping.
3. I think I'll do some window shopping and then I may go to the new bookstore. Of course, I could just go to the music store and look for some tapes. I just got a new car stereo.
4. I'll meet you guys at the mall entrance at five o'clock. I really need to get some new clothes and the department store is having a sale today. I'll be there for quite a while.
5. I read about that sale in the newspaper. I may see you there if I decide to look for some clothes. I might also go to the new clothing store. They're having a grand opening sale today.

LESSON 15—ACTIVITY 2

1. When I was younger I was very busy. I had a job and a family to take care of. Luckily, I was able to work late into the night to get things done. Now I can relax more so I spend time working on crossword puzzles.
2. Years ago, I was quite active in sports. For example, I was a pretty good tennis player and I could play tennis for hours. Now I like to do quieter things. I'm able to write poetry and I enjoy doing that.
3. Before I retired I was a super saleslady. I was able to sell things to all kinds of customers. Now that I'm retired, I can spend my time as a volunteer and work with people in a different way. In my job at the Public Defender's Office I'm able to advise people about their rights.
4. I can work with people too when I volunteer at the library. I enjoy getting out and helping people and I'm able to work the hours I like. In the past, I was able to work at a job I liked too, but that was full time and more demanding.

LESSON 16—ACTIVITY 2

1. **Driving Away from Home**
   You'd better find out about the driving laws where you'll be traveling. For example, you should know about speed limits and possible insurance requirements. If a police officer stops you on the road, you'd better pull over as soon as possible. You oughtta listen carefully, be polite and try not to argue.
2. **Renting a Car**
   You oughtta shop around to different companies to find the best price. You should ask about rental fees and insurance charges. If you do not buy insurance, you'd better drive carefully and watch out for other drivers. You should also find out about the rental company's gas policies. Some companies want you to return with a full tank. When you do not have a full tank, you fill up at the car return. You'd better ask the price of gas there; it could be very expensive!

LESSON 17—ACTIVITY 3

1. Hi Megan. This is Erica. What are you doing this afternoon? Do you want to see a movie?
   I'd love to, but I can't. I've gotta babysit my younger brother all day today.
   Do you really hafta do that? Can't your sister stay with him?
   No, she hasta go for a job interview this afternoon. Sorry. Maybe some other time.
2. Hi Garrett. This is Kayla. Did you do anything interesting last night?
   Actually, no I didn't. You wont believe what I hadda do. My parents made me clean my room! Do you believe it?
   I know what you mean. Two weeks ago I hadda stay in the whole weekend to clean up my room and to help clean out the garage.
   Boy, your parents are tough! All I hadda do was my own room.
3. Hello, Dan, this is Cameron. I called to ask about the homework for math class. Do we hafta solve all the problems on page 15, or just the odd numbered ones?
   I think we hafta do all of them, but I'm not sure. I missed half the class because I was at band practice.
   Oh. Well, I guess I'll call someone else to make sure. What about the science homework. Can you help me with that?
   Actually, I can't talk right now because I gotta eat dinner. My mom hasta go out tonight and we hafta eat right away. I'll call you back later.

LESSON 18—ACTIVITY 2B

1. Hello? Is this 549-2370?
   I'm sorry you must have the wrong number.
2. What's the fastest way to send this package to Saudi Arabia? It must get there no later than Thursday.
3. Good morning, I'm Mrs. Brady and you must be Arthur's mother, Mrs. Thomas.
4. I don't see Laurie and David anywhere, do you?
   They must be waiting for us in the next room. Let's go look.
5. The tire on the car looks a little flat. We must take it to a garage and check it before we leave on our vacation.

LESSON 19—ACTIVITY 2

1. Hi Ben, this is Peg. I was absent from class today and I need to get the homework assignments for math and history. Could you please call me and let me know what I missed?
2. Hi Marilyn, it's Aunt Irma. Can you babysit for me tonight? I know this is short notice, but I just found out there's an open house at Jimmy's school at 7 P.M. Please call me back and let me know.
3. This is the secretary at Doctor Stark's office. We need some information about your insurance. Would you please call me back today before five at 555-1234?
4. Hi, Mom. It's Jimmy. I'm at Billy's house right now, and he asked me to stay for dinner. Can I stay? I'll call you again in a little while.
5. Joe, this is Mom. I'm running a little late today and I have an appointment at the dentist at three o'clock this afternoon. Will you call that office and tell them I'm coming but I'll be a little late? Oh, and could you take the chicken out of the freezer so we can have it for dinner? Thanks a lot.

LESSON 22—ACTIVITY 3

1. Who's an Indian?
2. What's a reservation?
3. Why're some people referring to Indians as Native Americans?
4. Whaddya think about this information?
5. How's the image of Indians changing?
6. Where'd the Eskimos and Aleuts live?
7. Whaddya studying about the Indians now?

LESSON 23—ACTIVITY 2B

1. • Would you like to go out and do something with me tonight?
   • Sorry, I can't. I have four classes tomorrow. In fact, I really need to study tonight. I have to take three tests this week.
2. • I hear you're traveling to South America tomorrow.
   • Yes I am, but I'm not looking forward to the flight there. I have to take three different flights with two plane changes, and the trip will take a total of 18 hours.
3. • Did you take a business trip last week?
   • Yes, I went to three cities in five days and I had to visit two companies in each city. I'm exhausted.
4. • What did you buy at the department store today?
   • Well, I got three new knives for the kitchen and four towels for the bathroom.
5. • What can I help you with today?
   • I need two feet of lace, five buttons, and two sewing needles. Oh, and I also should get some marking chalk. Do you have any of that?

LESSON 24—ACTIVITY 2

1. I got the new Michael Jackson album at a music store in the shopping mall. I also bought a tape for my brother.
2. I bought a box of bandaids at the drugstore, but I forgot to buy aspirin. I guess I'll go out again. I still have a bad headache and need the aspirin.
3. I bought a new hammer from a new hardware store on Broadway. They were having an opening day sale, so I got it for a great price.
4. I bought a gold watch at the jewelry store in the mall. Usually the prices there are pretty high, but I got a good deal. It was the last digital watch and they wanted to sell it quickly. I was lucky.
5. I went to the new auto parts store near the mall. I bought an oil filter and some spark plugs.

LESSON 26—ACTIVITY 2

1. That company's profits have been increasing steadily.
2. Admission to all museums is free today in honor of the park's birthday.
3. I'd like to go to today's sale at that store, but it's a day's drive from here.
4. Take a boat to visit California's wine country.
5. That class is taking a field trip to the Children's Petting Zoo.
6. Try our Chef's Special—Frog's legs with orange butter sauce.
7. Take care of the earth's resources and recycle as much as possible at your neighborhood recycling center.

LESSON 27—ACTIVITY 3

1. Carol's aunt made trees for her family and her husband's family. She has the one for her husband but she can't find hers.
2. My friend and I were talking about our families yesterday. His grandparents are from Germany and mine are also.

3. My brother lives in a different part of the country, so we don't see each other too often. We try to spend our vacations together when we can.
4. Carol's family is what we call "blended." Her parents divorced and then remarried. Now Carol lives with her father, his new wife, and her two children.
5. My sister's children are young and mine are older. My kids are in high school, but hers are in elementary school.
6. Both of John's parents have large families. His mother has three brothers and two sisters and his father has two sisters and two brothers. Sometimes it's difficult to remember all of their names.

LESSON 29—ACTIVITY 2

1. The doctor says you need another appointment next week. Are you available on Wednesday at 4:00 P.M.?

    No, I have to work from 1:00 to 5:00 on Wednesday. I can come at 4:00 on Tuesday.

    Sorry. We're all booked up on Tuesday afternoon. What about Monday morning before 10:30 A.M. Are you free then?

    No, I'm afraid not. I have a class from 9:00-10:30 on Mondays and Wednesdays.

    Well, how about Friday. Do you have any time then?

    Friday morning I help at my son's school all morning from 9:00-12:00, but the afternoon is good. I can come any time between 12:00 and 3:00.

    Great, I'll put you in at 1:00 o'clock. Okay?

    Okay, see you Friday at 1.

2. Okay, Mrs. Statman, you need an appointment in two weeks. Dr. Barkett will be out of town on Monday and Tuesday of that week. And it looks like she's all booked up on Wednesday the 28th already. Are you available on Thursday the 29th or Friday the 30th?

    Hmmm. On Tuesdays and Thursdays I work from 8:00 A.M. to 3:00 P.M. and on Fridays I work from 8:00 A.M. to noon. Do you have anything on Friday after 12 o'clock?

    Let's see. Yes, I have an opening at 4:00 P.M. Is that good?

    Okay. Oh wait, that's not good. That's the day I drive for my son's car pool to basketball practice. I'm not available from 4:00 to 4:30 that day. You don't have anything in the afternoon before 4:00 P.M.? I'm free then.

    No, 4:00 P.M. is the only thing I have on Friday afternoon of that week. What about Thursday after work? We're here late that day. We leave at 6 P.M. Are you available at 5:30?

    Yes, I am. Okay. I'll see you on Thursday the 29th at 5:30 P.M. Thanks.

LESSON 31—ACTIVITY 2

Mr. and Mrs. George Simpson are happy to announce the marriage of their daughter Ann to Mr. David Graves. The couple had a small church wedding on January 5, 1996. The party was at the home of the bride's sister. Friends of the couple decorated the party with balloons and flowers. Some guests brought food for the party. The bride's sister baked a large wedding cake by herself. The bride wore a silk dress with a crown of flowers. For their honeymoon, the couple went by car to Las Vegas.

APPENDIX B: IRREGULAR VERB FORMS

base	past	past participle
bleed	bled	bled
feed	fed	fed
flee	fled	fled
lead	led	led
speed	sped	sped
find	found	found
have	had	had
hear	heard	heard
hold	held	held
make	made	made
sell	sold	sold
slide	slid	slid
stand	stood	stood
understand	understood	understood
lay	laid	laid
pay	paid	paid
say	said	said
bring	brought	brought
buy	bought	bought
catch	caught	caught
fight	fought	fought
seek	sought	sought
teach	taught	taught
think	thought	thought
creep	crept	crept
dream	dreamt	dreamt (or dreamed)
feel	felt	felt
keep	kept	kept
leap	lept	lept (or leaped)
leave	left	left
mean	meant	meant
meet	met	met
sleep	slept	slept
sweep	swept	swept
weep	wept	wept
build	built	built
light	lit	lit (or lighted)
lose	lost	lost
send	sent	sent
shoot	shot	shot
sit	sat	sat
be	was/were	been
see	saw	seen
lie	lay	lain
do	did	done
go	went	gone
run	ran	run
begin	began	begun
tear	tore	torn
wear	wore	worn
spin	spun	spun
win	won	won

base	past	-d/t/n
break	broke	broken
choose	chose	chosen
drive	drove	driven
freeze	froze	frozen
rise	rose	risen
shake	shook	shaken
show	showed	shown
speak	spoke	spoken
steal	stole	stolen
bite	bit	bitten
hide	hid	hidden (or hid)
ride	rode	ridden
write	wrote	written
beat	beat	beaten
eat	ate	eaten
fall	fell	fallen
give	gave	given
get	got	gotten (British: got)
forget	forgot	forgotten
blow	blew	blown
draw	drew	drawn
fly	flew	flown
grow	grew	grown
know	knew	known
throw	threw	thrown
become	became	become
come	came	come
overcome	overcame	overcome
drink	drank	drunk
swim	swam	swum
hang (an object)	hung	hung
cling	clung	clung
dig	dug	dug
sting	stung	stung
swing	swung	swung
ring	rang	rung
sing	sang	sung

ONE FORM ONLY:

base	past	-d/t/n
bet	bet	bet
burst	burst	burst
cost	cost	cost
cut	cut	cut
hit	hit	hit
hurt	hurt	hurt
let	let	let
put	put	put
read	read	read
set	set	set
shut	shut	shut
slit	slit	slit
spit	spit	spit
split	split	split

APPENDIX C: VERB SPELLING CHANGES

1. Spelling changes with *base + -ed* form.
   - If the base ends in **y** and the letter before it is a consonant, replace the **y** with **i** and then add **-ed.**

   stud**y**   stud**ied**   hurr**y**   hurr**ied**

   - For one-syllable words: If the base ends in a single consonant preceded by a single vowel, double the consonant before adding -ed.

   sto**p**   sto**pped**   hu**g**   hu**gged**

   - For words with more than one syllable: If the base ends in a single consonant preceded by a single vowel and the last syllable is stressed, double the consonant before adding **-ed**.

   contr**ol**/contro**lled**
   occ**ur**/occu**rred**
   pref**er**/prefe**rred**

   - If the base ends in **e** add **d.**

   nam**e**   name**d**   smil**e**   smile**d**

2. Spelling changes with *base + -s* form.
   - If the base form of the verb ends in a **consonant + y**, change the **y** to **i** and add **-es** for the **base + s** form.

   We stud**y** English.   He stud**ies** English.
   The students carr**y** books.   The student carr**ies** books.

   - If the **base** ends in **x, s, z, sh,** or **ch**, add **-es** for the **base + s** form.

   We wa**sh** in the morning.   He wash**es** in the morning.
   They fi**x** cars.   She fix**es** cars.

   - If the **base** ends in **o**, add **-es.**

   I g**o** to school.   She go**es** to school.
   We d**o** our homework.   She do**es** her homework.

3. Spelling changes with *base + -ing* form
   - For one-syllable words: If the base ends in a single consonant preceded by a single vowel, double the consonant before adding the **-ing**.

   jo**g**/jo**gging**
   cu**t**/cu**tting**

   - For words with more than one syllable: If the base ends in a single consonant preceded by a single vowel and the last syllable is stressed, double the consonant before adding **ing**.

   forg**et**/forge**tting**   pref**er**/prefe**rring**

   - If the base ends in **e**, drop the **e** before adding **-ing.**

   mak**e**/mak**ing**
   clos**e**/clos**ing**

   - If the base ends in **ie**, change **ie** to **y** before adding **-ing.**

   lie   l**ying**   die   d**ying**